A Life of Experimental Econ

Vernon L. Smith

A Life of Experimental Economics, Volume I

Forty Years of Discovery

Vernon L. Smith
Economic Science Institute
Chapman University
Orange, CA, USA

ISBN 978-3-319-98403-2   ISBN 978-3-319-98404-9   (eBook)
https://doi.org/10.1007/978-3-319-98404-9

Library of Congress Control Number: 2018951570

Cover image: © Vernon L. Smith
Cover design by Ran Shauli

This Palgrave Macmillan imprint is published by the registered company Springer Nature Switzerland AG
The registered company address is: Gewerbestrasse 11, 6330 Cham, Switzerland

Opulence, not poverty, puts the strain on the best there is in people.
—Arthur E. Hertzler, *The Doctor and His Patients*, 1942

Preface

In the ten years since I finished *Discovery* (2008), new learning and perspectives on earlier work prompt me to revisit its incomplete state. Re-visitation evokes a feeling expressed by C. S. Lewis: "The unfinished picture would so like to jump off the easel and have a look at itself." (*Letters to Malcolm*, 1964). I seem always to live with a certain incompletion, prompted by the obsolescence of earlier understandings. For me, returning to these pages is a pathway of renewal, consolidation, and rediscovery.

In *A Life of Experimental Economics* the inspirational theme continues—satisfaction and pleasure in whatever work one chooses. In *PrairyErth* (1991) William Least Heat-Moon visits the Tallgrass Prairie of Chase County, Kansas whose haunts I have also visited. There, he finds and interviews McClure Stilley, a Kansas quarryman, who expresses the sentiment in this theme beautifully: "Limestone is something you get interested in and something you learn to like. And then you become part of it. You know every move to make: just how to mark it off, drill it, load it, shoot it and then you see a real straight break, and you feel good."

Some of this pleasurable desire to reflect and reexamine has been implicit in a few of my standard scientific papers, whose format and style sucks (I addressed these pretentions more formally in *Rationality in Economics*, 2008, Chapter 13, pp. 296–308). Room for reflecting and expressing those sentiments in a scientific paper is limited to hints between the lines. I can do it here in a conversational style that I find more natural, wherein I can just sit and talk with you.

The new work revises and expands much of the earlier edition's content and continues the style of injecting in-context memories of social, economic, and political events in my lifespan. And it includes my recent ten-year learning and work experiences at Chapman University. The move to Chapman coincided with the economic collapse of 2007–2008, an event that revived childhood experiences enveloped by the Depression. It compelled my attention, not as a macro-economist, which I am not, but as an experimental economist long sensitized to incentives in human behavior, and its implications for society. Moreover, I had a stanch ally—Steve Gjerstad, whom I have long known—and we were well matched in our search for new insights. The turbulent housing crisis was as widely unanticipated as that of 1929–1930. Why did the severity of the recent collapse blindside everyone? We argue that in both episodes, housing and mortgage credit undermined our prosperity and then the recovery. I also include new insights into the characteristic differences between two kinds of markets studied in the laboratory: The rapid equilibrium discovery properties of non-re-tradable goods consumed on demand is manifest in the stability of expenditures for non-durables in the economy; the sharply contrasting bubble-like price performance of asset markets is manifest in durables—notably housing—a recurrent source of instability in the economy.

I discuss new perspectives on Adam Smith, known as the founder of classical economics. Smith's neglected contributions to the psychology of human sociability have brought unexpected new thinking and modeling to the study of human conduct, particularly in two-person experimental interactions, like "trust" games. Lastly, I expound on a theme in the prior edition that faith is at the foundation of religion; both concern our personal search for understanding; both involve thought processes in higher dimensional spaces than our sensory and instrumental observations.

Throughout I have tried to maintain the narrative style of writing from the memories of personal experience, introducing economics and other topical content where memory or context invoke relevant principles or experiences; as Tom Hazlett commented, I combine "biography, history, economics, and philosophy." Commenters and reviewers have approved of that style, as did Sylvia Nasar (*A Beautiful Mind*) whose invaluable commentary on an early draft of *Discovery* confirmed the tone to be sounded. That tone may slip in this work as I introduce new learning that cries out for informal expression, but is more narrowly the province of professional economics than personal narrative.

The new subtitles, *Forty Years of Discovery* and *The Next Fifty Years*, capture the perennial freshness of the experiences I want to convey—experiences well enough digested to be penned. I am especially encouraged to undertake this re-writing and research effort because of the warm acceptance of *Discovery* in reviews that have come to my attention, and for which I am grateful.

Recent years of experience have brought home to me even more vividly the perpetual human error of unconsciously seeking verification of our beliefs and thinking processes. The error is part of what Adam Smith called self-deceit. We have the habit, given our beliefs about anything—scientific propositions, political opinion, religion, the malevolence of an adversary—to seek further confirming evidence of those beliefs. We like to be, or to appear, right, to be comfortable in that state, and this leads to a certain sense of "righteousness." If contrary evidence surfaces, we tend to discount it or explain it away so that it is less likely to change our belief state. Most detrimental to learning and to intellectual growth is our protective reluctance to deliberately seek tests or data or circumstances that would challenge our beliefs, requiring us to re-evaluate what it is we think we know. Being open in this way need not imply that we will flip back and forth with unstable beliefs. Indeed, traditions will be stronger the more they survive challenging tests of validity, rather than the weak easily hurdled tests that only confirm and entrench what we believe we know. If your views are not changing, you are probably not learning.

Orange, USA   Vernon L. Smith

Acknowledgements

My personal debts run deep, beginning with John Hughes (*The Vital Few*), for 36 years my trusted friend and confidant until his death in 1992. His mark upon me pervades these volumes.

To Silvia Naser (*A Beautiful Mind*) and my dear friend of 38 years, Deirdre McCloskey (*The Bourgeois Virtues*), who read the earliest drafts of the manuscript and corrected, nudged and encouraged me in directions that shaped it to the end.

Tom Hazlett (*The Political Spectrum*) friend and cherished co-author. I knew Tom before he knew me because I was an avid reader of his columns that appeared in *Reason* magazine beginning in 1989.

Andreas Ortmann, economic theorist, experimentalist, and intellectual historian *par excellence* in all, who's comments, reviews—both published and private—have never failed to be rewarding to me.

Steve Hanke (http://sites.krieger.jhu.edu/iae/), wise counselor on monetary and fiscal policy, whose private and published reviews have encouraged and supported my dedication to these volumes.

Charles Plott (*Collected Papers on the Experimental Foundations of Economics and Political Science.* In three volumes), who, because I could outfish him, suspected that there might be something to experimental economics and became a co-conspirator in its development in the 1970s. Charlie invented experimental political economy.

Shyam Sunder (*Theory of Accounting and Control*), methodologist, experimentalist, whose passion in the search for foundations has long been an inspiration.

E. Roy Weintraub (*How Economics Became a Mathematical Science*), reviewer, whose wide-ranging interests included me.

My Amazon reviewers, each in his own tongue:

Paul Johnson, friend and colleague, University of Alaska, Anchorage;

Herb Gintis (*Individuality and Entanglement: The Moral and Material Bases of Social Life*) with whom I share gloriously radical roots and a passion for moral wisdom.

Roger Farley, investor and portfolio manager, whom I do not know. But we resonate well.

Pete and Jackie Steele, a breed of the many ordinary people that have made America. May we never lose their unwavering integrity, love of life, and of the good land.

Stephen Semos for his careful editing, fact checking, and many suggestions for improving style and content down to the final crescendo.

Candace Smith, devoted companion in our explorations of love, understanding, and faith developing.

And to co-authors and students galore—Steve Gjerstad, Dave Porter, Stephen Rassenti, Arlington Williams, and more whose imprint is in these pages.

And a very special debt to the Liberty Fund for inviting me to many of their Socratic colloquia, over the last forty years, on topics and figures in the philosophy and history of the struggle for liberty. I want to acknowledge my frequent use of quotations from Adam Smith (Dugald Stewart edition, 1853) and David Hume, published by Liberty Fund and that are available for quotation and free electronic download access.

You will encounter many more in these pages. "This is remembrance—revisitation; and names are keys that open corridors no longer fresh in the mind, but nonetheless familiar in the heart" (Beryl Markham, *West with the Night*).

Praise for *A Life of Experimental Economics, Volumes I and II*

"We learn from giants on whose shoulders we stand. There can be no doubt that 2002 Nobel Prize winner Vernon L. Smith is one of them. *A Life of Experimental Economics, Vol I: Forty Years of Discovery; Vol II: The Next Fifty Years*, is a much expanded version of his 2008 memoir *Discovery* in which he recounted his journey from birth until 2005. As many other reviewers did then, I called that earlier version a must-read and have recommended it to many of my colleagues and students as well as folks from other walks of life since. The new work reviews, and in places revises, that memoir and then adds several chapters that have been inspired by Vernon's more recent interests in the nature and causes of housing bubbles on the one hand and his attempt to draw out the insights to be had for modern economics from Adam Smith's *Theory of Moral Sentiments* on the other. The new volumes trace matter-of-factly the amazing journey from five-year old farm boy in the Great Depression to the towering, very public intellectual that Vernon is today. It does so—mostly—in the same conversational tone that made *Discovery* such a joy to read. (Yes, of course, the best pie this side of heaven is made from freshly cut rhubarb. And, yes, one should not mix strawberries with the rhubarb. Ever.) Be prepared to not agree with Vernon's opinions on all of the numerous issues discussed as we progress through the decades— many of his opinions are informed by a very libertarian streak indeed—but as provocative as they might be, they were formed in a lifetime of extraordinary achievements and extraordinary insights into human nature and institutions, as well as a deeply humanistic attitude."

—Andreas Ortmann, *Professor of Experimental and Behavioural Economics, School of Economics, UNSW Business School, Australia*

"This personal narrative guides the reader along a 90-year journey from a one-room school in Kansas through a career of scientific discovery, with a fairy-tail ending and a richly rewarding postscript. In contrast with other Nobel Prize winners in economics who often immerse themselves in their own "higher-level models," Vernon follows Adam Smith's methodology of detailed observation, with a special focus on human behavior in the lab and regulatory misbehavior in the wild. His intense love for life and research is conveyed in a sequence of colorful stories, presented against a landscape that switches back and forth from the American West to academic culture. The reader is treated to insights about how economics experiments and policy proposals are designed, interspersed with advice that ranges from relationships to making a good batch of chili from scratch."

—Charles Holt, *A. Willis Robertson Professor of Political Economy, University of Virginia, USA*

"Only Priests and Engineers populated Econo-Land. Priests spin theories without facts; Engineers collect data, give policy advice, and generally embrace only the most basic economic theory. Microeconomics textbooks the world over were filled with axioms and theorems, bereft of facts.

Over three score years ago, Vernon Smith, Engineer par excellence, set out actually to test economic theory! The Priests were horrified. Vernon put together a working laboratory, got amazing results having people play games of economic exchange, and started a movement that has radically altered the relationship of fact to theory in economics. Not only has experimental economics expanded a thousand-fold over the years, but leading journals now present models that attempt to account for the observed behavior of actual human subjects in field and laboratory.

Vernon changed my life in 1992, when I read an article he wrote in *Scientific American* surveying his work. I had thought that experimental economics was just a bunch of dimwits trying to show that Adam Smith's invisible hand really worked. I was wrong. Inspired by Vernon, I can honestly say that everything I assert with confidence about economics comes from either the result of experiments or observing the comparative performance of different real-life economic institutions.

Vernon Smith is larger than life. I recall vividly, as a young Associate Professor, meeting with Vernon at the American Economic Association meetings in New Orleans to try to convince him not to leave Massachusetts for Arizona. Vernon was dressed in a beautiful white Southern-style suit with a string tie and a stunning gold-embroidered vest. He was slim and gorgeous, with a big handlebar mustache. I had never met anyone like him in my life, and the experience was amplified by the fact that I, and my friends, veterans of civil rights and anti-Vietnam War struggles, dress uniformly in jeans and torn polo shirts with pictures of Ché on the back and the peace sign on the front. Vernon was a veteran of the same struggles, a conscientious objector, but absent Ché. He declined to return to UMass, and the rest is history. This two-volume set is a memoir that every young, creative economist should read, and the deadwood in academia should shun at all costs."

—Herbert Gintis, *Santa Fe Institute, USA*

"Vernon Smith's ingenuity in developing experimental methods to study "that which is not" has deepened economic analysis and enabled us to examine questions of institutional change and market design that would otherwise remain hypothetical. Combining personal and professional reflections with the arc of U.S. economic history in the 20th century, this heartfelt and engaging story uses economics and philosophy to analyze a life of intellect, curiosity, enthusiasm, and purpose. Professor Smith's life experiences, his creativity in developing new economic ideas and new fields of inquiry, and his dogged commitment to inquisitiveness are inspiring examples of a well-lived life of the mind."

—Lynne Kiesling, *Purdue University, USA*

"A Life of Experimental Economics, 2 volumes, provides a vivid picture of one of the most vibrant minds in modern social science, Vernon Smith—the 2002 Nobel Prize winner in Economic Science. That Smith is an outstanding theorist and innovator of experimental methods in economic science is well known. But, Vernon Smith is much more than a first-class economic scientist. His life story, as told throughout these volumes, provides an outstanding example of life-long learning revealed through his explorations into natural history, economic history, and all human endeavors, ancient as well as modern, to unearth deep scientific explanations. Smith's insatiable desire to discover the mechanics and meanings embedded in human sociability are displayed beautifully in the pages of this autobiography. Vernon Smith has indeed lived a wonderful life, and continues to live a life full of intellectual curiosity and creativity in his quest to understand the human condition philosophically as well as scientifically. What a fascinating and amazing journey of discovery we are privileged to witness in reading A Life of Experimental Economics. Read it, absorb its lessons, and most importantly, strive to follow its example and be a life-long learner."

—Peter Boettke, *University Professor of Economics and Philosophy,*
George Mason University, USA

"While the Marxist critique of political economy that constitutes the wheel-house of my work in the philosophy and sociology of education could not be further from the pro-market libertarian views of Nobel Laureate Vernon Smith, *A Life of Experimental Economics* is a book that I would highly recommend to all. It is a fascinating work that illustrates the life of a man blessed with a singular curiosity and creative mind, a man gifted with the grace of humility and endowed with a formidable intellect and yet, most impressively, a man who refuses to sacrifice wonder at the expense of classical logic. If you scratch any theory, you will find an autobiography underneath. With *A Life of Experimental Economics*, you don't have to scratch that hard to understand the myriad ways that the formative experiences of the young Vernon Smith have been carried forth throughout his life, ever steeling his desire to make the world a better place. Born into a family who worked on the locomotives of the Wichita and Southwestern and Santa Fe railroad companies that used to carry cattle to the stockyards near Kellogg Avenue, who labored in the rolling wheat fields and the oil fields of Kansas, and who were educated in the one-room schoolhouses that served the cattle ranches and farming communities, Vernon Smith recounts his pathfinding journey from his farmhouse in America's heartland to his trailblazing work in the classrooms of the University of Kansas, Harvard, Caltech, Purdue, George Mason University and Chapman University. A lack of dialogue across differences on university campuses has enabled superficial character-izations of intellectuals and activists on both the right and the left. *A Life of Experimental Economics* reveals the folly of such stereotyping. The self-por-trait that emerges from the pages of Smith's autobiography is filled with reflexive self-questioning, and a commitment to activism on behalf of racial, social and political equality. This is not a man ensepulchred in a brainpan filled with numerical abstractions and powered by a cold calculus of reason-ing, but a man whose is motivated by a reverence for life and a betterment of the public good. His life is a journey of discovery, minted by curiosity and wonder, and one that eventually took him through the gates of the Judeo-Christian tradition, where his Christian faith has challenged him to rethink the very foundations of science. It is a journey that will enrich us all."
    —Peter McLaren, *Distinguished Professor in Critical Studies, Chapman University, USA; Chair Professor, Northeast Normal University, China*

"Vernon Smith is one of our greatest living economists and at 91 years he is still active and strong. Along with others, he built an entire experimental science designed to reveal economic dynamics at the level of individuals that has global consequences. Vernon is as likable as he is deep. Who would have guessed he began employment as a drugstore delivery boy at age 12—and worked with the Congress of Racial Equality at 15? There is no better introduction to Vernon than himself, an organism who remembers his life as he lived it—simple, humble, unpretentious and with a bias toward honesty and justice."

—Robert Trivers, *Evolutionary theorist, sociobiologist,*
2007 Crafoord Prize winner and author, Wild Life

"Vernon Smith's autobiography is an incredible life story of the whole person telling the reader so much more than his development as an economist. His single-room schoolhouse, two difficult years on the farm during the Depression Era, transformation from a C+ high schooler to a straight A Caltech and Harvard graduate, and deep engagement with his family, friends, and faith, all played essential roles in sculpting his curiosity-driven way of life and discoveries. Smith's fascinating tale will resonate with all who are willing to let observation and experience change their minds. It is an essential reading for aspiring scholars."

—Shyam Sunder, *Yale University, USA*

"Nobelist Vernon Smith presents a riveting intellectual history of his life and his life's work. The creator of the field of experimental economics has crafted a superbly written two volume treatise that is loaded with provactive details. It reads like a novel. And like all great novels, it contrains one great character: the classical liberal Smith, himself."

—Steve H. Hanke, *The Johns Hopkins University, USA*

"The brilliance of Vernon Smith will not surprise the reader. What might, however, is the playfulness of his child-like curiosity, the richness of his experience, the easy flow of his thought, and his passion to grasp the next problem, tiny or vast. That this character led to intellectual discoveries that changed the world is a meaty tale, but it is very nearly a side show. This is a compelling human drama, filled with warmth, pain and love, honest and unretouched. It forces the reader to think about the greatest challenges of the human condition, and yet details the delicious secret of the perfect hamburger. I felt privileged to consume this beautiful tome, and be charmed by its author on every page."

—Thomas Hazlett, *Hugh H. Macaulay Endowed Professor*
of Economics, Clemson University, USA

Contents

List of Figures

1

Before "My"

Casey Jones, in the language of the time, was a crack twenty-six-year-old passenger engineer on the Illinois Central Railroad's Cannonball Express. On April 30, 1906, The Cannonball was approaching Vaughan, twelve miles from Canton, IL. Alan Lomax, the celebrated collector of American folk songs, prefaces "The Ballad of Casey Jones" with a report of the spectacular wreck of the Cannonball in *The Folk Songs of North America* (1960).

Casey and his fireman, Sim Webb, had not received any more orders and were bearing down on Vaughan, at the lower end of a "double *S*-curve." There was a switch in the middle of the first *S*, enabling a slower train to be sidetracked. A freight train had not pulled entirely onto the side track. Sim reports that as they roared down on the switch, he could see two big red lights indicating a train not in the clear, but "Mr Casey" couldn't see it because there was a deep curve to the fireman's side. Sim yelled "Look out! We're gonna hit something!" Casey shouted his final words "Jump Sim!" He kicked the seat from under him and applied the brakes. "I swung down ... and hit the dirt. When I came to ... Mr. Casey was dead."

The Cannonball's engine collided with the caboose of the freight and plowed into the next two cars—one of shelled corn and one of hay. When they found Casey, he had an iron bolt driven through his neck and on his chest was a bale of hay. The "Balad of Casey Jones" was composed by the roundhouse employee and "great Negro folk poet" Wallace Saunders, as he wiped up Casey's blood from engine No. 382.

Like Sim, Grover A. Bougher (1893–1918), my mother's first husband and the father of her two oldest children, was a fireman, who worked for the

Santa Fe Railroad. For those not brought up on railroad lore, a fireman puts in, not out, engine fires; he makes and stokes the locomotive's boiler fire by shoveling coal and maintaining the locomotive's steam pressure. A fireman was commonly an apprentice locomotive engineer who served time in the cab to master the engine's operations and learn from the engineer, who is essentially the captain of his train. This subordinate role of the fireman is clearly indicated in the exchange between the famous Casey Jones and his fireman, Sim Webb, who refers to Jones as "Mr. Casey." Sim Webb was "Negro" or "colored"—the polite ways of identifying "African Americans" in those days—and he may have been especially deferential for that reason.

At some point, after gaining experience in the cab, if he proved fit for the task and was of a mind to continue, the fireman would be promoted to engineer. An engineer lived by the maxim "Get her there and make time or come to the office and get your time (pay)."

I have a letter Grover wrote to his brother, George, a private in the American Expeditionary Force in France, dated October 3, 1918, and post-marked the following day in Newton, Kansas. Newton, which is twenty-odd miles north of Wichita, was a switchyard on the main line of the Atchison, Topeka, and Santa Fe Railroad. (None of the cities in the railroad's name was on its main line from Chicago to Kansas City to Los Angeles.) One day later, on October 5, Grover was killed instantly in a train wreck, an accident not uncommon at the time. A manual cutover switch had been inadvertently left open, diverting his passenger train onto the sidetrack, where it collided with a waiting freight engine. The accident was similar to the 1906 wreck of the Illinois Central Railroad's Cannonball Express, which killed Casey Jones.

The letter was returned to Newton, postmarked the following April, and forwarded to Wichita, where my mother had moved. A notation by the Command P.O. stated that George had been killed eight months earlier, shortly before Grover had written to him, on September 17, 1918, while fighting with the American Expeditionary Force in France. Thus, neither brother knew of the other's death. When Grover was killed, my grandfather to be, Asahel Lomax (1874–1945), my mother's father, had been laid up for some time with a serious leg injury caused by a railroad accident. He was an engineer on the Missouri Pacific Railroad (the MoPac, MP, or "MOP," as we affectionately called it, never made it to the Pacific, or even west of Denver). According to my recollection of the oral reports in my family from the 1930s, Grandpa Lomax was injured in a straight-track accident—not on an S-curve as in the celebrated Cannonball wreck—when a connecting rod on one of the great drive wheels broke loose at the front end and flailed up through the cab's wood flooring. Grandpa and his fireman jumped from their cab and survived. On a straight open track, a train will come to a stop without assistance from the engineer, and it's hard to be heroic inside a demolished cab. Grandpa often said that years later his leg still contained splinters from the wood floor of the engine cab.

I have not been able to document Grandpa Lomax's connecting-rod incident. I have, however, obtained a Missouri Pacific ICC report of a connecting-rod accident at Benton, ten miles northeast of Wichita, which is quite likely the one. It seems to be the only such reported incident in 1918 on the MOP, and the location, injuries, and time are fully consistent with the family information. Ray State, an online documenter of railroad history and data, generously provided me with a copy of the report:

"April 6th 1918 locomotive 2668 near Benton Kansas. Front end main rod strap bolt and key lost out permitting rod to drop: 2 injured." State comments, "Unfortunately, I have failed to identify 2668 as it does not appear in the 1920s number list. It may be an ancient 4-4-0 or 4-6-0 dating from before 1900 and condemned after the war." (I found these model designations in railroad history: the 4-4-0 was a popular nineteenth mid-century "American type" eight-wheeler with 4 axels; it was replaced by a "ten wheeler" with four leading and six power drive wheels, used for both freight and passenger trains.) He further notes: "Minor incidents of the type you describe never made it to the level of the ICC main reports. However, from April 1911 railroads were obliged to report locomotive incidents which killed or injured train crew. These were recorded by the ICC Bureau of Safety and published annually in their Locomotive Inspection reports. Until recently these lay unused by the public and in most cases un-catalogued in archives."

Here is the text of the letter Grover wrote to his brother in the vernacular of the time, complete with missing punctuation and misspellings and inaccurate word use. It captures much of the tenor of the war years, particularly the feelings that people had toward Germans, who were commonly and erroneously called the "Dutch" or, more derisively, "Krauts." Twenty-five years later, angry Americans would refer to the Japanese people as "Japs," and still later, they would refer to the Vietnamese people as "Gooks." As one conflict succeeds another, the objects of derision follow suit.

Newton, Kansas

Oct 3rd 1918

Dear Bro George:
Will write you a letter today. We got home the 1st & we sure had some swell time there in Indiana, all of us went & of course we had some time together the kiddies sure was some "girlies" when we were out on the farm [the farm was near

Paoli, where my mother was born and her father grew up] they wanted to know if you milked all the milk out the cows if you put it back in & all such questions they sure were amusing. Wish you had a been along

Well things in Old America bud are about the same old thing every thing fine & prosperous as ever & every body is working to there limit & now at present we have our 4th loan campaign & it will go over the top & above expectations I am sure & believe me the boys at the front are sure putting the -K- in the Kiser & it wont be long I hope till you all can come home & tell us your wonderfull experiences & how they correlled the "Dutch"

George have [you] been in eney active fighting yet & how do you like the noise it sure must be wonderfull believe me I wish I were there with you, Why don't you write to us more often I sure like to hear from you in fact we all do the kiddies often talk of Uncle George a soldier boy & gone to whip the Dutch you wont know those Babyies if you don't get home for long. Billyei you know will be five in the Spring & Eileen she will be 3 the 19th of this mounth.

I am now on a regular run I have 17 & 16 Newton to A. [Arkansas] City & back every day its the best job out of here in my opinion.

We are having fine weather here now. No cold yet & we have no stove up yet eather but must put up one soon cause it may turn cool most any time

I am now 5 X out for Eng Xboard [Grover is referring to his fifth time working the engine extra-board on call for any run as engineer] & will probably take the examination in the next couple mounths as they are hard up for men & we have no more promoted men hear now so you see I can nearlly have my pick of the jobs around hear.

Well Dad & Ma Lomax are hear with us & Dad's leg is not very much better he cannot walk on it yet he sure has had some hard luck, Ma she is going to work soon she has her a good job hear in one of the best stores, well I guess I'll leave a little for the rest to write so will say Good Bye for now & may the best of good luck be with you & all our boys over there & that the job will soon be done & you all can come home cause if every one is anxious to see their near ones as I am to see you they would all be wishing we were in Berlin now with the Kiser & his whole D---out fit hung to a phone pole Bye Bye Bud & Love

Grover

My mother appended a short postscript to Grover's letter:

Dear Bro,

Grover has written everything there is to write. I am a real busy woman now. Our family has enlarged. Mother and Dad are going to stay with us all winter.

I put another star in our service flag yesterday. Denny [her brother] is in training at Fairmount military school. He's had a time trying to get into service somewhere.

As ever—Belle

On October 5 and 7, *The Kansan,* the Newton daily published the following accounts of Grover's train wreck:

Newton, Harvey County, Kansas, Saturday, October 5, 1918

> *FATAL WRECK OF SANTA FE TRAIN*
>
> *Engineer B. McCandless and Fireman Grover Bougher*
>
> *Were Killed*
>
> *Santa Fe passenger train No. 17, which left Newton this morning a few minutes late shortly before 5 o'clock, crashed into a heavy freight engine, No. 1622, at Hackney, a few miles north of Arkansas City, at 8:00 this morning, resulting in the death of Engineer B. McCandless and Fireman Grover A. Bougher of Newton and Fireman C. E. Randolph of Arkansas City. It was stated in early reports that Engineer L. A. Dugan of the freight engine, of Arkansas City, and a few passengers, were badly injured.*
>
> *As soon as word of the wreck reached division headquarters here, Supt. H. B. Lautz had a special relief and wrecking train made up and it was speeded to the scene, and some accurate information regarding the cause of the wreck and other details were expected early this afternoon.*

Monday, October 7, 1918

> *Left Switch Open and Caused Wreck*
>
> *It is evident from information gained following investigations into the cause of the wreck of No. 17 at Hackney Saturday morning, that a brakeman of the freight crew failed to close a switch, which turned the passenger train in on a cut-over switch in such a manner as to side-swipe the big freight engine.*
>
> *The story is to the effect that the freight had a car from which the draw bar had been pulled. The crew had set this car on the house track, which is across the main line from the passing switch. The big 1622 freight engine had finished the work and returned to the passing track, by way of the cut-over switch, which crossed the main line. The brakeman failed to close the switch behind the freight engine, and when the 1451, pulling the No. 17, came along, she shot across the cut-over switch and struck the freight engine just about the cab. It was stated that Fireman C. E. Randolph of Arkansas City, on the 1622, was just climbing into his cab when he was hit, and only fragments of his body have been found. Engineer McCandless and Fireman Bougher of Newton, on the passenger engine, were instantly killed, the former having been thrown several feet. It is a mystery how Engineer Dugan of the freight train escaped, as he was in the cab.*
>
> *It was stated that the brakeman who left the switch open, was standing directly by the switch, and the instant he saw what happened, completely lost his mind,*

and it was necessary to restrain him and remove him to a hospital. So far as has been learned, no passengers were badly injured, though practically, the entire train was badly jarred and jolted.

The life insurance money provided to my mother by the Santa Fe Railroad, augmented by a retail job selling shoes, guaranteed a decent but modest existence to a twenty-two-year-old widow with two girls, three-year-old Aileen and four and half-year-old Billye. My mother, encouraged by her mother, had married at age sixteen. After she had been dating Grover for a short time, her mother had asked, "Why don't you marry Grover?" A woman's task was to find a husband, and earlier was better than later.

As in all earlier generations, aid to dependent children still came from family and friends. In this case, assistance came from my mother's parents, and she moved into their Wichita home at 201 West Eleventh Street.

My maternal grandfather and his twin brother had been orphaned at about age five. At the time, they were living on a farm in a Quaker community near Paoli, Indiana, where they were born. Their uncle John Stout had a nearby farm and was happy to raise them. Boys were especially adoptable because farm labor was always in demand. Asahel and his fraternal twin, Ezra, were among the youngest of nine children, a family that included another set of fraternal twins. Their mother was pregnant an eighth time, but no child survived. My mother always said that it was another set of twins, but this may be a family myth, as the genealogical record does not verify it. But, two sets of twins among ten children: No wonder the twin boys were orphaned so young! Asahel and Ezra's mother, who had married at twenty, died at age thirty-six of "consumption," as tuberculosis was called then; their father died of the same cause four years later. In the end, consumption accounted for the deaths of all but four of their father's family of ten surviving siblings.

In 1893, when the twins were nineteen, Ezra left for Kansas. Asahel married Ella Moore in 1895, and followed Ezra to Kansas in 1896, soon after my mother was born. Initially, the twins both worked for the Santa Fe Railroad. Asahel worked in the SF Shops in Chanute for $39.05 per month, according to a short history written by my Grandma Lomax when she was eighty-eight. He resigned from the Santa Fe in 1903 and went to Wichita to work for the Missouri Pacific in the roundhouse (an engine repair shop containing a circular turntable that could turn an engine 180 degrees to travel in the other direction). He was promoted to fireman after three months and to engineer just six months later. According to Grandma's narrative, his meteoric rise occurred because he was "one of the MOP's crack

Engineers." He served as an engineer until his retirement on August 19, 1937. Throughout the period preceding the Great Depression, engineers had been much in demand because of expansion in the rail business.

My grandfather was once stopped by a police officer for driving through a yellow traffic light. The officer asked, "Sir, do you know what a yellow traffic light means?" Grandpa replied, "Yes, officer. I've been an engineer on the MOP for twenty-five years; it means proceed with caution, and that is what I was doing."

Ezra was an engineer on the Santa Fe (as was the twins' older brother William). Both he and my grandfather much admired Eugene Victor Debs—"Gene Debs," as he was known in our family—who had been instrumental in organizing the American Railroad Union in 1894, and was a prominent leader in the Brotherhood of Locomotive Firemen. The hostility between management and the railroad workers is revealed in the following recollection: When I was about twelve years old, Uncle Ezra made one of his rare visits to Wichita. He and I were sitting on the front porch swing on a beautiful afternoon. He was reading the *Wichita Beacon*, whose front page carried news of the death of the Santa Fe Railroad president. Uncle Ezra, with a deadpan expression worthy of Buster Keaton, leaned over to me and said, "You know, Vernie, I would never knowingly piss on any man's grave, but if I ever were to do it accidentally I would want it to be his."

After researching Santa Fe Railroad history, I have concluded that Uncle Ezra was probably referring to Samuel T. Bledsoe, who became president of the Santa Fe in 1933 and died unexpectedly in 1939. Bledsoe had kept the railroad financially afloat during the hard economic years of his presidency, and he no doubt made many enemies in the process, including members of the Brotherhood of Railroad Engineers, such as Uncle Ezra. Moreover, he was the first Santa Fe president with a non-technical background, which would not have inspired respect from the Brotherhood. He was a lawyer.

Grandpa Lomax remained a supporter of Gene Debs for President on the ticket of the American Socialist Party until Franklin Roosevelt captured his loyalty in 1932. I still remember the portrait of FDR that he displayed proudly in his living room throughout the next decade. People often said that FDR saved America from socialism, but the American Socialists, particularly Norman Thomas—who became the leader of the Socialist Party after the death of Eugene Debs—always claimed that he won election by stealing most of the socialist platform. That was an exaggeration, but there was much truth in the Thomas quip. I am reminded of the U.S. military commander in the Vietnam War who, referring to a city U.S. forces were bombarding, said, "We had to destroy it in order to save it."

In those days, people did not have mild opinions about FDR. He was either passionately loved or bitterly hated. My friend Tris (H. Tristram) Engelhardt is a professor of medical ethics at Baylor College of Medicine and a professor of philosophy at nearby Rice University. Tris, a fifth-generation German Catholic Texan (who can say, "die-amm yankee sumbitch"), remembers that his family's priest refused to give last rites to his grandfather until he had confessed whether he had voted for Roosevelt.

The process of writing about the family railroad history motivated me to delve further into the events that produced the well-known Ballad of Casey Jones. The legendary folk hero emerging from the Illinois Central Cannonball wreck carried a bit of tarnish for Mr. Casey: His staying with the train to stop it was heroic, but he was found solely responsible for the wreck. Here are portions of the Illinois Central Report of the accident:

> *Reports received to date indicate that Engineer Jones of the passenger train, who lost his life in the accident, was alone responsible for the accident as train No. 83 which was obstructing the main track at Vaughan sawing ["sawing" refers to side-tracking one train to let another through on the mainline or "passing" track] by train No. 26 was properly protected by [the] flagman, who had gone back a distance of 3000 feet, where he had placed torpedoes on the rail; then continued north a further distance of 500 to 800 feet, where he stood and gave signals to train No. l; which signals, however, were apparently not observed by Engineer Jones: nor is it believed he heard the explosion of the torpedoes as his train continued toward the station at a high rate of speed, notwithstanding the fact it was moving up a grade; collision occurring at a point 210 feet north of the north passing track switch. It is also stated that Engineer Jones of train No. l failed to sound the whistle for the station when passing the whistle board. … Flagman J. M. Newberry of No. 83 … signaled No. 1 to stop; and although the engineer of that train had a unobstructed view of the flagman for l l/2 miles, he failed to heed the signals, and the train was not stopped until the collision occurred.*
>
> *The explosion of the torpedo was heard by the crews of trains at Vaughan Station; by Fireman S. Webb (colored) on No. l, and by the postal clerks and baggageman on that train. Fireman Webb states that between Pickens and Vaughan Stations, after putting in a fire, he was called to the side of Engineer Jones … and they talked about the new whistle which had been put on the engine at Memphis; Jones stated that going into Canton it would arouse the people of the town. This was the first trip with the new whistle and Jones was much pleased with it.*
>
> *Fireman Webb states that after talking with Jones, he … heard the explosion of the torpedo … went to the gang-way on the Engineer's side and saw a flagman with red and white lights standing alongside the tracks … saw the markers*

of Caboose of No. 83 ... called to Engineer Jones that there was a train ahead, and feeling that the engineer would not be able to stop the train in time to prevent an accident, told him that he was going to jump off, which he did about 300 feet from the caboose of No. 83. ... He also states that had he or Engineer Jones looked ahead, they could have seen the flagman in ample time to have stopped before striking No. 83. ... Engineer Jones ... had a reasonably good record, ... not having been disciplined for the past three years. ... Jones' work up to the time of the accident had been satisfactory.

Upon reading the full report, it occurred to me that I might learn a lot more about my Grandpa Lomax if I could get access to old MOP railroad reports. So I emailed Ray State the following question: "I have noticed that the Illinois Central reports—at least for Casey Jones's wreck—contain information on the engineer's record; specifically, suspensions and the reason. Jones had nine suspensions, five to thirty days each for various infractions, but none for three years prior to his wreck. Is such detail common in any other reports?"

His response emphasized that it was unusual for internal railroad inquiry reports to be made public. In the Casey Jones wreck, the ballad was drafted immediately after the accident, and someone was motivated to make it available. At the time, the company inquiries into accidents remained private, along with the previous disciplinary record. In prior years, the Interstate Commerce Commission would have commented on these documents. Later, however, Commission policy changed and the matter was left to the railroads after an inquiry conclusion had been reached. As the records changed hands through bankruptcies and railroad mergers, very few of these records survived destruction.

Ray mentioned that discipline could be harsh in dealing with infractions of the rules: "Time lost to a train was [a] serious offence and would be a disciplinary measure as was running ahead of time, speeding, failure to read orders and forgetting to take your watch on duty. A watch that was not showing the correct time was also a serious offence.... The operating rules were complex and there was in most cases little infrastructure to aid the engineer...When the weather was bad or the engine wasn't steaming or one did not feel well then the slightest slip and a disaster was presented.... It is probable that the true position of the conditions existing in the first two decades of the 1900s will never be fully known."

Most major rail lines were single track, not double track as today. Hence, a train had to be sidetracked to accommodate oncoming trains, or those whose speeds overtook it. All this activity had to be coordinated manually by employee on-the-ground knowledge of schedules and accuracy-approved timepieces. There is little wonder that accidents were commonplace. The twins had left a far harder life experienced by their parents and prospered economically. They even had steady work during the Depression years, faring far better than was common for other working-class people.

I sent Ray State Grandpa's engine identification, MOP #1478 (see the accompanying 1937 picture of Grandpa and his train crew). After accessing an engine list, he replied that it was a huge locomotive, and that my grandfather would have achieved top MOP seniority in order to have gained the right to operate such a machine. Of course, to me he was just a regular guy who was thoughtful, well read, quiet, and very unassuming. He was also the guy who said that if there was anything to reincarnation, he hoped to return as "a bull out there in the pasture with all those heifers." It was a neat ending to my explorations, and a remarkable, if only tiny, bit of Americana and family railroad lore.

Enjoying myself, I was reluctant to end my explorations. So I googled "Railroad history, engine list, 1937, Missouri Pacific 1478," and I hit pay dirt. At the top of the list was the Denver library Web site, and there, in the midst of a long series of Missouri Pacific engine-train pictures, appeared a shot of number 1478—"mighty tall and handsome"—at work five years after my grandfather's retirement. The picture, taken on October 18, 1942, displays number 1478 "Eastbound near Pueblo, Colorado pulling 38 cars" [short by contemporary standards in which 100 car trains are commonplace powered by 2 to 4 diesel engines]. Number 1487 was a locomotive type 2-8-2 whose configuration was known as the "Mikado" which, according to Wikipedia, "saw great success in the United States, mostly as a freight locomotive." The "class name 'Mikado' would become a popular English name for things Japanese in the nineteenth century, such as the Emperor of Japan. Also, the Gilbert and Sullivan opera *The Mikado* had premiered in 1885, and achieved great popularity in both Britain and America."

Gilbert and Sullivan were part of my childhood, so there will be more to be said about them later (Fig. 1.1).

Fig. 1.1 MOP engine 1478 Grandpa Lomax center right and crew in 1937

Part I

Beginings and Launching

I, too, was blessed by not being protected by child labor laws. B-29s – Dad flew 29s, as a flight engineer, and was based in the Mariana Islands, actually on Tinian. He had pictures of them loading the big one. He flew many missions over Japan – some through typhoons which pulled damn near all the rivets out of those 29s. The experience left him a life-long pacifist.
—Steve Hanke, email letter sent to me dated May 30, 2010; later he slightly edited the text in giving me permission to quote him.

Candace, "Why the traffic delay? Cabdriver, "Oh, somebody jumped off a building; it's common." "Why is that," asked Candace. "They have everything; and want for nothing."
—Conversation with a cab driver in Stockholm, 2004. Candace and I were bound for our hotel when traffic was diverted around a cordoned-off block.

What I have recorded in Chapter 1 is a reconstruction based on external documents, and a story I've only experienced through family lore. What I write now is indeed autobiographical re-visitation. Everything I write will be revisited dozens of times, sometimes for an hour, for a day, in Tucson, in Orange, in planes or hotel rooms, between meetings of some kind, but each time it involves accessing an inner world. It's like entering through a wardrobe of old memories, inaccessible unless I open those doors, pass through them, and close them behind me. I attend to nothing else, not noise or distractions, nor other thoughts remote from the experience of that world. It is satisfying, peaceful, spiritual, alive with feelings vibrant, present, yet otherworldly. Perhaps it is akin to what Sarah Flower Adams was experiencing when she wrote "Nearer My God to Thee." Or perhaps it is similar to what Arthur E. Hertzler, the famous Kansas surgeon meant, near the close of his book *The Doctor and His Patients* (1940), when he hears the strains of that hymn on a distant radio and feels "nearer my Agnes to thee." Agnes was his daughter and only child, who died on the surgery table in Hertzler's desperate attempt to save her life in flagrant violation of medical protocol. But, no other available surgeon was his equal.

2

You *Can* Go Home Again

The world stands out on either side
No wider than the heart is wide
Above the world is stretched the sky,
No higher than the soul is high.
The heart can push the sea and land
Farther away on either hand;
The soul can split the sky in two,
And let the face of God shine through.
But East and West will pinch the heart
That cannot keep them pushed apart;
And he whose soul is flat—the sky
Will cave in on him by and by.

—Edna St. Vincent Millay, *Renascence*

I was born Vernon Lomax Smith shortly after lunchtime in Wichita, Kansas, on January 1, 1927. Wichita is on the flat Kansas prairie, but it is peopled by souls who are anything but flat. And I come from my childhood not "as though it was my homeland," as I believe Antoine de Saint-Exupéry once said, but because it *is* my homeland. I have never had any other. In returning to it in memory, I discover myself anew.

It was good year, 1927. Babe Ruth hit his 60th home run on September 30. As a Red Sox fan, I find it hard to fathom that they sold Ruth's contract to the Yankees in 1920, and the next year he hit 59 home runs!

© The Author(s) 2018
V. L. Smith, *A Life of Experimental Economics, Volume I*,
https://doi.org/10.1007/978-3-319-98404-9_2

Georges Lemaître, the Belgian physicist and priest, derived the first model of the expanding universe, later to be known as the Big Bang. Also in 1927, Charles Lindbergh was the first to fly the Atlantic. And Julia Lee began her run as a locally popular Kansas City blues singer with her unique trademark songs like "King Sized Papa"; "Come On Over To My House"; "Snatch and Grab It." 1927 was the 200th anniversary year of the death of Isaac Newton.

I was the only one of my mother's three children born in a hospital. My older sisters had been born at home in Newton, Kansas. I was brought from the hospital to the home I would live in until our 1932 move to a Kansas farm. We would return from 1934 to 1945, and again for the summers of 1946 through 1949.

Let me guide you through the house of memories as it looked in those early years after I was born.

The house at 143 N. Sedgwick Avenue is modest, situated in the company of similar houses, on the west side of the tracks, and far smaller than I will richly remember it. Some might say that it was on the wrong side of those tracks, but I will be in high school before I fully appreciate the hierarchical social distinctions associated with house locations in the city, a topic that I will learn little about from my family. It is a home that will provide such warmth and opportunity for me that, decades later, I will still treasure it in memory and anticipate with suspense driving past it whenever I visit Wichita.

The house is on the west side of the street, facing east. You approach the front of the house on a paved walk. Next to the front porch, on either side of the walkway, are tall *Spirea* bushes with their large semispherical clusters of white blooms. You ascend steps to a roofed porch. The porch is ringed by a wood railing, with a swing on its right, and the front door in the center. Years later, the porch will be remodeled and the front steps moved to the driveway, the railing removed, and the porch screened. Walking through the front door, you enter the living room. You see my mother's old, but always tuned, solid walnut upright piano and bench on your left, facing north in the southeast corner. When you sit at the piano bench, there is a window on your left, bathing the piano and sheet music with daylight, even on one of those rare cloudy days in Kansas, a condition that has already attracted the attention of the great entrepreneurs who would make Wichita the world center of the light airplane industry. Sitting at that piano bench, I would learn left from right.

Children are not programmed to autonomic-ally acquire knowledge of left ver-sus right. It is not acquired naturally (without explicit instruction) in the same way that children learn up versus down, or, after age three, to add *s* to plu-ralize a regular noun in English (see S. Pinker, *The Language Instinct*, 1994). Sitting on that bench, I will make the associations from which I will learn left hand from right—a deliberate, conscious, memorization process—when taking piano lessons. "The left hand for the bass clef," I will think to myself, "is always by the window." Later, I will still identify, visualize, and remember "left" as being on the same side as the hand next to that window until, finally, I would internalize the memory and no longer relate it to the window.

Lifting the hinged lid on the piano bench, you find it stuffed with music by Mozart, Bach, Beethoven, Stephen Foster, and Hoagy Carmichael, as well as the complete scores of Mascagni's *Cavalleria Rusticana* (his only sig-nificant operatic success; you heard it's enchanting strains throughout much of Godfather III); and Gilbert and Sullivan's *HMS Pinafore* and *Pirates of Penzance*. These list in name only a few of my favorites from that treasure chest. Decades later, as I write my memoir, I will still have a wine box full of that music. If I pull out three of those yellowing old scores and read lines like, "I am the builder, come walk with me"; "I am the very model of a modern Major General…Stick close to your desk and never go to sea and you all may be rulers of the Queen's naiveee"; or, "When the deep purple falls over sleepy garden walls," the memory of that piano bench will be fresh and sharp. As a child, I am sitting on that bench in one of the picture inserts in this book.

Upon entering the front door, to the right on the north wall of the living room, is an open ceramic grated gas fireplace; a mantel; and glass-enclosed bookcases containing my father's set of rust-red Harvard Classics and the complementary black-bound set, the Harvard "shelf of fiction." My father had an eighth-grade education and has always needed to work long hours for a living. He aspired to read more, but he actually read little that was not related to earning a living. For me, however, these books will come to sym-bolize the immensity of the knowable, and I will keep them all my life. One of the Classics, volume 17—which contains tales by Grimm, Hans Christian Andersen, and Aesop—will become severely worn and frayed, its binding shredded as a result of my frequent readings.

In my early childhood years, I will think of libraries as infinite exten-sions of my father's bookcase that surely contain all that is known, and I will aspire to go to college because that is where one learns everything. I will believe that nothing is unknowable. One has only to seek knowledge. I will know little and be hungry to know more, but I will gradually learn that the action—all the learning and understanding—occurs in the pursuit of knowledge and that the questions multiply faster than the answers. Every answer sprouts multiple questions so that knowledge becomes an unending, never arriving, quest. Therein constitutes its charm and its challenge. I will learn that any three-year-old can force you to the outermost limits of your knowledge, on any topic, by asking, "Why?" three times in response to an answer. It is a sobering observation that all children pass through a short "repeat-why" stage, pressing to identify the borders of what is known, before they learn to stop asking and arbitrarily accept living with less, a state that I will find troubling again and again throughout my life, and find it unacceptable.

I will learn to read early and well, and Harvard Classics 17 will become one of my two childhood treasures. The other will be *Tal: His Marvelous Adventures with Noom-Zor-Noom* (1929, 1937, and 2001) by Paul Fenimore Cooper, whose great grandfather was James Fenimore Cooper, novelist of the American wilderness and devotee of liberty. I will read *Tal* to all my children, and this copy, as well, will come to have no binding left to dangle, so thoroughly will it be loved and enjoyed. My oldest daughter, Deborah, will name her son Tal (Taliesin). Sixty years after first reading *Tal*, I will conceive of the idea of having the book reprinted at my own expense, believing that no one else would have such an interest. I would procrastinate and be pleasantly surprised to discover that a third edition, inspired by the author's nephew, Henry S. F. Cooper Jr., appears in 2001, with an introduction bearing testimony to its loyal and dedicated readership. I will have no idea that I was far from alone in loving that book.

Fantasy is important to the child. Dreams are fashioned of fantasy, and out of dreams come the desire for adventure, the desire to learn, and ultimately the realization that learning to learn is what is most important. In dreams and fantasy, nothing is unattainable; this is not only a model for seeking, overcoming, and coming to know, but is also, and most importantly, a model for living.

To the left of the fireplace is a light oak open staircase that you ascend facing west, circling south. The staircase leads to a landing with a balcony overlooking the living room. Two or three years later, each night you might look down from that balcony and see my father standing in the living room, facing the bedrooms behind you, singing an Irish ballad for me just after I have retired to my bed upstairs. At the balcony landing, you turn and ascend to an upstairs landing. My bedroom is on the right, while my parents' bedroom is on the left, the doors always open. I will be raised by parents for whom nudity in the family will not be avoided as an embarrassment. There are no upstairs bathrooms, and the closets are very small, closely matching our budget for clothes, toys, and "things" generally. I will learn to design and make toys much as my father learned to design and make machine tools.

If you walk through the living room entryway, straight ahead through an archway, on the south side of the house, is the dining room, where my sisters, Billye and Aileen, and Billye's husband, Carl, would join my grandparents and me for Easter, Christmas, New Year's, birthday, and Thanksgiving feasts. . The woman with the most to give becomes the matriarch of any family. Family celebrations will almost always be at my mother's house, which seems to provide a natural equilibrium to which everyone wants to return.

As you continue west through the dining room—much light flows in through the window on your left—you see the kitchen straight ahead. In Kansas—almost anywhere in the temperate northern hemisphere, for that matter—the primary living areas of the house should face south, thereby allowing the low-elevation winter sun to flood through the windows for warmth and good cheer, but ensuring that those same windows will be shaded from the blazing summer sun, high in the sky. I will eventually have children, and my youngest daughter, Torrie, and her husband, Jim, will use that principle in locating their first "earth ship" (off the grid) home in Colorado's San Luis Valley, with a window wall facing almost south but rotated 15 degrees east to catch the light and warmth of the winter sun at the moment it rises over the Sangre de Cristo Mountains on a bitter winter morning.

In the far right corner of the dining room is a door that leads to a hallway. Across that hall is the only bathroom in the house and down the hall to the left is the door to the downstairs bedroom in the northwest corner of the house. After you enter the kitchen from the dining room, you see a door on your right that also enters that corner bedroom. At times, the downstairs bedroom will be occupied by a sister, a sister and husband, or either of my two grandparents living with us between moves, or sometimes for extended periods to save somebody money.

I will be the lone family member to escape living constantly in each other's pockets. That will shape my view of the importance of children's desire for independence, a view that will inadvertently contribute to my children's resentment. More generally in this regard, however, is the fact that I will grow up to be a loner, protecting myself from distractions, but thereby projecting an image of aloofness that was never part of what I felt inside.

In the southwest corner of the kitchen is a built-in dinette nook. I will come to love that nook because it is like a restaurant booth with built-in wood benches. I will be nine years old before I know what it is like to eat in a restaurant.

If it is a hot summer day, the "evaporative cooler" may be set up and running in the middle of the kitchen floor, or in the dining room or living room. The cooler consists of an ancient oscillating fan with a line strung between two chairs on which wet tea towels hang. The air blowing from the fan evaporates the water from the towels and cools the room. This is an effective air cooler in 1930s Kansas, with its single-digit humidity, but the towels require frequent re-soaking. You cannot help but notice that our "tea towels" are made of cotton flour bags. We were poor, I would later discover, and lived by the maxim "Waste not, want not."

Straight ahead, across the kitchen to the right, are a door and a stairway leading down to a landing. To the right of the door is an icebox (fifty-, seventy-five-, or hundred-pound blocks of ice are delivered regularly by the iceman, who wears a leather vest and uses ice tongs to carry the blocks on his shoulder)—which years later will be replaced by a round, coil-top Frigidaire. For decades thereafter, refrigerators of all makes will be called Frigidaire. From the landing below, you can either go through a back door to the west or descend a staircase facing east into the basement, where I will often play with friends during inclement weather, make toys, and constantly tinker with mechanical and electrical things. This is where I will discover a miracle of sorts: I will disassemble, piece by piece, a discarded alarm clock that no longer operates, then put it all together again, and it will start running. As I will learn much later, it was no miracle; my disassembly and reassembly simply reduced, for a time, the coefficient of static friction in the gears and bearings.

If you walk through the rear door to the backyard, immediately behind the screen door on your right is my mother's trellis, heavy with the ripe, rich smell of honeysuckle, and buzzing with bees that will never bother to sting me. At age seventy-six, I will read an entry in my mother's diary dated February 26, 1944: "Had a man working in yard; tore down the old Honeysuckle trellis—been there 22 years; hated to see it go but needed it no longer." [Re-reading the diary in early February 2018, I find the entry, "Verne (my father) and I went to see M. Curie in eve. Marvelous picture— Greer Garson and Walter Pidgeon." I called my wife, Candace, she found it we watched and Mom was right!]

A few years later, while I am still very young, if it is a hot summer night, my mother may put a pallet of blankets on the thick Bermuda grass so that I can sleep, cool, and comfortable under the stars, after watching the fireflies flit about and being sung to sleep by the "locusts," or cicadas. Still later, when we can afford one, I will sleep on a canvas cot in the yard. In either case, the cost in aggravation will be no more than a few chigger bites.

Behind the trellis, with full southern exposure, is the trademark Midwestern backyard three-wire clothesline.

To the left, just outside the rear door, is a walkway to the garage, just big enough for one car, a manual lawn mower, and hand gardening tools. Due west of the back door, behind the clothesline, is a chicken yard running from left of center to the right side property line. The corner gate to the chicken yard is behind and northwest of the garage. The gap between the garage and the chicken yard gives access to a space somewhat wider than the garage; just behind it, there is space for a garden.

You will wonder why there is a large chopping block behind the garage with a big axe stuck into it. That is for dispatching one of the chickens for a Sunday or special occasion dinner. Behind the garden, at the very back of the long, narrow lot, is an alley traversing most of the block. Behind the garden, on the Fourth of July, my playmates and I will use firecrackers to blast roadways for our toy cars. In the late 1930s, it is here that we will use our homemade beanies to launch July 4th cherry bombs so that they explode high above us.

One day, it will become my chore every Saturday to clean the chicken coop: scrape up the excrement on the night roosts, rake up the straw on the floor, sprinkle lye on the floor and roosts to control bacteria growth, and scatter clean new straw. Each day, I will also gather fresh eggs from the nests, replenish the feeding trays with grain at feeding time, and fill the watering trays. Sometimes, I will help my mother by carrying the basket of damp clothes upstairs from the basement into the backyard to the clothesline, and I will help my father mow the lawn until I learn to do it on my own (Figs. 2.1, 2.2, 2.3, and 2.4).

Fig. 2.1 My house, 143 N. Sedgwick

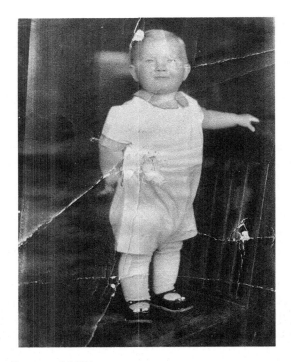

Fig. 2.2   Vernon first stand 1927

Fig. 2.3   Mom, dad below oak stairway landing to bedrooms

Fig. 2.4 Billye, Aileen, Mom

3

Enter My Father

When large numbers of laborers are unable to find jobs, unemployment results.

Attributed to Calvin Coolidge[1]

It's a truth, if a cliché, to say that fortune smiled broadly for us all when my father, Vernon Chessman Smith (1890–1954), a machinist who had apprenticed in Cleveland, Ohio, met my mother, Lulu Belle (Lomax) Bougher (1896–1957), in Wichita and was delighted to find a warm and caring woman who already had a family. They met at a dance, I know not when, and were married on August 16, 1921, three years after Grover was killed. A simple and beautiful entry in my mother's diary, dated August 16, 1944, states,

Our 23rd wedding; thought of it Monday—forgot it today. Vern remembered today. A wonderful 23 years. I love him.

In this book, I write often of my parents and what kind of people they were, but this closet diary entry, a private and unadorned personal message of affirmation, says almost everything of importance.

My mother often mentioned that she had not intended to have any more children, but my father so loved children, particularly her two young daughters, that she came to view it as unthinkable not to have a child by him. I

---

[1]John Ise, *Economics*. New York: Harper & Brothers, Revised edition, 1950, p. 388.

© The Author(s) 2018
V. L. Smith, *A Life of Experimental Economics, Volume I*,
https://doi.org/10.1007/978-3-319-98404-9_3

was born some five years and four months after they were married. If I had been a girl, my name would have been Verna. Billye and Aileen often said that they never thought of my father as a stepfather.

My father had two siblings. His brother, Norman (1888–1946), was a wildcat driller who followed their father, a "tool dresser," into the oil fields, and a younger sister, Harriet Izella Smith (1892–1918), who died in the great flu epidemic of 1918, two months after Grover Bougher widowed the woman who would become my mother. Norman had one child, Bill Smith, my only first cousin, whom I have never met.

I have only a few memories of my first five years in Wichita. When I was nine months old, we acquired a fox terrier puppy, named after Gloria Swanson, the actress. Glory was my constant companion until she died of old age when I was sixteen, and I experienced my last childhood tears— those since are a man's and are even more essential. My earliest memory is of watching passersby from our front yard, with Glory at my side. Sitting by me, she would bark fiercely at any stranger; alone, she would ignore them entirely.

I vividly recall seeing my neighbor, Max Clark, about four or five years my senior, departing for school or returning to his home next door. He, and later I, attended Martinson Elementary School, which was only a few blocks from our homes. Max was athletic and handsome. As a teenager, he became an accomplished baseball pitcher, with a great mix of fast-breaking curves, a sinker, and a fluttering knuckleball. He became my hero and a role model to me. I was a pitcher, too, and I played in the same American Legion Baseball League. I was younger, though, and played in the Junior League.

I watched intently when Max practiced with his catcher, Ed Hullitt. My catcher, Jimmy Randall, lived just across the street with his older brother Jack.

The league often played at Cessna Field, next to the Cessna Aircraft Plant on West Second Street, about half a mile from where we lived. I remember watching Max play for his team, the Trojans. Runners were on base, and Max was in the process of drawing an intentional walk. Defiantly, he hit a home run, but the umpire claimed that Max had reached (stepped) across the plate to hit a high outside pitch, and the runners were called back. That led to a really emotional argument.

Max joined the Air Force about 1940 and became a pilot flying the Lockheed P-38 Lightning, a very hot twin-engine, single-seat pursuit fighter. He became an exceptional pilot and was assigned a commission as an instructor during most of the war. Late in the war, however, as the fighting intensified after the Allied invasion of Europe, Max was transferred to a fighting squadron. In preparation for action, he needed to update his gunnery training. He was killed on a domestic practice sortie when his aircraft encountered mechanical problems, and he was unable to bail out. My mother made the following diary entry on February 15, 1945: "Word came yesterday that Max Clark was killed in training. Oh God! Will it never end?" Just a year earlier, on January 18, 1944, she had already written, "Darlene Clark's [Max's sister's] husband going across [to Europe]," and on January 24, "Word has come that Dean Vetten was killed in Italy Dec. 20; as a navigator on B24." Dean was a childhood playmate of mine and a classmate through twelve grades. Again, on July 5: "Darlene's husband has been wounded—hospitalized in Italy."

For many years, the war would touch every life in America.

Many years later, with my wife, Candace, I would visit the Smithsonian Air Museum near Dulles airport. No air museum worth its salt would be without a Lockheed P-38 Lightning on display, and I anticipated finding that sleek, beautiful flying machine. In spite of that, I was unprepared for the tears that flowed as I stood, entranced, my eyes riveted on that plane, acutely aware that Max had died in the same machine, sixty years earlier. The plane seemed less sleek, less beautiful than I had anticipated, and I just stood there, alone, wondering what Max's last minutes of terror were like, until the tears gradually receded and I was ready to move on. With trepidation, I made my way to the B-29 display, expecting to see one of the planes that I helped to make. It was the Enola Gay, the B-29 that dropped the bomb on Hiroshima and ushered in a changed world. I was relieved to see that it had been manufactured by Martin, not Boeing. Some other kid had helped to make the instrument that delivered such destruction and pain. I still remember one of the news items after the defeat of Japan: Near the impact point of the bomb, a human's "shadow" had been "fire-stenciled" into the sidewalk. Shit!

In January 1932, at age five, I began kindergarten at Martinson Elementary. We all liked our teacher, Miss Pontius, and looked forward to the trademark graham crackers and milk on which we snacked at recess. Yet the only lesson I recall was being taught to "tell time." There was an old-fashioned round-faced alarm clock on the table at the front of the room. Each day Miss Pontius called a child to the front of the room to announce the time in hours and minutes. Then, Miss Pontius asked where the hands would be pointing if it were noon, or 6:00, or some different time—that was our only test. There was no homework, but for my children kindergarten homework was standard.

I once opened the rear door of our 1927 Oldsmobile and stepped smack in the middle of a chocolate cake that my mother had put there to keep it from sliding off the seat. She had planned to deliver it to Don Eaton's first restaurant next door to Lloyd's Barber Shop, near the northeast corner of Meridian and Douglas. Don was a restaurateur who had been known to my family for many years. Throughout the 1930s, my mother home-baked desserts that Don bought for his restaurant—beautiful cakes and cream pies—for a quarter each, or by slice for a nickel. My mother baked cakes for several restaurants, but Don, her largest and most loyal customer, raved about her baking skills and spread word to other owners. You cannot imagine the flavor of her chocolate devil's food, the best of her most frequent bakes. It had that deep, rich, "death by chocolate" shine and the spectacular taste to go with it.

Many wonderful memories stem from my privilege of eating one ice cream cone per week. Every Thursday, I was given a nickel to buy an ice cream cone from the ice cream man—later known as the "Good Humor man"—but I don't recall being aware of that designation. I remember sitting on the curb in the street listening, watching, and waiting anxiously. Ice cream was so good.

When I was learning to talk, I could not pronounce one of my first words, *spoon*. Instead, I said, "*Sa-poon.*" My sisters would instruct: "Vernon, it's not *sa-poon*, it's *spoon*. Now say it," and I would say, "*Sa-poon.*" "No, say *ssss.*" So I said, "*Ssss.*" "Good, now say *poon*," and I said, "*Poon.*" "So now say *sssspoon.*" And I said, "*Ssss-apoon.*" "NO!" They tried repeatedly without success.

So much for a rational constructivist attempt to teach natural language. As I think Yogi Berra should have said, "If you're not ready, you're not ready." Natural language acquisition proceeds on a neurobiological timetable as predictable as the loss and replacement of baby teeth, and the less certain production of third molars.

I still have all my wisdom teeth, in spite of suggestions from dentists, beginning with the first appearance of my third molars at age nineteen, that they were large, would be hard to keep clean, and should be pulled. My dental adviser was always Carl Snell, longtime husband of my oldest sister, a dental laboratory technician and skilled professional who mistrusted all dentists for whom he fabricated bridges and sets of false teeth. He told me that you should never pull a healthy tooth, and that he had anchored many a partial plate on wisdom teeth. It was good advice, and to this day, I insist that dentists justify any of their proposals to work on my teeth. If they suggest pulling one, I just reply that I hire dentists to save teeth, not pull them. I also avoid routine full-mouth dental X-rays. When a dentist says that it's time for my "regular" X-ray, I say that I am not a regular X-ray patient. "The risk is negligible." I reply, "Then why does your assistant cover the patient with lead and leave the room?" Silence. I once had a dentist who was so pissed off that he sent me a letter to sign and absolve him of all liability for his work because he could only X-ray me after I heard his reasoning and approved his request. So he got himself fired. Some don't seem to understand that I hire them as consultants, and I am not obligated to follow their advice. This has a cost: Recently, I experienced a molar decay that could have been detected earlier with X-rays. One in 60 years is good odds for saving all that X-ray exposure, and I still did not lose the tooth. I have a great dentist, who respects my bizarre views. He understands that at my age, in ownership of all my teeth, I can afford to risk losing one!

No wonder the healthcare system is perpetually in bad economic straits. The supplier is in the enviable position of recommending what the customer should buy and then proceeding to supply it. Moreover, when a third-party prepaid payer is added through insurance, there is no economic equilibrium, and healthcare costs spiral out of control. I've described the problem more fully elsewhere. (See my "The ABC Dilemma of Health Reform," *Wall Street Journal*, October 16, 2009)

Why is it so difficult to find the private and public means, that combination of markets and government assistance, to enable better healthcare outcomes to emerge? This question has a simple answer that plagues health care everywhere. The healthcare provider, A, is in the position of recommending to the patient, B, what B should buy from A. A third party—whether the insurance company or the government—is reimbursing A for it. This structure defines an incentive nightmare. When phrased in this way, you do not have to be an economist to realize that nobody knows how to solve this problem. Hence the many experiments, all of which have been deemed unsatisfactory.

I don't know whether this problem has a solution. If it does, I think it requires us to find mechanisms whereby third-party payment is made to the patient, who in turn pays the provider, supplemented with any co-payment from the patient who has skin in the game, and an incentive to shop. Hence, from the moment a patient seeks services, both provider and patient know who is paying for the service. Each party wants what the other brings to the table. Patient control of payment and re-imbursement better nurtures the relationship between patient and provider. Most important, the patient is empowered to become better informed about the services recommended by various providers, and the providers might find it particularly important to build good reputations with patients. The same principle applies to those of us involved in the delivery of public education and to escalating education costs. Higher education does much better than lower because students can choose among colleges, private and public, which provides some measure of discipline. Perhaps there is some restraint in the medical profession arising from the Hippocratic Oath, which seeks to limit the delivery of iatrogenic (physician-induced illness) treatments. The maxim dictates, "first, do no harm." In public education and health care, the seller recommends to the buyer what should be bought, and a third party—government or a regulated insurance company—pays for it. This tells you everything necessary to understand their economic problems, and why medical and education costs rise so much faster, year after year, than other commodities and services. If these problems have solutions, they will surely involve reimbursing the customer directly via insurance claims, coupled with consumers taking more responsibility to become better informed. This would be equivalent to giving vouchers to the customer, in the form of payment allowances for the ailment. Vouchers, together with any additional personal funds, can be used to shop around for a doctor. Only in this way might it be possible to orient suppliers toward customers rather than toward the payer. It's simple: He who pays the piper calls the tune.

Wichita was a treasured home that my friends and family could not escape. Home was important to me. I left, and yet I carried it with me everywhere. Why?

My mother often said that when I began talking, I used the pronoun *my*, rather than *I* or *me*, when referring to myself. In particular, instead of saying, "Let me do it," I said, "My do it." (Hence, the title of Chapter 1) "My" is possessive. A thing could be mine, such as "my toy truck," so why could not an action of doing or deciding be mine as well? In the normal course of language development, I stopped saying *my*, but then began saying, "Dingy do it." I started calling myself Dingy all the time and soon everybody in the family, thinking that it was cute as all hell, started to call me Dingy. My mother put a stop to it, however, telling my smirking sisters and grandparents that she would not tolerate it, not wanting me to be known as Dingy.

I am in the back of the Oldsmobile. It's a cold day, but I roll the window down. My sister says, "Vernon, it's too cold, now roll the window up." I do nothing. She reaches over and rolls the window up. I roll it down. She rolls it up. I sit there and the car starts moving. Shortly thereafter, I roll the window down and she rolls it up. "Dad, make him stop." Now I sit still, but with my hand on the knob, and soon I roll it down some. She rolls it up. My hand is on the knob, and I move it down ever so slightly, watching her. I see no reaction, so I inch it down just a wee bit more, and then still more. Here comes the outburst. "Stop it." I do, but she rolls the window up, and so on.

I am said by some to have symptoms of Asperger's Syndrome, but more on that later. When my mind is immersed in concentrated thought—mentalese, or composition mode—all my circuits seem to be sharply focused on that experiential world of mental creation, and I cannot switch out of it and into something different without the complete loss of those self-ordered trains of thought that make for coherence. I lose the emerged state of whole-vision unity, and later, if I reestablish that mental state, it is only after a considerable start-up cost in mental time and energy. Afterward, I have a lingering sense of permanent loss in recovering only an approximation of my initial comprehension. As I write this autobiography, I return to each earlier experience and relive, with total absorption, the sequence of experiences within each of those self-contained worlds. I am almost completely unaware of my surroundings as I move through these long-past historical sequences, which are alive and well in my mind. But it's the same when I write or mentalize about anything else.

The psychologist who gave me a battery of psych tests in 1995 thought that I probably had the celebrated disease of the 1990s, Attention Deficit Hyperactive Disorder (ADHD). Perhaps this was correct. I have always had a substantial problem switching out of concentration mode, diverting my attention to something else, and then switching back. In time this mental "deficiency," or characteristic, earned me a reputation as an absent father with my children—particularly the three oldest—and my former wives. I married Candace after I began the self-examination that led to the psychological evaluation. She has been tolerant in accepting my mental handicap. Occasionally, however, I still have to remind her that she has to think of me as handicapped. I became aware of this deficiency only because people pointed it out, reporting that I was "not there," or that they felt they had to serve as my "social interpreter." I was never able to relate my experience and memory to any of those external reports. I do not recognize myself in those descriptions, but the psych tests do confirm that I have a switching problem. Perhaps mental hyper-focus is an unconsciously learned avoidance response to the high switching cost of ADHD brains.

It is a good working hypothesis that the performance properties of every mental characteristic are realizations from a frequency distribution across such individual traits in the population. In the tails of certain jointly distributed genetic and phenotype characteristics, one observes phenomena described as Asperger Syndrome, bipolar disorder, schizophrenia, autism, and so on, and all but this very small percentage carry sub-clinical manifestations of those properties to a highly variable degree. Hence, the notion that there exists a stochastic order in which one of Einstein's sons is schizophrenic and his second cousin has autism. There is good evidence from twin studies that these properties have both inheritable and experiential components.

My mother, her father (according to Billye), and her youngest daughter, Aileen, were afflicted by symptoms of depression. Mother and Aileen were treated for it, and Aileen's only son was schizophrenic by his early twenties and spent almost all his life trapped in state mental institutions. I was never depressed—at least never for more than a few minutes and neither, I believe, was Billye, with whom I became very close in the last twenty years of her life. I have, however, had the feeling that I could easily become depressed if I do not begin a new project after having just finished the last. My work style is to have several projects that I cycle through, back and forth, so that if one is finished there are still others in process. Currently (2008), for example, I am writing two books, and from time to time I spend several days away from both, expanding an article or a lecture that was liked well enough to motivate me to write it up in full.

The great poet Kahlil Gibran wrote, "Work is love made visible." Perhaps that is why work is an effective form of continuous therapy.

During the Christmas season, the city of Wichita always put colored lights and tinsel on a large pine tree on "The Hill" at the confluence of the south and north forks of the Arkansas River, referred to locally as the Big and Little Arkansas Rivers. (I do not know why Wichitans pronounced Arkansas *Arkansas,* complete with audible final *s,* when referring to the rivers and to Arkansas City, but *Arkan-saw* when referring to the state. Speaking of that river confluence, it was part of local folklore that the Indians claimed that a tornado would never strike Wichita because it was located at the junction of two rivers. (To my knowledge none has, but probably no city in tornado alley is particularly likely to be hit.) The tree was a great focus of my attention, and I am told that I stood in the front seat of the car when I was two years old looking eagerly for the Christmas tree, and that I shouted, "Tisten-tee, daddy, tisten-tee," over and over when it came into view.

My father's study of voice led him to develop a considerable repertoire of songs about which I will have more to say. There was a period, probably when I was between two and five, when at bedtime he sang me a song. I remember being ushered upstairs to my bedroom at 7:00 p.m. After mom tucked me in, he stood below the balcony downstairs in the living room and sang—often it was an Irish ballad. I learned many of these songs, and I know fragments of them still.

Mother Machree

There's a spot in my heart which no colleen may own.
There's a depth in my soul never sounded or known.
There's a place in my memory, my life that you fill.
No other can take it, no one ever will.
Sure, I love the dear silver that shines in your hair,
and the brow that's all furrowed, and wrinkled with care.
I kiss the dear fingers so toil worn for me.
Oh, God bless you and keep you, Mother Machree.
Every sorrow or care in the dear days gone by,
was made bright by the light of the smile in your eye.
Like a candle that's set in a window at night,
your fond love has cheered me, and guided me right.
Sure I love the dear silver that shines in your hair,
and the brow that's all furrowed and wrinkled with care.
I kiss the dear fingers so toil worn for me.
Oh, God bless you and keep you, Mother Machree.

Anticipating my father's tenor voice put me in a mood to sleep, in spite of my great resistance to going to bed. I remember wanting to go to bed much later than bedtime, which always interrupted something I had going. I think that set the stage for me to feel irritation when I am in deep mentalese and someone succeeds in diverting my attention. Bedtime was one of those fixed rules that my mother enforced, ostensibly because children need sleep. In later years, however, she confessed that, "Parents have to live too."

I still have dad's word-prompts for the solos he performed, cribbed on three-by-five cards in my mother's familiar handwriting, cards that his large hands easily covered while he sang.

My father was a machinist for the Bridgeport Machine Company prior to 1932. I do not know when he started to work for Bridgeport, but according to the Tihen Notes in the *Wichita Beacon*, it opened July 25, 1922. The plant had been built in the 1880s by the Burton Stock Car Company, which made railroad cars. Eventually, the Burton Company closed, and the buildings were used to make the first Wichita automobile—the Jones Light Six—at the turn of the century. Jones invited Clyde Cessna to build the first two airplanes in Wichita in 1916 and 1917 as part of a promotion for his automobile. In 1927, Stearman Aircraft took over the original Burton facility to manufacture airplanes, but soon left for new facilities. The Bridgeport Machine Company operated there until April 3, 1940, when they were replaced by Culver Aircraft. Later, after World War II, the rapidly expanding Coleman Company used those buildings as its north plant.

According to the online In Flight USA Aviation History: "In 1929, Al (Mooney)…start(ed) a company of his own in Wichita, Kansas, the 'Air Capital City' – already home to Swallow, Cessna, Stearman and Walter Beech's Travel Air, the largest civilian plane maker of that year. Mooney opened shop in the old Burton Car Works (then the factory of his backer, Bridgeport Machine Co.) – the same plant where Clyde Cessna built Wichita's first plane and Lloyd Stearman began his company. …the stock-market crash of 1929 ushered in the Great Depression, and the collapse of American industry, including aviation. Mooney was bankrupted…"

The sturdy walls of "Bridgeport" housed Burton, Jones, Stearman, Mooney, Coleman, and Culver in sequence—entrepreneurs all. I remember clearly the great buffalo (sic *Bison*) billboard mounted atop the Bridgeport Plant, visible, one weekend, as my father and I turned east off US 81 North and approached the plant where he worked. I once had a treasured pocket knife with that same *Bison* symbol on it.

In 1932, my father was laid off for lack of work and became one of the many who fitted Cal Coolidge's definition of unemployment. The three of us moved to the farm near Milan (pronounced *mile-n,* not *mil-awn*—and certainly not *mil-awno*), Kansas. My two older sisters remained in Wichita. Aileen was finishing high school, living with her grandparents not far from Wichita High School North. Billye left high school and married Carl in 1931, at age seventeen. Billye's early marriage, as well as my mother's at sixteen, illustrates how my family had four-generation portraits before I became a teenager. Eventually, I learned from my mother that grandma had urged her to marry Grover not long after they began dating. Mother's strong impression was that grandma wanted the additional freedom that her daughter's marriage would give her (Figs. 3.1 and 3.2).

Fig. 3.1 Dad a new father

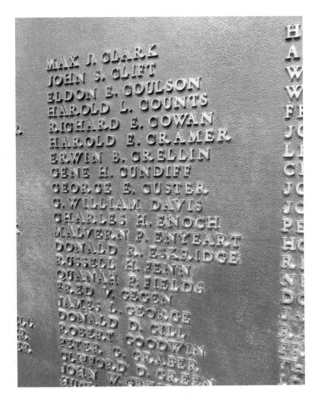

Fig. 3.2   Max Clark childhood neighbor and idol killed in p-38

4

From City Lights to Starlight

A Fire-Mist and a planet,
A crystal and a cell,
A jelly-fish and a saurian,
And caves where the cave-men dwell;
Then a sense of law and beauty,
And a face turned from the clod,
Some call it evolution,
And others call it God.

A haze on the far horizon,
The infinite tender sky,
The ripe, rich tint of the cornfields,
And the wild geese sailing high,
And all over upland and lowland,
The charm of the golden rod,
Some of us call it Autumn,
And others call it God.

Like tides on a crescent sea-beach,
When the moon is new and thin,
Into our hearts high yearnings
Come welling and surging in,
Come from the mystic ocean,
Whose rim no foot has trod,
Some of us call it Longing,
And others call it God.

© The Author(s) 2018
V. L. Smith, *A Life of Experimental Economics, Volume I*,
https://doi.org/10.1007/978-3-319-98404-9_4

A picket frozen on duty,
A mother starved for her
Brood.
Socrates drinking the hemlock,
And Jesus on the rood;
And millions who humble and
nameless,
The straight hard pathway plod,
Some of us call it Consecration,
And others call it God.

—W. H. Carruth, *Each in His Own Tongue*

Of all the persons ... whom nature points out for our peculiar beneficence, there are none to whom it seems more properly directed than to those whose beneficence we have ourselves already experienced. Nature, ... which formed men for their mutual kindness, so necessary for their happiness, renders every man the peculiar object of kindness, to the persons to whom he himself has been kind.

—Adam Smith, *The Theory of Moral Sentiments*

After my mother and father were married, they parted with some of the life insurance money from Grover's fatal Santa Fe train accident and invested in a farm, roughly forty-five miles from Wichita. The farm was to become our sole means of survival in the difficult years 1932 (when I was age five) to 1934. Except for occasional visits by sisters and grandparents, dad, mom, and I lived alone. Grandma Lomax built a small house behind the main farmhouse, but her stay was very short. We were not a seasoned farm family— my father was a machinist, not a plowman—but the justification for taking up farming was that we could at least grow most of our food and participate in a subsistence economy.

We became part of a reverse migration from urban to rural areas that has been discovered in migration statistics to have occurred at many times and places, though the overall trend is in the other direction. For example, during the last half of the twentieth century, Alaska experienced a net out-migration from the rural villages to the urban and regional centers. Essentially, this is because of the greater employment opportunities in cities than in villages, where unemployment is high. But paradoxically, as I learned from Lee Husky, a professor at the University of Alaska in Anchorage, some people still move to the villages. Part of the explanation is that people reduce their dependence on wage income by engaging in hunting, fishing, and trapping. If employment conditions are hard in the cities, it's possible to move to a rural area where employment prospects are even worse, but where one can live without wages by subsisting on wild foods. My family hunted rabbits, grew vegetables, picked fruit, and canned much of our food needs for winter consumption.

The farm brought new dimensions of hard work and hard times for my parents, but also survival for two years during a time when there was no acceptable alternative. Farming near Milan was not yet hydrolyzed, electrolyzed, or mechanized, and neither was our house, which had no indoor drinking water, no electricity, no central heating, and no indoor toilet.

We lifted drinking and cooking water from a well, located thirty to forty feet outside the kitchen door, using a stand-up hand pump and a galvanized bucket. In bad weather, we avoided leaving the protection of the house unless necessary. We tried to anticipate bad weather and carry enough water into the kitchen to last until better weather arrived, but in Kansas that was a crapshoot. We had a cistern that collected roof runoff water, but that was undrinkable because of the critters that collected in it. Rather, a small pantry room off the kitchen had a table-mounted hand pump that enabled water to be drawn from the cistern and heated for washing and mopping. The cistern contained "soft" rainwater, which made good suds for washing and cleaning things in an age when detergents did not exist and the standard bar soaps needed all the help they could get. My mother always used rainwater to wash her hair. If she had to use "hard" water, as she did when we lived in the city, she added lemon juice or vinegar.

For washing (pronounced *warshing* in Kansas) clothes, my mother always used Procter and Gamble laundry bar soap—which was much cheaper than soap flakes—she cut it into pieces with a paring knife. She used a washboard to scrub dirty clothes by hand, without rubber gloves. She used hand cream whenever we could afford it, and I do not recall her fingers ever looking "toil worn," as in "Mother Machree." We all bathed once a week, every Saturday—a strict rule, whether we thought we needed it or not—in a heavy-gauge galvanized tub, after water had been heated on the stove. In warm weather, the tub of water was often left in the sun until it warmed up and then moved under one of the fruit trees so that it wouldn't burn our hides.

All laundered clothes were squeezed damp-dry through two adjustable rollers operated by a hand crank. We dropped them damp in a clothes basket, and when it was full we carried it through the kitchen to an outdoor clothesline which consisted of three parallel heavy-gauge wires, strung between the cross T's atop two poles anchored in the ground. Before hanging the first batch of clothes, we had to clean the accumulated film of rust and dust off each wire. Otherwise, the freshly cleaned clothes were stained wherever they were pinched around the wire by the clothespins. We wiped each wire clean by wrapping a coarse cloth around the wire, squeezing it in a fist, and walking the twenty-foot or so length of the line. Then we folded the gunk on the cloth to the inside to clean the next wire and so forth.

It was so dry, clear, and sunny in Kansas during the 1930s that my mom's clothes-drying routine was as follows: She filled one of the outside wires with clothes; next, she moved to the middle wire; and finally, filled the remaining wire. Then she returned to the first wire and felt the clothes. Sheets, shirts, flour-sack towels, and other such lightweight cotton items were already dry. She took them down and put them back in the empty clothes basket, by which time the pants, towels, and other cotton items would often have dried.

With no electricity on the farm, indoor lighting depended on the use of what everyone called "coal oil" lamps, which they were not. These were the lamps one often sees in old antique stores, which have been used to model electric lamps to give them a period feel—a feel that I am sure my mother could not relate to very warmly, as she worked very hard on that farm, but if there were complaints, I have no memory of them.

Two decades later, I would learn that it was not "coal oil" that we burned in those lamps, as my parents and grandparents always called it, but kerosene made from petroleum. Still later, I would learn that "coal oil" derives originally from a process invented in the 1840s by a Nova Scotian medical doctor, Abraham Gesner, who was looking for a mineral oil to use as an illuminant. By distilling lumps of coal, he produced a clear liquid that produced a clear white light in an oil lamp equipped with a flat absorbent wick. The product was costly, but cheaper and far superior to the smoky light produced from burning whale and other animal and vegetable oils, which were commonly used at the time. He called his fuel "kerosene" and founded the Kerosene Gaslight Company in Halifax, Nova Scotia. Coal, however, as the source of kerosene would last only until petroleum was discovered and became a far cheaper source for lamp oil. But the name "coal oil" persisted into the 1930s.

By the 1840s, the cost of whale oil for lamps had climbed as sperm whales became scarce. By 1859, more than fifty companies in the USA were manufacturing kerosene from coal, and they were thriving in the competition with more costly whale oil. A plant in Pennsylvania produced six thousand gallons a day. Even so, the demand for kerosene drove the price from seventy-five cents to two dollars per gallon, setting the economic stage for the first oil well in Titusville, Pennsylvania, in 1859, where the Seneca Indians and later settlers had long skimmed oil from Oil Creek. Kerosene was distilled from the oil, and this far cheaper source of lamp oil rapidly wiped out the "coal oil" industry.[1]

If only presidents, congressmen, the Department of Energy, and political environmentalists like Paul Ehrlich could understand that when the price is right, there is no problem extracting fuel from coal, the sun, wind, fuel cells, or shale (the early settlers learned from the Indians how to heat western shale rock to "sweat" lamp oil out of the rock, a far cheaper source than hauling in whale oil from the coast). Expect no long-term shortages of energy over the next two hundred years, any more than there have been in the last two hundred, because demand will respond to price changes, inducing substitution and innovations to economize on the higher-cost scarce materials. As Julian Simon's remarkably clear scholarship demonstrates, the long-term historical trend has been down, punctuated by temporary upward spikes, in real (inflation-adjusted) resource prices as economizing technologies allow more fuel (or material) to be extracted with less effort and expenditure. The finitude of resources does not give rise to any corresponding finitude of the products and services yielded by those resources. As fossil-energy resources become scarcer, their rising prices *enable* higher-cost renewable sources—sun, wind, and tides—to become cost-efficient and to be employed. As iron mines become deeper, the ore more scarce and of lower quality, the price of ore rises, and finally it pays to mine surface junkyards for scrap to recycle into new steel.

In place of indoor flush toilets, we had the outhouse, or "privy,"—sweltering hot in the summer, and icy cold in the winter, with the Kansas wind howling through the cracks—where we performed essential excretory functions. We quickly learned to sphincter up and minimize the number of exposures requiring us to brave the elements. For indoor winter nights, there was, of course, a crock or pot in each bedroom with a lid so that we did not have to suffer the outdoor wind and cold at 3:00 a.m., but without heat in the bedroom, we had no desire to use that pot either. At age five, I had no difficulty learning to hold my urine until wake-up time in the morning. Toilet training began early and was learned well on a Kansas farm.

For me, the farm yielded memories of personal inconveniences that were trivial. The reason was simple—I knew of no alternative. That was life, and we were there to make the most and best of it without bellyaching. I minimized any discomfort from most things that were less than the best. The farm was exciting, and it was a great place and time to be a kid looking for

---

[1]See "Edwin L. Drake and the Birth of the Modern Petroleum Industry," Pennsylvania Historical Museum Commission, http://www.phmc.state.pa.us/ppet/edwin/.

adventure. For me, it was not hardship; it was more like high-class camping out. It was a rich time of discovery.

My significant memories were those of adventure, of learning about chickens, milk cows, threshing machines, binders, haylofts, "cricks" (creeks), horses (we had just one), hogs, rats in the hog pen, fruit trees, gardens, wheat, corn and "cafricorn" (it's not in your dictionary; it looked like small white BB shots, and you could pop it! It grew in bushy heads like sorghum), rabbit hunting, priming well pumps, Coleman lanterns, and nights with bright stars clean down to the unobstructed horizon—a phenomenon that can only be experienced, not imagined—in a great expanse of "infinitely tender" sky that seemed uncannily like the open sea. That marvelously tender sky was punctuated and contrastingly defined by Kansas lightning storms that, for eons, had kept the landscape treeless, and by dust storms and the incredible "gully washer" rainstorms where water poured down like "a cow pissing on a flat rock," as the locals liked to say. At night in a lightning storm, it was possible to read newspaper print during those flashes—if you could afford to buy a newspaper, of course.

Riding in a wagonload of wheat, farm kids put handfuls of raw wheat in their mouths and chewed without swallowing; eventually, the wheat turned into chewing gum. Wrigley's three gum flavors were luxuries that we never bought with our scarce cash! The tradition of simple homegrown or homemade products—toys, foods, sundries, games, remedies—during a period of limited specialization through market exchange—provides an incredible prehistory of business innovation. I could not begin to guess how many seemingly "new" and very successful products, from chewing gum and skateboards to ice cream and rubber guns, were simple manufactured versions of home-industry products that generated cash savings when wage work was limited.

Our only cash income, except for a skimpy annual wheat harvest, was from the sale of the Jersey Cow cream we made using a hand-cranked centrifuge separator. My mom often made reference to the fact that this cash from cream sales amounted to only eighty-five cents per week! The by-product—skim milk—was fed to the hogs. We also made butter in a two-gallon jar with a hand-cranked paddle wheel. When the paddle wheel was rotated in chilled cream, butter precipitated out on the paddle, building up until it could be scraped off into a jar. The residual buttermilk contained flecks of butter and was the standard form in which milk was drunk. After returning to Wichita in 1934, we continued to buy bulk buttermilk from the local dairy for ten cents per gallon. It was buttermilk, rather than milk, that we used in bread, biscuits, pie crust, pancakes, waffles, gravy, and mashed potatoes, as well as for drinking.

We raised chickens from our own nest-hatched eggs. When we could afford them, we also bought chicks from hatcheries, because they had a higher survival rate. Even a short period of observation of chickens gives a clear meaning to the term *henpecked*. As chicks grow, they lose the downy yellow birthday coat that makes them so cute, and they begin to grow feathers. The feathers sometimes grow erratically, and a chick's patches of exposed skin area may attract the attention of others in the flock, which peck at them whenever the hapless chick passes by. I remember one chick whose exposed butt was pecked raw, and this attracted even more henpecking. The little fellow would try to stay clear of the others, keeping his little ass turned outward toward the fence, but he was skinny and not able to eat like the others because he was constantly harassed. I rescued him, keeping him fed and watered far from the chicken yard. He thrived after I befriended him as a pet, and he followed me everywhere. I used to put him in my red wagon and haul him around until he became accustomed to my racing fast with him in that wagon. He loved it, and so did I. I remember making fast, tight turns with that chick perched on the side of the wagon, holding on tenaciously, but never refusing to ride in that wagon, because it was so exciting.

Unfortunately, his penchant for following us into the house killed him. One day, as my mother brought in a basket of clothes, the screen door slammed shut behind her, with him not quite hot enough on her heels, and the door broke his neck. He knew that screen door well, but he seemed to prefer living dangerously to being isolated. By this time, he was old enough to harvest, so my mother cut off his head, and we ate him, the pieces mixed in with those of another chicken so that no one would know which was which. We never wasted food out of sentimentality, and on a farm it was a completely natural part of life for animals to be milked, their eggs gathered, or their meat eaten. Dogs, horses, and cats each had their own important contributions to make.

People on the local farms would have been horrified, however, at the idea of eating horsemeat, a thought that occurred to me when I ate horse meat for the first time twenty-five years later at the Harvard Faculty Club, where horse tenderloin was a treasured delicacy and a leading topic of conversation.

The farm proved to be an invigorating childhood environment with ample opportunity for daily fatherly and motherly lessons in the details of how things work—an interest I have retained throughout my life. I learned when and how to help milk cows and put them to pasture; feed the hogs, chickens, and horse (we could afford only one horse and had to borrow another for plowing, but one was enough for harrowing and cultivating); and to tag along, hold tools, and watch my father repair fences, gates, hog sheds, and barn doors, store hay in the barn loft, and shoot rabbits with my grandfather's 1890 vintage lever-action Winchester twelve-gauge shot- gun (unfortunately, he sold that gun to a collector after World War II). I remember watching my father, frustrated by many unsuccessful attempts to catch a really big bass in the creek, and try unsuccessfully to shoot him with his .32-caliber revolver. Beginning about age twelve, I used dad's shot- gun to hunt rabbits in the pastures a couple of miles west of our home in Wichita, long before that area was urbanized.

In the meantime, I was learning from my mother about stoking a wood cook stove, cooking and baking on that stove, planting and tending a gar- den, and all manner of house chores. When we moved to the farm and ate our first rabbit dinner, we all sat down at the table and my mother asked which piece I wanted. I said, "the breast meat." She did her best to stifle her laughter and explained that a rabbit was not built like a chicken and there- fore had no breast meat. It was all so new at age five. Live and learn.

I learned to milk a cow, but not nearly as effectively as my dad could. The standard procedure is to grasp the teat by making a loose fist around it. Then you squeeze the index finger and the inside of your thumb tightly around the teat, then the middle finger and the next fingers in a smooth sequence. This creates suction in the teat duct that siphons the milk down from the storage udder. Once you get the milk moving, you maintain the flow by grasping the top of the teat between the thumb and either the index or the middle finger, slide your thumb and tightly squeezed finger down the teat, then repeat the action in a rhythm that maintains the flow. You can't lose the rhythm or you lose the siphon effect, and you go back to a restart. From scratch, an expert could do the routine with two fingers, but I could never make that work. I could never master the two-finger rhythm protocol and could only milk by applying the fist action, over and over, which was slow and tiring for a six-year-old, but I found an entertaining challenge in trying to switch to two fingers and maintain the flow.

Occasionally, a heifer would have a sore teat, scratched by sharp branches or barbed wire. In that case, you had to be very gentle, and sometimes you had to skip milking that teat. Otherwise, the animal could kick you, or worse—since your bruise would heal—kick over your bucket of milk (which would bring on the barn cats for cleanup). Dad would guard against that— and the vagaries of a temperamental heifer that did not require a sore teat to get into a kicking mood—by holding the bucket firmly between his knees as he milked. This procedure was well beyond the competence of six-year-old legs, but it was one of a host of little tasks that you yearned to learn because they were what you came to identify with being an adult. Somehow, you knew that the state of adulthood was all-important; it was defined not by age, but by all those things you could not yet do and did not yet know, but wanted to do and to know.

I forgot to mention that when milking a cow, you squat on a T-stool. Dad made ours by nailing an eight- to ten-inch two-by-four, vertically, to the center of a second of similar length. Believe me, milking on a T-stool, bucket locked between your knees, took skill, balance, and good physical conditioning. So did fence mending, wood chopping, and plowing and planting potatoes and garden vegetables. An exercise room at that time in those parts would have been as worthless as teats on a boar.

The cows had to be milked very early in the morning. I don't know why—it was probably the need to relieve the overnight accumulation of milk before putting the cows out to pasture for the day. Anyway, it was often dark at milking or feeding time, whether morning or evening, and we used our gasoline-burning Coleman lantern. City folk have no idea what an incredible invention that simple device was for the farm. It extended the workday by literally, it seemed, converting night into day. A Coleman lantern casts a very bright white light in a great circle. Here is one for Ripley: "Fairmount College (now Wichita State) played the first night football game in the Midwest under Coleman lanterns in 1905" (*Wichita Century*, 1870–1970). If Coleman had a competitor making lanterns, no one seemed to know about it, because everybody wanted his lantern.

The lantern was easy to start once you mastered the technique of working the small air pump (initially manufactured separately, but later built into the fuel tank), adjusting the fuel jet, and occasionally attaching new little silk bags to the burners, which facilitated the chemical conversion of the heat-evaporated gasoline into high-intensity light energy. The old-fashioned wooden kitchen matches made by Diamond Match were essential because the stick was the perfect tool for adjusting the L-handle and the jet.

William C. Coleman brought his company to Wichita in 1901. His son, Sheldon, took the company into the camping-supplies business after World War II, a brilliant move that caused the company to grow like never before and continue an incredible record of innovation and customer service for well over a century. The widespread reputation of the Coleman name on lamps and cooking stoves was transferred by management effort into an image of premium-quality camping gear of all kinds.

Billye introduced me to Sheldon Coleman sometime in the 1960s, and I rightly felt that I was meeting one of the numerous great Wichita entrepreneurs, whose company had served as an engine of wealth creation by satisfying people's wants all over the world. This is what globalization is all about—entrepreneurship, technology, and trade. The political problem is to let this process do its thing with minimal interference from national governments, the World Bank, and the International Monetary fund. Governments, if they would only recognize it, are in competition with each other to provide stable monetary and fiscal environments, stable human, including property, right régimes, and opportunities for their people. Those that best achieve these ends and allow wide-ranging economic and political freedom will have the most prosperous people. By changing its policies, Ireland has transformed its economy from Third World levels of per capita income to the sixth highest in the world, well ahead of the United Kingdom, which is sixteenth (2008). Regrettably, the Irish growth miracle was temporarily devastated by the Great Recession, but key bank failures contained the balance sheet damage. Astonishing changes for the better have also occurred in New Zealand since 1980 and recently in China, as their governments turned from their past to allow greater economic freedom.

And trade promotes peace, although there is no guarantee it can overcome strong political winds for escalating hostilities. In the current (Spring 2014) conflict between Russia and Ukraine, western attempts to sanction Russia for their interference into Ukrainian affairs have met with business opposition, thanks to growth in trade between Russia and other countries. German business has been particularly vocal: "If there's a single message we have as business leaders, then it's this: sit down at the negotiating table and resolve these matters peacefully," urged Eckhard Cordes, a former Daimler AG executive who now heads the Ostauschuss, the Eastern Europe lobbying arm for German industries.[2]

When we milked the cows, a cat or two always showed up for a squirt of fresh milk. My dad would usually hold a teat up on its side and, at a three-to-four-foot distance, hose down the cat's face, and we would watch how the cat licked up every drop of that warm Jersey milk. Barns always have cats hanging around. We never interfered with that because cats guaranteed rat and mice control. At least, since the dawn of agriculture, mice and rats have imposed an incredible cost in grain loss to humans. They colonize in pairs and families that just keep expanding—Malthus style—to press upon the available food supply. They spread throughout the Pacific Ocean as stowaways aboard the migration boats of the Polynesians as they eventually occupied all the habitable islands; together with rats, mice became the first two mammals of consequence to be imported into New Zealand about 900 years ago.

---

[2]See http://online.wsj.com/news/articles/SB10001424052702303948104579535983960826054.

But cats take rats and mice out wholesale—they collect them the way I collected marbles. We had a black house cat named Mandy—how's that for a little racism by contemporary standards of political correctness? When Mandy died, she was replaced by another black cat, Sambo; my mother would have been mortified if she had thought any racist interpretation was implied. (The hundred-year history of the children's book *Little Black Sambo* ended in the 1970s when it was banned in an expression of political correctness, although Sambo was a hero worthy of emulation in the story.)

My home education on racial matters was that Negroes—blacks would have been an unspeakable term of derision—and all of the races of humankind were just like us except for the skin color; it was the "we are all brothers under the skin" directive. I would later learn that the most credible hypothesis, supported by archaeological and DNA data, is that all of us are descended from our common Cro-Magnon ancestors, originating some 150,000 or so years ago, who were certainly full out-of-Africa black. It is said that skin color adapted fairly rapidly by means of natural selection as populations moved into northern Europe: The diet changed, and with less daylight, light skin became essential for the generation of adequate vitamin D in the human body. (Many genes have been thought to contribute to skin color. However, *Science* [2005, pp. 1782–1786] reports the discovery of a single-gene mutation found to be shared by people with light skin in populations of European and African ancestry. Hence, it seems that a gene mutation contributed to the survival of people living in more temperate and northern climates and became fixed in these populations.)

Newly uncovered evidence, however, shows that skin color can adapt to white in only about 8000 years.[3]

An international research team compared DNA components across 83 ancient peoples from various archeological sites. Today's Europeans are a genetically blended mix of three migrant populations arriving over the last 8000 years. Later migrants from about 4500 years ago are thought to have brought Indo-European languages from the steppes above the Black Sea.

The team found strong evidence for the natural selection of highly favorable traits that spread rapidly through Europe in only the last 8000 years. Five genes were related to changes in skin color and diet. They confirmed earlier findings that these peoples could not digest lactose in milk. That tolerance did not develop until it began to spread quickly about 4300 years ago.

The new evidence suggests that three separate genes produce light skin; that 8500 years ago settlers in Span, Luxembourg, and Hungary had dark skin. Two genes associated with light pigmentations were missing. But to the North in Sweden, both of these light-skin genes were present in a 7700-year-old site.

[3]Ann Gibbons, "How Europeans Evolved White Skin." *Science*, April 2, 2015. https://doi.org/10.1126/science.aab2435.

These samples also had a third gene which causes blue eyes and is thought to contribute to blond hair and light skin.

The bottom line is that this is a story about rapid biological adaptation to changes in sunlight exposure when that exposure is critical to survival.

Mandy even harvested cottontail rabbits that were larger than she was and of course dragged them proudly back to the house. I don't think we cooked and ate them, though! Decades later, in Indiana, my dogs caught a pheasant before it could make it out from under a hedge-apple tree (Kansans sometimes called them Osage orange trees, after one of the tribes which made strong and flexible bows from the wood) to become airborne, and I rescued it from the dogs so that we could cook it for the table. Mandy also harvested rats that had colonized the hog pen, but she was smart enough to stay clear of the barn. In the cat world, there is a divide between house and barn cats that cannot be crossed without an incredible fight. When such a fight occurs, most people want to hightail it out of the area and not interfere, as should the house cats, but they learn that rule the hard way.

A really memorable event for me was when my dad decided to harvest one of the big sows that we raised. The technology for dispatching and bleeding the animal was of great interest to me. In order to load hay into the second-story barn loft, there was a rope-and-pulley arrangement. The loft had sliding doors on the front and rear of the barn. One pulley hung on a rafter above the front door, connected by a rope across the rafters to a second pulley that was similarly positioned above the rear door. With a wagonload of hay below the front door, the rope was attached to a hinged, double-pronged hayfork. At the rear door, the rope was pulled tight from the pulley to the ground and attached to the horse: To pull a big fork load of hay out of the wagon, we giddy-upped the horse until the load was positioned above the storage area and then released the fork by hand and returned it for another load.

The farmers adapted this apparatus, minus the fork, to slaughter and dress out the hog. With the help of neighbors, the sow was positioned outside the barn under the second-story sliding door. The rope, ordinarily fastened to the hayfork, was looped firmly around the sow's hind legs at the ankles while the other end, strung through the pulleys, was tied to the horse on the other side of the barn. When all were ready, my father shot the sow between the eyes with his .32-caliber revolver, normally kept under his pillow—a routine form of security at the time that no one questioned—and to my knowledge never before fired by him except unsuccessfully at that cagey bass. Immediately, a waiting helper with a long butcher knife approached the sow and sliced her throat deeply.

The horse pulled and lifted the sow by the hind legs until she was vertical. The blood flowed down and into a galvanized metal tub placed under the hog by another helper. In this manner, the body was bled dry to yield the best spoil-resistant meat. The hog's belly was slit from rib cage to tail and the entrails removed. The heart, liver, kidneys, and sweetbreads (pancreas) were saved. A skinning knife was used to remove the hairy hide. The head was removed, and the body was split first into two hanging sides and later into quarters, ready for home processing.

The one thing I could never eat was the "head cheese" made by removing the bullet and cooking the sow's head. After it is cooked, the meat is picked off the skull, mixed with the gelatin that comes from cooking the bones, and formed into lunchmeat size loaves to be cooled, hardened, and sliced for sandwiches. Ugh. "Waste not, want not" is a useful saying, but I was willing to go wanting when it came to head cheese, especially after I had seen it made.

From my mother, I learned about cooking on a wood stove in the Kansas prairie where there is precious little wood—cottonwoods lined the few streams, and the pastures and grain fields were barren of trees. We supplemented by burning dried corncobs and dried, sunbaked "cow chips." One of my jobs was to collect the chips.

As I noted earlier, each time I revisit this manuscript, I enter into the world of deep memory—especially childhood memory—and on this reading I recalled something of the procedure that any 6-year-old farm kid can learn to apply when sent out to gather cow chips. My father, or perhaps my mother, would have taught me the routine. The Kansas wind and clear days of bright sun ensure that, within a couple of days, cow splats will dry to a hard fedora-sized round disk about 1 inch thick in the center and tapering to half an inch at the edges. If, however, they have been unloaded for only about half-a-day, then the wind-sun treatment will have dried them on the top, but not yet in the middle. Deceptively, they look cured, but they are not. Rather than to stoop over trying to pick one up to put in your shoulder collecting bag, you learn to kick it on its disk edge. If it does not move, and merely crumbles, leave it be for further curing. If it jumps up, perhaps spinning or cartwheeling, it's ready to harvest; pick it up, put it in your bag, and get on with your business. When your bag is full, you return to the house and divide your precious cargo of stored Kansas combustible energy between the wood box by the wood-burning kitchen stove and the larger wood box in the family room by the big pot-bellied heating stove. Then get on with your next duty.

The early European settlers had burned *Bison* chips, as had the Indians before them. Decades later, I learned that the first Americans, who most likely crossed the Bering Strait stretching from Siberia to Alaska, burned mammoth chips, the only source of fuel on the dry, windswept plains of northern Siberia and northern Alaska. I felt intimately and warmly connected to those ancient peoples of 15,000 years ago, whose ancestors had settled the entire North American continent some 11,000 years ago, perhaps earlier.

The date for the earliest settlement of North and South America has been pushed further back because of new archaeological finds in the Americas. The laws of probability make it plain that there is no reason to expect that the first archaeological finds will be the oldest—the earlier ones will emerge later with more intense fieldwork. Hence, for later excavations, dates on a particular cultural material will tend to be pushed into earlier periods.

Also, always keep in mind the incentive structure of scientists: You do not become famous by replicating existing dates; fame comes with a breakthrough in which the scientist is able to establish for the first time a more ancient date for a particular cultural marker (and sometimes a more recent benchmark; e.g., one showing that Neanderthals co-existed with our Cro-Magnan ancestors, well into more recent times; or that the mammoth survived on Wrangle Island, off the coast of artic Siberia, until 5000 years ago). This incentive structure explains the skepticism of seasoned archaeologists when dramatic new dates are discovered. Vance Haynes at the University of Arizona always withheld judgment on date revisions until replication; sometimes that replication involved a site visit by independent teams sent to verify new claims.

While I was learning from my father about machines, animals, and crops, I learned from my mother about cooking, a process that fired my interest and imagination from our first days on the farm. Mother never discouraged me from wanting to learn about cooking. I watched her in the kitchen, and she never tired of explaining why and how her culinary products were created. The kitchen pantry was stacked with Mason jars for home canning. We had fruit trees and a large garden and ate both fruits and vegetables year-round. It was fresh fruit and vegetables from late spring until early fall and canned fruit, green beans, and corn in the winter. Mom also canned sausage, about which everyone, visitors, and locals alike, raved. I watched it all, very much aware of everything that was in process and how it was being done. She taught me simple tasks, such as how to make popcorn, heat syrup, and boil eggs; as I grew older, she taught me to make peanut brittle and caramel candy. Later, I graduated to cooking the full line of breakfast items. Typically, boys bond with their fathers by learning to repair and make things. It was the same way for me with my father, but also my mother with foods and their preparation. In memory, it seems that my indoor time at the farm was mostly in the kitchen, where there was always warmth, activity, and new experiences. This was natural preparation for my first wage work, dispensing drugstore fountain drinks, and later work as a restaurant fry cook.

I can still taste in my memory the fresh buttermilk pancakes and hot buttermilk biscuits—both made with lard—that were cooked on the top, or in the oven, of that ancient iron stove. And homemade sausage and cured bacon! If the kitchen egg basket was empty, I was sent to the chicken coop to gather eggs, some so fresh that they were still warm from the hen's body, occasionally containing two yolks, for frying or for pancakes served steaming hot, smothered in home-churned Jersey sweet butter, and covered with homemade corn syrup boiled from corncobs before the latter became cooking fuel.

> If you are curious about two-yolk eggs, go to a Trader Joe's, if there's one near you, and buy jumbo brown eggs. A dozen may contain several that have two yolks. (Alas, in recent years, I have not found any, but if you regularly buy brown eggs from a local farmers market, you will occasionally get a double-yolk gem. I opened one just this morning, May 26, 2014). You don't find double-yolk eggs in your commercial grocery store because the eggs have all been "candled" (an ancient term from the days when an egg was literally held up to a candle and visually determined to have one or more yolks. I never had an explanation for this pre-occupation with sorting them out—perhaps from some ancient superstition against breaking a two-yolk egg. The husbandry purpose of candled eggs was to determine if they were fertilized, not see if they were double-yolk-ed. Your pen has an active rooster who regularly mounts the hens. So, you candle them to sort the ones that are not fertilized and can be eaten—the others incubated for chicks). I am biased in favor of brown eggs, the only kind our Rhode Island Red hens knew how to lay, so I do not hesitate to pay a premium for them.
>
> My discourse on sorting out double-yolk eggs motivated me to research the candling of eggs for double yolks. There is indeed—or so it is claimed—a superstition about breaking a double-yolk egg: "Eggs themselves have their own lore...The discovery of a double yolk within is cause for terror or celebration depending on which school of thought is followed — some say it presages a wedding, others a death...its shell must be broken up lest a witch" obtain power over the one who ate the yolks.[4]

---

[4]Read more at http://www.snopes.com/holidays/easter/easterlore.asp#vfB8TgmEHFev80dh.99.

I also remember my mother, many times, chopping off the head of a chicken for the table. You could tell from her grim wooden face that she did not relish the chore. The protocol was to begin with a bucket of boiling-hot cistern water, carry it out to the backyard, and set it next to the three-foot-diameter sawed-off cottonwood chopping block that was about knee high. Next, she would go into the chicken yard and choose a young three-to-four-pound chicken, grab him or her around the ankles, and carry the squawking and flapping bird out to the block. She would take the axe out of the chopping block with her right hand, holding the bird by the ankles and legs in her left hand, and position it so that the neck and head were on the chopping block. This was no trivial feat because the bird, at this point, was wiggling and squawking and shifting and bobbing its head all over the place. At some point, she took aim and down came the axe; off came the head, she dropped the bird on the grass, where it flopped around all over the place like, well, a chicken with its head cut off.

An alternative method required no axe. One simply grabbed the bird's head in your right fist and whirled the bird clockwise like a sling, twisting off the head. My mom thought that was completely disgusting and refused to learn it. No matter which procedure one applies, it's necessary to wait until the flopping bird's body comes to rest—always seemed like an eternity to me—before plunging it neck first into the hot water, immersing the entire carcass, and dunking it up and down like a doughnut. The hot water loosens the feathers, and then it's time to begin plucking them out until the bird is naked to the skin. If it's a Rhode Island Red, the chore is pretty much over at that point; but if it's a Black Australorp, the skin has black feather follicles that do not look very appetizing and must be squeezed out like blackheads. That was all scummy business, to say the least, but it never seemed so at the time, as it was all part of a typical day on the farm.

The benefit was crispy fried (breaded with flour and buttermilk) or roasted chicken, sometimes with buttermilk dumplings, but always with buttermilk mashed potatoes and my mom's incredible buttermilk gravy; there was buttermilk everywhere.

Times have really changed. Try ordering a glass of buttermilk in a restaurant. For starters, the waiter or waitress may not even know what the hell it is. Suggest that the cook may have a cooking supply. You probably won't succeed; but if you do, they will enter into conference to figure out what to charge you. When you get it, it will not be buttermilk at all. It will be regular milk that has been cultured and is called buttermilk, but is not nearly as tasty as the real thing.

Yes, my parents' lives were hard, and their workdays were long, but for a five- or seven-year-old, every new day dawned with fresh excitement. I didn't have a care in the world in those days, and there was so much to learn and witness—that sense of not being burdened by care followed me for decades into the future. Years later, when I took up hiking and camping, it brought back memories of the farm days, which did indeed seem like upscale full-time camping out.

Our farmhouse had three rooms downstairs: a kitchen, an adjoining sitting room (today called a family room) with a potbellied wood- and cow-chip–burning stove, and, to the east, a living room with a front porch and a swing. The kitchen and porch faced south, with the porch to the east and the kitchen to the west on the other side of the porch wall. Almost every day, we had that warm Kansas winter sun streaming into the kitchen to help heat the first floor. Upstairs were two bedrooms with no heat, and believe me they were as cold as a witch's teat, as I learned early to say. On cold winter evenings, my mother placed bricks under the potbellied stove. When they were thoroughly heated, she wrapped them in towels, took them upstairs, and put them under the covers at the foot of my bed. When the bed was warmed up for my feet, I would be taken up the narrow staircase to get into that toasty warm bed. My bed had so many blankets and comforters that when I rolled over in the night I had to hold the covers up with my hands, so I could turn my body underneath them. But was it ever cozy, warm, comfortable, and secure? To this day, I prefer to sleep in a cold room with lots of covers.

When walking the only path to the barn, due west from the house, you passed between the chicken yard to the north and the storm cellar to the south. (This is roughly where my Grandpa Smith, visiting from the city, caught up with me, at a dead run, after I struck him squarely in the head with dried navy beans blown from my homemade blowgun. Having twice warned me to lay off, he blurted out "Vernie, damn it, you did that on purpose." Indeed, I had. I could hear the daybed springs squeak in the dark northwest corner of the sitting room as he bounded off it fast and hit the ground running. I knew that I was in deep shit, and bolted out the kitchen door, headed for the barn.) The storm cellar on every Kansas farm was a small, L-shaped dugout cave covered with a homemade wood door slightly inclined above the flat ground. Under the door was a short staircase leading underground. The cellars were cool in the summer and warm in the winter, relative to the above-ground temperatures. We stored home-canned fruits, veggies, and sausage on the shelves and had no problem with vermin invasions because we had two very efficient house cats—Lady and Mandy—that were always up for a fresh kill in the territory east of the storm cellar and north of the hog pen. Mandy was the expert; she provisioned Lady, who usually just waited until she returned from the hunt and expropriated Mandy's kill. Mandy did not mind, as there was plenty of game for both, and the thrill was clearly in the stalking and capturing, not in the eating. The cats avoided the chickens. Occasionally, an unconditioned cat would try to prey on a chicken or the chicks. When that happened, we killed the cat; its genes had no value for humans, so we stopped the lineage right there. Chicken-killing cats could not be tolerated.

Lady was Mandy's mother. The two of them always got pregnant at the same time and gave birth within a day or two of each other. They were assigned separate boxes in which to whelp and care for their kittens, but the assignment was never accepted. Within a few days of having her litter, Lady would carry her kittens, one at a time, from her box to Mandy's box. We tried to discourage her behavior by placing the boxes in separate rooms, but to no avail. Lady's maternal instincts were short-lived, and she was off for adventure. Mandy always nursed both litters and did not seem to mind it at all.

Both cats were characters. In the summertime, after moving back to Wichita, Lady had a novel way of opening the screened front door to go out. She raced through the house at a dead run, became airborne as she approached the door, hit the screen four to five feet off the floor with her full body weight, and clung with all four sets of claws to the screen. Her momentum opened the screen door, and she hit the ground running and was out of there. It's called "cat folk physics."

It was in that storm cellar that we took refuge if we thought tornadoes were in the air. There were no tornado watches and no broadcasts, and in any case we had no radios. There were no warnings, but we could feel the tension of tornadoes in the air. We could sometimes see them to the west and south as they snaked down from a squall line, with bright light and clear sky beyond the line, black boiling clouds overhead and behind, and faster-moving white clouds just below. Normally, they would snake back up to the sky and disappear into the squall line. I never saw one that came to earth, except in the Judy Garland movie.

When tornadoes were in the air, we were up against the one thing that was really, really, scary. We kids could see it on the faces of the adults, who pretended that they knew that everything would be OK. Fortunately, in the two years that we lived there, it always was.

If you want to get a sense of it, and you just happen to be passing through Topeka, Kansas, go to the Capitol building and enter the main floor rotunda. There you will find the magnificent John Stuart Curry mural circling the room, depicting the essence of Kansas and its history. In one scene, you will see the tiny, insignificant figures of a farm family, clutching the children, and rushing from their house to the storm cellar. Behind them is an immense, towering cone snaking down into a twister from a sky of black clouds above.

In the autumn of 1932, at age five, I took my place in the first grade, alongside more seasoned farm children, in a classic rural one-room schoolhouse. On the first day, I showed my city-boy naiveté. Someone was pulling a binder (a mowing and bailing machine for wheat) down the road with a horse, and we all rushed to the window. I said, "Oh, look at the threshing machine," and a little girl with long blonde curls next to me fainted, collapsed to the floor, and had to be revived with cold well water. I learned to keep my mouth shut until I knew one piece of machinery from another, because I thought that getting it right was so important that people would faint if you failed.

A neighbor, Mr. Hemberger, who was part of the local German community, had the distinction of being able to speak, read, and write English. He knew arithmetic as well and so was deemed fully equipped to be our grade-school teacher. It was a wise decision, I think, although my mother was always a bit irritated when he used the word *ain't*, a completely grammatical contraction of which English has many; Mom was something of a language maven, as Steve Pinker (*The Language Instinct*) would say. Each morning my teacher-neighbor faced rows of old-fashioned desks with lids that could be raised to store books, notes, and paper. "Homework" was farm work, as we were never asked to take home any schoolwork. After all, what the hell was the classroom for, if formal education could not be fully and completely accomplished there? A quarter of a century later, when my own children were in public school, I found myself naturally resistant to the concept of homework in the first grade. Of course, I had books that I read at home— *Tal* and Harvard Classics No. 17—but that was purely for personal joy.

The first row on Mr. Hemberger's right, where I sat, was grade one, the second row grade two, and so on for all the grades. I sat in the front seat of row one because I could not see the blackboard—no one knew yet, and it would be two years before anyone knew that I was myopic, and nothing written on that blackboard had any apparent meaning to me. Each morning, after some first-row recitations and an assignment, I had the opportunity to listen in on the second- and third-grade recitation lessons. Those students were seated closest to me.

As I later became aware, this classroom implemented the original "progressive system," in which you were part of a single seamless community consisting of all elementary grades conducted in the same space. At the end of grade one, in the following Spring, Mr. Hemberger gave me a note to take home to my mother. Addressed to Mrs. Smith, the note went immediately to the point, stating unceremoniously, "Vernon can read the second-grade reader and therefore next year he will be in the third grade." There were, of course, only three subjects: reading, writing, and arithmetic. What else was there to learn? Reading seemed to be the litmus test; if you were less strong in arithmetic or writing, the next year you could still participate along with those in the row to your left. The whole purpose of this management style was to move each person along at her own pace of accomplishment and get her through school and into farm work, where she could be useful to herself and her family.

I understand that the earliest achievement tests showed high performance in Kansas and Nebraska because of these rural schools. It's no wonder to me that Kansas bred the Eisenhowers, William Allen Whites, Beeches, Cessnas, Garveys, Kochs, and so on by the hundreds, maybe thousands.

I should not leave the farm without saying something about the harvest, and about the in-kind personal exchange, or reciprocity, which is the substance of the second quotation from Adam Smith that opened this chapter. Personal exchange is so much a prominent part of the unconscious socioeconomic folk fabric that it would be decades later before I and my co-authors would appreciate its role in our reinterpretation of experimental findings in two-person extensive form games. I will deal with these issues—Adam Smith and personal social exchange—at greater length in Chapter 21.

> As I recall events and experiences in writing this memoir, I try to record my experienced memory of them. But I now see each episode through the eyes of my understanding of prehistory, institutional change, and experimental learning. Although the memories of my experiences are refreshed in the context of the earlier time and circumstances, the intervening years have given them new meaning for me, and I will not speak or write of them unvarnished by the mind's eye as transformed by what I have understood since I had those experiences.

As noted earlier, my family had only one horse because we could afford only one. When we "borrowed" a second horse because we needed two to plow, it was part of an exchange, even if it was not explicitly or contractually recognized. The horse was to be borrowed, not rented. Borrowing entailed an implicit promise that you would return the favor in some appropriate way. For example, my dad might spend a day helping the owner of the borrowed horse to install new windows in his house or do repairs on his barn. When we returned the neighbor's horse, we were likely to say something like, "When can I help you with those windows?" And so, we acknowledged a debt, if in no other way, by the generic refrain "I owe you one."

In 1932, precious few farmers in Kansas could afford mechanized farm implements. This was before the combine, and therefore mowing the wheat and binding it into sheaves was an operation distinct from threshing it. A binder, such as the one I miscalled a threshing machine on that fateful first day of school, was a mowing machine that cut the wheat a few inches from the bottom of the long stem. The long stems fell onto a conveyor belt on the binder as it moved through the field. As wheat collected at the end of the belt, binder twine was threaded through a mechanism to tie the stems into a cylinder-shaped bundle, roughly a foot in diameter (imagine a big bouquet of flowers tied in the middle). The tied sheaf then rolled off the end of the conveyor and onto the cut field stubble. One or two other men walked behind each binder and stacked sheaves of grain upright into shocks. The shocks stood there in the sun for a few days to reduce the moisture content of the wheat. (Can you visualize the Grant Wood painting of wheat shocks standing in the field?) The price we received at the storage elevator in Milan varied inversely with the moisture content of the grain. Elevators don't like to buy water at the price of Kansas No. 1 hard red winter wheat, the premium grade that yields semolina, so richly and deservedly prized for fine Italian pasta.

When the grain was dry and fully ripened, it was threshed, an operation that separated the wheat grains from the chaff. The threshing machine was stationary; the sheaves were hand carried to it with a pitchfork and then pitched into the thresher. After a time, the threshing machine was moved to a new location in the field. As the grain was threshed, it emptied into a truck or horse-drawn wagon. When the truck bed was full, the grain went to the Milan elevator while a new truck was filled.

Even with those machines, the harvest was a labor-intensive process. In our area, only the patriarch of the Hemberger family owned a thresher. He provided the machinery for our harvest, and in return my father and the neighbors provided labor to help with his larger harvest. Accounts were balanced with extra labor or a share of the wheat or some other in-kind transfer. Money might be used as a standard of value to arrive at a wage ($1 per day was common) or the rental value of equipment on an hourly basis, but it was rarely used as a medium of exchange among neighbors. Everyone conserved scarce cash for imports of gasoline, kerosene, seeds, and manufactured goods. Even flour might be milled for us and bought with some of the harvested grain. No one seemed to have money after paying for essentials; very few things were "store-bought," when you could make them or do without.

The memory of all this makes me more than a little skeptical of national income accounts that measured national product at market prices or at factor cost, especially during the 1930s. In those days, people traded wheat equivalents for flour, and labor for the rent of "borrowed" assets: harvest labor for threshing machine hours, carpentry for horse days, etc. In the 1940s, when there was more cash around, all these patterns would have been influenced, with money as an exchange medium replacing many bartered deals. Thus, previously bartered exchanges would have started to show up in the measured accounts for national income.

The wheat combine merged the operation of mowing and threshing. When the tractor-drawn combine was introduced, after World War II, it was expensive and family farms were still the standard 160-acre quarter sections privatized under the Homestead Act. The labor and equipment savings of the new technology, however, completely dominated the old, and the ecologically rational response was the highway convoy train of trucks carrying combines. Contractors traveled ahead and lined up farmers to perform the harvest for less than it would cost them using the methods of the mid-1930s. The old thresher-binder harvest culture was wiped out as surely and as quickly as was the coal oil industry after Colonel Drake's Pennsylvania petroleum discovery three-quarters of a century earlier.

Perennially, the highway combine trains started in Texas in April and May, harvesting the earliest, most southern hard red winter wheat, the premium wheat for high-quality flour and the best pasta. The combine convoys moved north into Oklahoma, then Kansas (June harvest), Nebraska, South and North Dakota, and finally across the border and into Saskatchewan in August and September. Winter wheat must be planted in the autumn, have good germination, and be sprouted before cold weather arrives. The wheat grows all winter during the intermittent warm spells, but is hardy and weathers frost and periodic freezes. North of Nebraska, the fields yielded to soft summer wheat as the winters become more severe and hostile to planting in the autumn and harvesting in the spring and early summer. Farmers in those northern frozen-ground communities plant in the spring or early summer and harvest in the late summer or early autumn.

By 1947, the highway combine trains were so prominent that it produced a well-rated movie, *Wild Harvest*. For you old-movie buffs, this one is a classic bit of Americana documenting a market response to fill a niche that did not last many years. The cast is one of Hollywood's best for those years—Alan Ladd, Dorothy Lamour, Robert Preston, and Lloyd Nolan—with the good guys pitted against the bad guys in conflict over business and sultry women. It's a hard-to-get oldie but worth a try for history, drama, and laughs.

I worked on a land-clearing project thirty miles north of Carrot River in Saskatchewan, Canada, in the summer of 1947. The land, never before farmed, was being cleared of all "bush" by Canadian veterans, under the Veterans' Land Act, 1942, in preparation for planting wheat. That far north it was not possible to plant until June, but the wheat grew incredibly fast in the long daylight, and the ripe grain was ready to harvest about ninety days later. This was flat bush country, potentially rich in agriculture once the bush and the wolves were cleared, and the heavy soil was plowed and planted with soft summer wheat.

In our part of Kansas in 1932, the much smaller corn harvest was not mechanized—we grew no corn on our farm, as it was difficult enough to grow wheat. A man in a horse-drawn wagon, with a high-walled side and a low-walled side, reined the wagon slowly along the rows of corn. Two or three men walking parallel on the low side of the wagon husked the corn; that is, they stripped each ear off the stalk, tore off the dry husks, and threw the naked ear of corn into the wagon. The opposite side of the wagon was high to keep the ears from being thrown over the other side. Corn-husking tournaments were actually run as social events, with the winning wagon team weighing in with the most husked corn at the contest finish.

For a six-year-old in 1933, the excitement was not only in watching all these procedures in action, but in joining eighteen or so people for breakfast or lunch in June for the winter wheat harvest (I was far more into big social events back then than I am now, seventy plus years later). There were pancakes, bacon, eggs, biscuits, and homemade bread sandwiches to be eaten, and water to be pumped and carried to thirsty men—that was one chore that any young farm kid could do (Figs. 4.1 and 4.2).

Fig. 4.1 Milan Farm, Creek below

Fig. 4.2 Farm Creek, 84 years later

5

City Lights Again

This division of labor … is not originally the effect of any human wisdom, which foresees and intends that general opulence to which it gives occasion. It is the necessary, though very slow and gradual, consequence of a certain propensity in human nature which has in view no such extensive utility; the propensity to truck, barter, and exchange one thing for another.

—Adam Smith, *The Wealth of Nations*

… the same age, which produces great philosophers and politicians, renowned generals and poets, usually abounds with skilful weavers and ships-carpenters.

—David Hume, *Political Essays*

In 1934, my father returned to the Bridgeport Machine Company, first for alternate-week work, and subsequently for full-time work. This was fortuitous, as we lost "ownership" of the farm to the mortgage bank—with which we had always shared ownership—because we were unable to meet the loan payments. We would have had to move back to Wichita, whether dad had employment or not. It is likely that we would also have lost our home in Wichita, but my parents recognized this possibility earlier and had temporarily deeded the Wichita house to Grandpa Lomax to keep it from being added to the default obligation, so the issue never arose. That was probably some kind of horrible criminal (I exaggerate, actually it would only have been a civil) offense.

© The Author(s) 2018
V. L. Smith, *A Life of Experimental Economics, Volume I*,
https://doi.org/10.1007/978-3-319-98404-9_5

Sixteen years later, I would have summer employment at the Bureau of Business Research at the University of Kansas. I recall doing research on land title holdings in western Kansas during the 1930s. We were constructing maps coded with shadings and stripes to identify classes of owners. I remember that prominent on these maps were large holdings by financial institutions, particularly in western Kansas. People lost their farms to foreclosures, but the market value of the land was commonly less than what was owed on the mortgage, and thus, there were many insolvent banks. It would be at the University of Kansas that I would first learn of the banking crisis caused by a rigidly and inappropriately structured Federal Reserve System in which it was thought that the central banks had to tightly rein their reserves and those of the member banks when the latter were losing reserves to customer withdrawals. The central bank, however, cannot fail like a private bank because it is the lender of last resort. It can create the deposit funds needed to strengthen member bank reserves. It did the opposite, which leveraged even more the private bank incentive to retrench and protect reserves. Consequently, much of the inelasticity—indeed, perverse elasticity—of the banking and monetary system was the direct consequence of inappropriate rules caused by the misunderstanding of credit creation and the principal roles of central banks. It was another in a long list of unintended and disastrous consequences of inappropriate public policy. Capitalism and profit-seeking by greedy bankers, rather than the ignorance of policymakers and their consultants, would be blamed. The knowledge gleaned from that experiment was costly indeed.

Only in recent years have I come to understand that in 1934 we were in the fifth year of a balance sheet crisis; its severe economic consequences would not be repeated until the five years, 2007–2012 (see my discussion in Chapter 19, Volume II of this book, based on *Rethinking Housing Bubbles*, 2014). Although the failure of the Federal Reserve to act has long been considered the "cause" of the Depression, I now see it as originating in the booming expenditures for new housing (1922–1926) followed by a steep decline (1927–1933), precipitating a housing-mortgage market crunch, and leading to household-bank insolvency which was, without a doubt, exasperated by the failure of the Fed to provide liquidity. This failure was prominently documented by Milton Freidman and Anna Schwartz in *A Monetary History of the United States, 1867–1960*, Princeton University Press, 1971. But providing liquid balances to an insolvent system merely suspends it and cannot be a stand-alone solution. Believing its inaction had been a key failing in 1929–1930, the Fed did not repeat that perceived mistake in 2007–2008. Nevertheless, we still had a collapse second only to the Depression, and subsequently a massive rescue operation, in 2008–2009, mounted by the Central Bank and the US Treasury. Hence, in retrospect Fed action in the Great Recession, while appropriate, was quite insufficient to prevent the collapse. Both episodes involved household-bank balance sheet crises for which neither monetary nor fiscal policy was fashioned. I revisit these issues in depth in Chapters 19 and 20.

In 1934, we were leaving the world of local personal exchange and returning to a world of market exchange. As indicated in the quotation from Adam Smith, far more of our needs would be met by store-bought goods in a world that would gradually emerge, reinvigorated, from the Great Depression.

Taking inventory, my parents now had little if anything left of the original Santa Fe Railroad life insurance asset. Of course, losing the farm just confirmed my mother's political commitment to socialism—for her the proof of the pudding was in the eating—but my father, certainly disappointed, seemed to take it in stride. At some point in the 1930s, I remember that dad flatly refused to apply for public employment in the WPA (the Works Project Administration). Grandpa Lomax always said that WPA meant "We piddle around," and that IWW meant "I won't work" instead of International Workers of the World. This from the railroad engineer who admired Gene Debs (who founded the IWW), but who had even greater admiration for a strong work ethic. Similarly, dad considered "working" for the WPA demeaning, which was a point of contention with my mother, who thought he was being completely unreasonable. Yet, in spite of all of her socialist rhetoric, she was ingrained with the same ethic of hard work and savings.

As I think back on these matters, there were contradictions all over the place, but they were not evident to any of the principals at any time. My mother was as fiercely independent and productivity-oriented as she was collectivist-minded, yet she had not a clue that collectivism completely destroys the freedom needed to nourish productivity. That required far more understanding of the nature of humans and what they can accomplish through the extended order of market exchange than an otherwise sensible person like my mother could muster. Implicitly, she saw the productivity, work, and saving ethics as a fixed and unchangeable characteristic of people that would be unaffected by income redistribution under socialism. But the true policy challenge was to somehow find ways to nourish a stable economy without destroying its proven capacity for ever-increasing human economic betterment. We have enough freedom that human betterment processes manage to thrive and continue without being widely understood, but the same cannot be said about economic stability, a continuing challenge to political economy.

Wichita and farm life were separated by location as well as by intellectual and economic activity. The city was home to a surprising number of prominent businesses. Beech, Stearman, and Cessna Aircraft, Coleman Lantern Company, Dold Meatpacking, and the Fred Koch and Jack Vickers petroleum companies, and others provided tangible initial evidence of the machinery of markets, specialization, and globalization. Bold and independent actions by Coleman, Cessna, Beech, Koch, Garvey, Innes, and many others instilled a Plains Midwestern sense of freedom and entrepreneurship in Wichita.

Clyde Cessna had been brought up on the Cessna family farm at Rago, Kansas. He was skilled with farm machinery and became fascinated by the airplane, later building a series of monoplanes between 1911 and 1913. After World War I, two other aviation pioneers, Lloyd Stearman and Walter Beech, who had left the Swallow Airplane Company, invited Cessna to join them in their start-up, Travel Air Manufacturing Company (Walter Innes, President and Treasurer; Cessna, Vice President; Beech, Secretary), and he designed a plane for mail services. The company manufactured mail planes of the same kind that Antoine de Saint Exupéry and Beryl Markham flew in the 1920s and 1930s from Spain to Africa. (Read Saint Exupéry's beautiful *Wind, Sand and Stars; The Little Prince;* and *Night Flight;* also Markham's, incomparable, *West with the Night.*) But, restless and intent on forming his own company, Cessna sold his shares in Travel Air and, in the summer of 1927, opened a workshop on Wichita's west side near my home. I was six or seven months old at the time and would grow up unaware that I was surrounded by people who were as fascinated by making things work, go, or fly as my father was. Believe it or not, Stearman's original plant was built in the Depression year 1930 with funds advanced by Walter Innes and other Wichita business leaders.

As if to further defy the popular view that after 1929 economic activity had ground to a halt, in 1932 Walter and Olive Ann Beech co-founded Beech Aircraft, which would continue the tradition of Travel Air, taking over the Travel Air facilities in 1934. After Walter Beech (1891–1950) died of a heart attack, his wife became president of Beech Aircraft and has been recognized as one of the truly great early female executives, and a great aviation pioneer, as well. She was the first female president of a company listed on the New York Stock Exchange. Olive Ann Beech grew the company into an internationally successful manufacturer of light planes and continued to be active on the Board well into her eighties. A parallel story can be told of Olive White Garvey, the matriarch of the Garvey family, who built the largest grain-storage facility in the world. These were two of a small army of women who settled the West and then helped to industrialize it. In the process, they defied the prevailing views of a woman's "place." Many would also operate the dangerous new air machines: Amelia Earhart, lost in her historic flight around the world, and Jackie Cockran, the ace racing aviatrix. They were joined by Beryl Markham, who came out of Africa to become the first person to fly the Atlantic from East to West.

I reentered school in grade 2B at Martinson Elementary Public School in the fall of 1934. Had we stayed on the farm, Mr. Hemberger would have placed me in 3A, skipping grade 2 altogether, but Martinson's principal,

Mrs. Burrite, balked at a full grade advance. I am grateful for the favor she did me.

These were good years, not least because I was discovering girls! In grade school, Leona Dusenberry was the first girl I liked. That must have been in the third or fourth grade. Jean Buck was next. She always reminded me of Stephen Foster's "Jeanie with the Light Brown Hair." She was a sweetheart. I had other friends at Martinson, such as Elizabeth Brubaker, and Betty Dooley, for whom I had no special feelings—they were just girls, as we put it in those days. Many of us at Martinson went through public school together and would graduate from North High at the same time. I saw many of them at my twentieth high school reunion. The funny thing is that I don't remember any boys from my Martinson days except my neighborhood playmates, such as Jack and Jimmy Randall, Clinton Reser, and Dean Vetten, from long hot summer days of rubber guns and street hockey.

I do not know what became of Jack; Jimmy Randall became a park ranger and died in 2012. He had a great athletic (and academic) record at North High and subsequently in college. Here is an excerpt from his obituary in the Estes Park News, also carried in the Green Valley News in Arizona, where he had a winter home:

"James Arthur Randall was born September 29, 1928 in Wichita, KS...He graduated from Wichita High School North in 1946 where he was a member of the National Honor Society, played the snare drum in the band and earned athletic letters in baseball, swimming and football. Jim enlisted in the U.S. Navy and served from 1946 to 1948, where he was a flight deck air craft director on the USS Boxer...He received his B.A. in Forest Recreation from Colorado A&M (Colorado State University) in 1952. While there, he lettered in football and baseball and was named in the Who's Who Among Students of Colleges and Universities... He was awarded the Department of Interior's Meritorious Award and was a founding member of the Association of National Park Rangers in 1976...Jim and Ruth (wife) retired to their Estes Park home in 1989, but in 1989 he worked with the National Park Service's Incident Management Team on the cleanup of the Exxon Valdez oil spill in Alaska. In 1994, they started spending winters in Green Valley, AZ..."

My great childhood memories of life on the farm are followed by strong memories of growing up in the city. In Wichita, I had many playmates; I had none during our years on the farm. We played outdoor games every evening after school, during weekends, and all throughout the long Kansas summer. We played street hockey with homemade hockey sticks and a tin can as a puck. The goals were wooden boxes set at the south and north ends of a section of street. We had dirt-clod fights in the empty lots of not yet planted gardens.

> We manufactured all of our own toys, except skates and bicycles. One improv-isation proceeded thusly: Take a pair of discarded roller skates made to clamp around the soles of your street shoes. Remove the bolt that adjusts the skates to size, and the front wheels will separate from the rear. Take a hammer and flatten the raised edge at the rear. Next, align one set of wheels at the front and one at the rear of a two-foot-long two-by-four; screw them firmly to the bottom. Now turn it over, wheels down. It's a homemade skateboard! To make a cool scooter; you perform the same operation with the other skate, but use a three-foot two-by-four. Next get a wooden crate out of the trash bin down at Cole's grocery and nail it to the top front of the two-by-four, wheels down. For handlebars, fasten a one-by-two crossbar atop the orange crate, and you're ready to race.
>
> We let nothing go to waste, including discarded items scavenged from the trash cans of the rich kids who were careless enough to throw away skates and other valuables that could be repurposed as other toys.

Life was not all playtime. I had to mow the lawn, help mom carry the baskets of clothes, hang and take in the laundry from the clothesline, and so on. Some farm tasks moved with us to the city. As already noted, we had a chicken pen and coop between the backyard and the alley behind the house. Every Saturday, it was my job to clean out the chicken coop, and in par-ticular to scrape off the roosts with a hoe and wash them down. The adults assigned this task; they never did it themselves. I dreaded it, but perhaps it was intended to have some character-building value. If so, I must have really great character, so much did I hate that detail. But garden planting and tending were much different. I really enjoyed these tasks. We planted to save money and obtain high-quality vegetables, but nurturing seeds in the soil also instilled a habit of creativity.

> I have always kept gardens whenever possible, as I did when living in Kansas, Indiana, and Arizona. You can't obtain better tomatoes anywhere than home-grown varieties in Indiana (except that Peter Dougherty at Princeton University Press has broken through my insularity by pointing out that New Jersey toma-toes are awesome starting around mid-August). My favorite was and is the Ponderosa, or "beefsteak," variety, but since Ponderosas require up to one hundred days to mature, you need also to plant some early-maturing varieties to stay your impatience. People dependent on store-bought tomatoes (and most varieties of fruit, such as peaches and apricots) have no idea what a real tomato should taste like. Onions, muskmelons, and beans also do well in the

rich soil of Indiana, where on summer nights you can actually hear the corn grow, I deceive you not, as the corn stocks randomly snap noisily in a large field when all else is quiet in the heavy night air.

Gardening in Arizona is year-round: leaf veggies, broccoli, green onions, radishes, and sugar snap peas in fall and winter; cantaloupe, squash, all manners of peppers, and tomatoes in spring and summer. Herbs can be grown almost anytime.

Only gardeners tutored by my mother or another natural-born horticultural chef know that a beet tuber is an engine for growing tops for salads and stir-fries; that squash yields can be improved by hand pollination of the female blooms freshly opened in the early morning; that you eat the male blooms in salads, or deep-fried in batter, after they have been spent servicing the newly opened females; that tomato blossoms won't set tomatoes if it's too cool or too warm; that the best pie this side of heaven is made from freshly cut rhubarb, and that NO strawberries should be mixed with the rhubarb—shades of catsup on a finely crafted hamburger; and what can be done with the huge crop of green tomatoes left on the vines when the first killing autumn frost occurs—the vines are at peak production at frost time and are heavily laden. The squash-blossom routine I learned on my own, but countless hours with my mother in the garden—preparing the soil, planting, weeding, nurturing, and harvesting—enabled me to move and think seamlessly, from seeds to the stove to the table, as did she. Making green-tomato relish, cooking fried green tomatoes, and the art of storing green tomatoes in the dark for a rich ruby red harvest at Christmas were things my mother taught me. Mother, like my father, was a storehouse of knowledge about how things worked, and she taught practical procedures for garden and kitchen.

In the 1920s, my Grandfather Lomax one day announced to my mother, "Belle, I think I have found a church for us." It was the First Unitarian Church, located at the southeast corner of Central and Topeka, just east of Cathedral High School. Grandpa read Ralph Ingersoll and other religious skeptics and was essentially an agnostic. Western Unitarianism leaned strongly toward humanism, but used a rich mixture of sacred and secular music and poetic forms in the Sunday service that I grew to love and respect. On the slanting walls on either side of the choir loft, behind the center pulpit, appeared both secular and sacred inscriptions: Part of the quotation at the beginning of this book from Edna St. Vincent Millay's *Renascence*, the scripture "He who loveth not his brother whom he hath seen, how can he love God whom he hath not seen?" and others that I no longer recall. It was to the liking of both my parents, and I was raised in that church and am therefore a third-generation Unitarian. My children would be afforded the same Unitarian upbringing. I have rarely attended Unitarian churches since my children grew up. That early experience provided an openness to the spiritual and mystical; eventually, I became a more traditional Christian.

My mother studied piano and had a very good soprano voice. My father studied voice and sang many solo tenor performances around the city. Both sang solo in the church and in the choir, and my mother directed the choir for many years after returning from the farm. These interests drew them to classical music, which they were otherwise unlikely to have studied. Also, for many years before leaving for the farm and after returning to the city, my parents were active in the Wichita Opera Society. They sang in the chorus production of *The Pirates of Penzance*, *HMS Pinafore*, Mascagni's magnificent, unparalleled melodic opera, *Cavalleria Rusticana*, and others. (Remember *Godfather III*, with the opera performance as background to the final scenes? That was a collector's production of Mascagni's classic work.) Dad sang the tenor part of the Prospector in the local production of *Sunset Trail*.

My parents' musical dedication and experience had a big influence on me, although I have no instrumental performing talent. But I have no difficulty singing on key, and I can pick out a tune on a piano by reading sheet music or from my mind's memory of sound. In those days, no one used babysitters, so I attended all practice, rehearsal, and performance sessions, often falling asleep during a rehearsal. To this day, I recall many of the refrains and even the words of some of the operas in which they sang (From *HMS Pinafore*):

> *Now landsmen all, whoever you may be,*
> *If you want to rise to the top of the tree,*
> *If your soul isn't fettered to an office stool,*
> *Be careful to be guided by this golden rule —*
> *Stick close to your desks and never go to sea,*
> *And you all may be rulers of the Queen's Navee!.*

My Unitarian upbringing left me completely naïve about what religion meant to others. At Martinson Elementary School, there was a standard Bible school program under which classes were escorted to a local church for Bible instruction. One day I brought home an announcement and consent form for my mother to sign that would allow me to attend Bible school every Thursday morning at a nearby Baptist church. The teachers encouraged all the children to go, since if any did not, the teacher had to stay and supervise the children who did not participate. Mom asked if I wanted to go and I said, "Sure." All of my peers would be going, and in those days, I never was one to miss out, so she signed. A few weeks later, curious about what I thought about it—I was never, then or now, one to volunteer anything—she asked how I liked Bible school. "Fine," I replied. Mom asked,

"What is it that you like about it?" I said, "The stories." "What stories?" she asked. "All those stories about God and Jesus," I replied. She many times related to others this account of my first brush with the Bible. I understood the Bible lessons as recounting stories no different than those I had read in the Grimm and Andersen tales, volume 17 of the Harvard Classics, or in *Tal*. No one ever explained to me that, to many, the Bible was considered to be of a completely different nature than these fictional works. I remember being involved in an argument with Max Clark's younger sister, Darlene. The Clarks were Catholic, which meant nothing to me, and Darlene was telling me about how the biblical accounts were all true. I said that they were never intended to be true, that they were just supposed to be good stories. I do not know how old I was, but mom explained that many people, including the Clarks, did indeed believe that the Bible is a record of true events that happened just as reported. By and large, as we now know, the Bible as history is surprisingly accurate and provides a pretty fair guideline for Middle Eastern archaeological explorations.

In 1920, my mother cast her first vote for Eugene Victor Debs, socialist candidate for president, who was campaigning from his jail cell where he had been sentenced as a result of his opposition to World War I. Debs drew just under one million votes, giving a rough idea of the popularity of his opposition to the Great War; his first candidacy for president as a socialist was in 1900, when he received only 96,000 votes! Debs was convicted under the Espionage Act of 1917.

His supporters mounted a court defense of his conviction, ending in the Supreme Court case *Debs vs. United States* (1919) upholding his conviction. In our time, Daniel Ellsberg was charged under this act for leaking *The Pentagon Papers* to the *New York Times*. (For more on Ellsberg, see Chapter 8.) Although sentenced to a term of 10 years, President Warren G. Harding—his Republican opponent in 1920—commuted Debs' sentence in December 1921 along with 23 others imprisoned for their opposition to World War I.

According to the N.Y. Times:

"Announcement was made at the White House late this afternoon that President Harding had commuted the sentences of twenty-four so-called political prisoners, including Eugene V. Debs, who were convicted under the Espionage Act and other wartime laws and sentenced to from two to twenty years. Debs will be released from Atlanta Penitentiary on Christmas Day. 'The President expressed the wish that it be stated that the grant of clemency in the cases acted upon does not question the justice of any action of the courts

in enforcing the law in times of national peril, but he feels the ends of justice have been fairly met in view of the changed conditions. The vast majority of so-called political prisoners still imprisoned are the I.W.W group, are rarely American citizens and have no good claim to Executive clemency. A number of convicted citizens have never been imprisoned, owing to appeals under bond. There are also many thousands of indictments under war legislation still pending. These do not come under Executive consideration." (See "Harding frees Debs and 23 others held for war violations." *New York Times*, December 23, 1921)

It had been an unpopular war, a major departure from a policy of American isolationism dating back to the founding and was seen by many as a disastrous break from a successful policy of avoiding European conflicts—Harding's pardon was a healing act in recognition of changing attitudes, while respecting the rule of law. Opposition to the war was now seen as respectable. The Sedition Act of 1918, passed as a series of amendments to the Espionage Act, had made it illegal to use disloyal, profane, or abusive language to criticize the US Constitution, the government, the military, the flag, or the military uniform. The "thousands" referred to by Harding were arrested for sedition. The Sedition Act was repealed in 1921. The official attitude on war was entirely reversed in less than three years.

The national revulsion to the war would haunt Franklin Roosevelt with the rise of Hitler and the growing inevitability of World War II. Bertrand Russell, a British pacifist opponent of World War I, said that there had been only two wars worth fighting: the American Revolution and World War II. Russell died in 1970 and saw the Vietnam War added to his list of those not worth fighting.

As I write in 2014, Americans are once again turning against foreign military intervention: "Americans in large numbers want the U.S. to reduce its role in world affairs even as a showdown with Russia over Ukraine preoccupies Washington, a Wall Street Journal/NBC News poll finds."

This is a major change from decades of polling. Almost half of the people surveyed now want the USA to be less active in global affairs; less than 20% would call for a more active involvement. This anti-interventionist trend is bipartisan, with approval of President Obama's handling of foreign policy reaching a low for his presidency. Only 38% approve, in the face of improving scores for his overall job performance. Various polls combine to indicate a public tired of getting mixed up in foreign entanglements. The 47% of respondents who want a less active role is up from only 14% in 2001. Ironically, in sympathy with the feelings thought to have elected Donald Trump in 2016, over half felt that the country was no longer a place where everyone, regardless of background, had an opportunity to get ahead, with the system stacked against "people like me."[1]

The simplistic socialist claim that capitalism promotes war through the armaments trade ignores the proposition that "If goods don't cross borders armies will." (Unknown author)

I can't remember my mother being politically committed to anything except the American Socialist Party. In Kansas, the socialists had difficulty fielding a complete slate of candidates, and my recollection had been that her name regularly appeared on the ballot for Kansas State Treasurer, although she never did anything that resembled campaigning. My son Eric and his wife Laura were unable to confirm that she was a registered candidate for the 1936 election, but I remember well that presidential campaign when I was not yet nine years of age. Bob Beloof and I handed out programs at the Wichita Forum when Norman Thomas, the Socialist candidate, came to speak. Bob was the son of Mrs. Beloof, the absolute bedrock of the Kansas Socialist Party and a Quaker activist in the labor and antiwar movements.

Robert Lawrence Beloof (1923–2005) would have been 12 years old in the fall of 1936 when Norman Thomas visited Wichita to campaign. I lost track of Bob after the 1930s, and writing this autobiography motivated me to track him down. He became a Professor of Rhetoric and was on the Faculty of UC Berkeley for 41 years. You will find a touching statement "In Memoriam" at university Web site.[2]

Here is an excerpt that directly relates to the remembrances I have been recording here, with many parallels in our two independent careers:

Born in a poor neighborhood in Wichita, Kansas, on December 30, 1923, Robert Lawrence Beloof was raised by his mother, Ida Beloof, an outspoken political agitator and Kansas delegate to the 1919 Socialist convention in Chicago, Illinois. Mrs. Beloof operated a boarding house for cowboys and ran for governor of Kansas on the Socialist Party ticket in 1938; along the way, she also took in laundry to pay for elocution lessons for her youngest son, who grew up proud to tell generations of students about his activist mother and her profound influence upon him.

A lifelong Quaker, Robert enrolled in Friends University in Wichita in 1940, but his education was disrupted when he was drafted for military service during World War II. As a pacifist and conscientious objector (C.O.), he opted for

---

[1]Hook, Janet "Americans Want to Pull Back From World Stage, Poll Finds." *Wall Street Journal*, April 30, 2014.

[2]http://senate.universityofcalifornia.edu/_files/inmemoriam/html/robertbeloof.html.

internment in a labor camp in North Dakota and was later assigned to work in a state mental hospital near Philadelphia. His undergraduate education became a hit-and-miss affair of attending classes at Haverford College and Swarthmore College while serving out his C.O. sentence and writing poetry. In 1946, Friends University awarded him the B.A. degree in absentia. That year his achievements as a poet also won him the Atlantic Monthly prize for best poem, a tuition fellowship to the Bread Loaf School of English at Middlebury, Vermont, and the Elinor Frost Scholarship, which Robert Frost awarded for achievement in poetry.

Interesting that Bob is represented as having been born in a poor neighborhood. So was I—we all were, I guess—but I never thought of myself in those years as poor. I discovered that later.

Ida Beloof held party meetings regularly in her home (the "boarding house") and spoke against the capitalist profit system that she believed to be the root cause of war, poverty, unhappiness, and all other ills of the contemporary world. She was a self-styled Marxist through and through, although most American socialists were very pragmatic, I think, and did not feel ideologically connected to Marx. (They knew the more famous Harpo, Chico, Groucho, and Zeppo better than Karl.) When Norman Thomas visited Wichita, we met with him in the Beloof living room, and he came to our home once on another campaign trip, probably in the 1940s. Thomas was a very impressive person with a New York accent who referred to the *saowshi-list* movement. Tall, articulate, quick, and very knowledgeable about current events and trends, Thomas was a man of great compassion. He had been a Presbyterian minister achieving international fame as a socialist, pacifist, and six-time presidential candidate for the Socialist Party of America. He had been secretary of the Fellowship of Reconciliation before World War I and became one of the founders of the National Civil Liberties Bureau, the precursor of the American Civil Liberties Union that had been a stanch and uncompromising defender of free speech and First Amendment rights in the 1930s and 1940s.

As a candidate, he was always challenging Roosevelt, Landon, Communists—few were more anticommunist than Thomas and the Socialists—and other candidates to debates, to which bait they never rose. This brought out the showman in him. At the Wichita Forum, he debated Roosevelt anyway, placing an empty chair center stage, where "all can see that the president has, as always, accepted the challenge." Thomas fired both the questions and answers back and forth. At one point, he offered no response for the chair to a sensitive issue, his query was met with silence, and the audience much enjoyed the resulting sport. After World War II, Thomas traveled, spoke, and campaigned continuously to create the United Nations, and he made the news often as a peacenik and antiwar protester. He surely must have received many nominations for the Nobel Peace Prize, but he had a formidable competitor in my Caltech teacher, Linus Pauling, who—having already won a Nobel Prize in chemistry—was much better known in Oslo where the Peace Prize is awarded.

Mrs. Beloof always thought that Thomas' efforts for peace were irrelevant diversions; peace, she believed, was unattainable until the world was rid of the capitalist profit system. She believed Thomas ought to hold true to this basic socialist faith. But he was not a doctrinaire Marxian socialist. After the war, I recall that his message as an American Socialist became tempered by an expressed concern for what he had come to recognize as an incentive problem in the government operation of enterprise. With a better understanding of how an economy works, Thomas could have been a very effective political force, but not as a socialist, for with any such understanding he could never have been a socialist! But he was a great American, in the tradition of Gene Debs; both were very much products of their particular time.

When I entered the voting booth for the first time in 1948, at age twenty-one, I repeated my mother's history of 1920 and cheerfully voted Socialist, for Norman Thomas. I doubt that I have voted for any one since who approached Thomas's incredible integrity and compassion for humanity. Remarkably, I still have a warm memory of that experience, although I now know, of course, that command and control systems do not and cannot work, and demonstrably cannot manage the economy. They perpetuate poverty, destroy freedom, subordinate the individual to a mindless bureaucracy of doublespeak, and in their worst incarnations, brutalize their most imaginative and independent citizens, all the while purporting to stave off those very conditions. This, of course, is why Thomas was anticommunist, but he did not appreciate that it was impossible to rely upon well-meaning socialist politicians to avoid the corruptions of increased state control of the private economy.

An understanding of why I could feel warmly toward that first voting experience would go a long way to explaining why, in the name of freedom, fairness, and justice, we realize less and less of all three; why market liberalization efforts often break through the political process—for example, the worldwide privatization and decentralization movement of the 1990s—but the pendulum also swings back and gradually undermines wealth-creating, and poverty-reducing, reforms.

The answer, based on ongoing behavioral research with my colleagues, is found in an inherent tension between the individual's personal experience in social exchange and the requirements of freedom in the external order of impersonal exchange through markets. As I have written in my research, you can make the case that the collectivist impulses of the individual are nourished by human perceptions and understanding that come, experientially, from what the economic historian and Nobel laureate Doug North calls "personal exchange." Personal exchange is what I described earlier, on the farm, as trading favors and barter in close-knit communities based on trust and reliability. In this more intimate environment, our individual experience is that good comes from reciprocity—doing good and receiving good in return—being cooperative, and being a good neighbor. At the level of the family, extended family, and our social groupings, our direct experience is that good intentions produce good outcomes.

In impersonal market exchange through prices, we do not see that it involves—functionally, but not emotionally—the same reciprocal benefits for buyer and seller that characterize personal exchange. Neither do we see that specialization—or knowledge and task subdivision—derives from and is supported by markets; that each of us is empowered by markets to specialize in some field of knowledge and skills, increasing thereby our value to others through market exchange, and to use our higher earning capacity to enjoy the products and services of others who also specialize in activities different from ours. Without markets, no one can specialize in the acquisition of unique high-value skills and knowledge while simultaneously benefiting from the uniquely valuable skills and knowledge of others unknown to us. We do not directly experience the fact that millions of people, with differing cultures, languages, skills, and resources, cooperate through long networks of interdependence connected by prices; we all benefit from the immense wealth created by this invisible cooperation. These facts are not part of an experience of warmth, as in our deliberate acts of neighborhood sharing. If the price of gasoline increases, our immediate perception is that the oil companies get more money and we get less, and that is not "fair." We do not see that some remote disruption of a source of supply or an increase in demand has caused the price increase, and that this sets in motion an adjustment process that will provide incentives for supplies going elsewhere to be diverted to us. We experience the effect while not knowing its cause, or the equilibrating adjustments set loose by the original disruption.

Consequently, we readily come to believe that markets perform badly and that by means of better planning and intervention we can make them work better for everybody—and make us feel better because we have taken action—but such a myopic policy has unintended consequences, making us worse off, and these consequences are invisible to our experience. Emotionally, we easily and warmly relate to programs of redistribution and control in political economy. Yet those programs, unintentionally, so often do far more harm than good wherever the natural state is both efficient and in equilibrium. Any human good that is claimed to flow from some interventionist scheme will seem to ring true, but the creeping and accumulating harm it causes in limiting the growth of wealth and welfare is not plainly visible to our experience.

Periodically, there is a moment of truth. Under the Democrats, we had the John Kennedy tax reform in the 1960s, when Kennedy said: "Our tax system still siphons out of the private economy too large a share of personal and business purchasing power and reduces the incentive for risk, investment and effort–thereby aborting our recoveries and stifling our national growth rate." The highest marginal tax bracket fell from 91 to 65%, and, far from lowering tax revenue, it rose.[3]

Under the Reagan Republicans, a similar House and Senate coalition led to the tax reforms of 1986. But these sporadic truth moments did nothing to change the incremental process that had culminated in the high marginal taxes and tax subsidies for farmers, real estate, and so on that created the distortions in the first place, and required reform. For instance, with the breakdown of the Cancún international trade meeting (September 2003) the less developed South Asian countries have revolted against the subsidies and protectionist agricultural policies of the USA, Europe, and even nonagricultural Japan (in rice production). Good for them; may they help turn the tide against such policies and open the globe to freer multilateral trade, not more of these regional bilateral half measures in which neighbors solemnly agree to beggar their other neighbors.

Similarly, New Zealand's socialism created an economy in crisis by 1980. Extensive, perhaps unprecedented liberalization and reform of taxes and state ownership were undertaken with demonstrated economic benefits. Yet by the late 1990s, many of those reforms were being compromised. New Zealanders are a caring and egalitarian people—I have experienced it—but this leads easily to policies in which people unintentionally shoot themselves in the foot. The New Zealand economy came out of World War II with the third-highest per capita income in the world—tied with Switzerland—and then pissed away this accomplishment because it was unable and unwilling to compete in growing world markets. A small country competing in world markets cannot afford socialism and its wastefulness; a large country can afford it only for as long as it has the resources to sustain the wastefulness. A small country rich in oil, diamonds, and other extractive resources can afford it only so long as the revenue from basic commodity exports continues.

The crux of the socialist disease and its destruction of community were captured for me in 1978 in a taxicab trip from the Wellington airport to my hotel. The driver was friendly, and I said, "Tell me about your country." He replied, "It's really wonderful. I don't like paying half my small income in taxes, but we receive so much that is free: healthcare benefits, prescriptions, free education through college and advanced graduate study. I am just a cab driver, but my son is going to be a medical doctor. He has finished his medical degree and internship and will begin practicing next year." In recognition of his obvious pride, I said, "How wonderful. You have every right to be proud. Is your son going to practice in Wellington?" He replied, "Oh, no, he's going to Australia. You can't make any money here." The New Zealand economic crisis occurred two years later, and the socialist system was replaced—by the Labor Government

---

[3]http://www.ontheissues.org/celeb/John_F__Kennedy_Tax_Reform.htm.

that had once championed it. In the 1930s, amidst the flush of enthusiasm for socialism, Labor's forbearers had believed that centralized command over the economy would work so long as the control process remained democratic.

I tell the taxi-driver story in talks around the world on the topic of markets, globalization, and prosperity. It triggers a wave of audience laughter. In private discussions afterward, from Iceland and Scandinavia to Mexico, people tell me their own brain-drain stories and their worry that opportunities at home are not adequate to hold their best and brightest. I am told that it's less of a problem in Iceland, because those who leave tend eventually to return for love of homeland, but even there those wonderfully dedicated people are flirting with danger. Essentially, state policies that inhibit, restrict, or control private development levy a tax—the forgone higher incomes available elsewhere—on the goodwill that Icelanders create for each other in their home country.

Occasionally, but only rarely I am happy to report, after my speech someone will suggest the need for a rule that requires those educated at home to stay at home. Thus emerges the authoritarian mind, looking for a fix that will make the impossible possible, but failing to see that this "solution" is at the core of the problem. First, you do some great and obvious "social good," such as free education through advanced degrees. Then, after it becomes clear that what you have done is flawed because of "ungrateful citizens" you crank up the policing power of the state to plug the leak. It says a lot about New Zealanders that they could not bring themselves to take police action before or after the crisis hit. Instead, they opted for greater freedom.

The Berlin wall was Communist East Germany's attempt to forcefully retain its best and brightest who wanted to migrate to one of the many places that offered greater opportunities. American policies guard, Berlin-wall-like, the US border to keep out people who seek opportunities unavailable at home. This is bad policy based on the premise that the individual exists for the good of the group, rather than that the group exists for the benefit of the individual.

Here is a concrete illustration of how East Germany shot off its legs by causing people to leave, and how we, through strict immigration policies, hurt ourselves by keeping out people who are seeking a better life. When he was a teenager, my friend Bill Oschewski walked out of East Germany with his uncle, with only the clothes he was wearing. This was shortly before the Berlin wall had been built, when people could still get out but could take no valuable possessions of any kind. He managed to immigrate to the USA, attend school, earn an engineering degree, and afterward he worked in Tucson for Burr-Brown. Eventually, he left the company, founded Apex Micro Technology, in part self-financing the start-up by selling his spacious home. Eventually, he sold this successful electronic manufacturing business. He was part of a wealth-creation process that might have occurred in his homeland but for its failed commitment to freedom and opportunity. Sadly, over the decades, he saw in the USA a growing number of regulations, taxes, and bureaucratic interferences that made it increasingly difficult to conduct his operations and to do good for others while doing well for his family as part of an international market system.

In early 1940, my father lost his job, permanently, when the Bridgeport plant was closed. My father always said the independent entrepreneur owner of Bridgeport, A. A. Buschow, closed his factory rather than cede control of his oil-field equipment factory to President Franklin Roosevelt's defense industry production. I have not been able to confirm this story, but I have been able to verify that A. A. Buschow was president of Bridgeport. Also, The Wichita Eagle reports, September 15, 1940, that the "Culver Aircraft Company yesterday closed a contract for purchase of the Bridgeport plant in North Wichita and will move their airplane factory here from Columbus, Ohio about October 1. Entire plant and airport, about 43 acres, is included. Price was around $100,000."

My father went to work for the Coleman Lantern Company, but stayed there for less than a year. Then, on October 24, 1940, he was hired at Stearman Aircraft, which had been purchased by Boeing in 1938, the year before Hitler marched into Poland. I remember the larger-than-normal headlines in the *Wichita Beacon* announcing Hitler's unopposed invasion, September 1, 1939.

Lloyd Stearman manufactured the famous PT-13 and PT-17 Kaydet biplanes that served as US Primary Trainers then and throughout World War II. The Navy had adopted Stearman's plane in 1934. If you are driving in the West, occasionally you still see a Stearman biplane providing its high-maneuverability service as a crop duster. In 1941, Boeing started the construction of Plant II, where the B-29 was to be built, and the Stearman plant (built in 1930) was renamed the Boeing-Wichita Plant I. By 1945, more than 1000 B-29s and 10,000 Kaydets had been manufactured by Boeing-Wichita for the war effort. My father moved from Plant I to Plant II when the latter was completed, working as a supervisor in the Machine Tool Department, where he was employed until his death in 1954 at age sixty-four, a few months before his planned retirement.

Sometime in the 1940s, to increase war production, the USA converted to "Roosevelt time"—or Daylight Saving Time. In Kansas, it was said that Roosevelt time replaced God's time. There was no concept of an arbitrary standard time, created by humans, in Kansas folk physics.

Wichita became the national, then international, center for light plane manufacturing. Why? I always heard that it was because Kansas had more clear flying days than any of the other competing states. The industry's rapid growth and the stock market bubble in the 1920s and 1930s were part of a classic economic surge with many new products in strong demand. In 1929, Wichita had some fifteen different airplane manufacturers: Travel Air, Stearman, Cessna, United, Laird, Swift, Lark, Knoll, Bradley, Yunkers, Wichita, Watkins, Mooney, Sullivan, and Buckley (*Wichita Century,* 1870–1970). A decade later the surviving company names would be Beech, Cessna, and Stearman (Boeing). Three companies (some might also count Culver, which did not stay in Wichita) rose like the phoenix from the bankruptcies and consolidations of the many early century beginners that were financed by exuberant investors. Clyde Cessna, Walter Beech, and Lloyd Stearman had been essential to the entrepreneurial survival process. Incredible long-term value was created from those risky experiments in new technology, technology management, and the process of determining who should be among the survivors of the fifteen start-ups, after the shakeout commencing in 1929. Every new product bubble and crash, each fueled by a wave of innovation, from steamships, railroads, and mass retailing in the nineteenth century, to the computer, communication, and Internet revolution of the 1990s, writes a similar story.

Along with a story of entry and expansion, there is exit, decline, and retrenchment. Hence, the end of Boeing's 85-year history in Wichita was reported by *The Wichita Eagle*: "End of an era: Boeing in final stages of leaving Wichita." By Molly McMillin. July 29, 2014, 05:42 p.m.

After my stellar first-grade academic achievements, I continued to perform well in the city elementary schools—except for penmanship from Mrs. Hadley at Martinson, which was never my forte. (The psychologist who gave me a battery of tests in 1995 suggested that I had dysgraphia. Come now, doesn't every physician exhibit this disease when he writes prescriptions?) My school performance, however, deteriorated beginning in the eighth grade and all through high school. I found high school studies very uninspiring—girls were far and away more interesting—but I always expected to go to college. My inspiration was just temporarily diverted, as is common with teenagers. I vividly recall that my mother helped me with my English homework when we were learning to diagram sentences in the tenth grade, and complained about the deterioration in the quality of the public schools, circa 1941–1942. She had learned to diagram sentences in the eighth grade. It was not evident to me why one should learn it in any grade, but what did I know? I never got the point of diagramming, nor did I ever understand what language was all about, until fifty-odd years later when I had the great pleasure of reading Steve Pinker's *The Language Instinct* (1994).

I have often wondered whether my mother's socialist constructions would have survived her pragmatism, and the reality of poor performance under socialist-controlled production, including public education. Much later I would learn from economics books that education was a public good that "needed" to be supplied by the government. This is one of the many things you learn in economics that are not true: Public goods, including education, can be and are routinely provided privately; it is entirely feasible to have privately provided education even if much of it is publicly financed, as with the voucher system. I wonder what Mr. Hemberger would have thought of the idea that he was working for the government, not his neighbors, and producing a public good!

I began seventh grade at Allison Intermediate in January 1938. I had a big crush on Virginia Hill, who was cute as a bug's ear. Plenty of others had a crush on Virginia. She and I were in the same class. In the summer, probably following the seventh or eighth grade, I used to ride my bike way down on South Seneca to Harry Street. Clinton Reser went with me sometimes. On the northeast corner of Seneca and Harry was a big lot, but not such a big house, considering that it was home to a large family. The lot was large to accommodate Hills Nursery; Virginia's father ran a greenhouse and nursery business. She had two older sisters, whose names have long been obliterated from my memory, an older brother, Dale, and a sweet-as-sin younger sister, Rosemary, was very nearly up to Virginia's pace-making standard. You could have eaten Virginia with a spoon. The Hills had a big mulberry tree in the front yard, and we used to climb it and pick mulberries to eat until we were stuffed. Decades later I drove down on the south side of town, and Dale was running Hills Nursery. The others had scattered. Virginia had moved to California. Why does everyone end up in California?

I must have had a crush on Virginia for two years, but there was no visible evidence of reciprocation. Perhaps Virginia felt similarly, but I was just too socially inept to see it. In those days and at that age no one ever revealed feelings, but that may have been me. I may have been the principal "no one" who had not a clue that others were on a frequency different from mine and that their messages were not received. Anyway, after we all transferred to North High, I no longer saw much of Virginia. She was popular at North High, dated the football heroes, and all that. I was never part of the social scene at North. You are born to your caste in high school. Virginia was cute enough to overcome both her caste handicaps—she was born on both the west and south sides of the tracks. That was really Oblivion-Ville in Wichita, but you can overcome oblivion if you're a sweetheart, and she was. I did visit Virginia in the hospital once, where she was recovering from surgery on her tailbone. The upshot is that my crush passed to Rosemary, who was a year younger than Virginia and in the class behind ours. That made her my age—you do what you have to do. Remember: I was the youngest in my class, thanks to Mr. Hemberger back in the first grade. Being the youngest in your class and male are not conditions calculated to enhance your social status in high school.

From Rosemary, my ongoing need to be in a state of crush passed to Juanita Brockert. She was something: The sweethearts were getting sweeter!

It was almost exactly a mile from my home to my intermediate school on Seneca Street, one block south of Douglas. On the way you passed the Nu Way Restaurant and Drive Inn on the north side of Douglas Avenue, a street that at the time was paved entirely with bricks. Tom McEvoy opened the Nu Way in 1930. It is still in operation at the same location, where I stopped to eat a Nu Way with my wife Candace, my niece, Marlene (Billye's daughter); and Marlene's husband, Harold Shapley, on another of my life-long sequence of lucky days, April 13, 2003. And Candace and I visited the Nu Way again—on our Way from the airport to the hotel—in June, 2014. None of the earlier pictures of Tom McEvoy had survived on the walls since our visit in 2003. But it makes sense to me that, with the arrival of catsup or ketchup on the tables, Tom would disappear! We are talking about a legend: How many restaurants have operated continuously at the same location for eighty-four years, based on a single new product that has not changed? Tom McEvoy was a great Wichita entrepreneur. Not being rich was his deliberate choice.

A Nu Way was and is a type of hamburger sandwich that was made in an entirely "new way." I ate precious few of them from 1938 to 1941, because—even at five cents each—we could not afford them except as special treats. The ground hamburger is not fried in the form of the standard hamburger patty. The meat is stir-fried so that the finely ground ribbons of beef are separated like rice and kept hot in a steam table until served. It is cooked with onions and mild spices (secret?) that give it an exceptionally rich beef flavor that radiates from the large exposed surface area of the ground meat. In a typical hamburger, the beef is compressed into a single large patty with much less surface area for the same volume. For a Nu Way, a hot hamburger bun is spread with a thin layer of mustard, a layer of thin slices of dill pickle is added, and the cooked beef mixture is scooped on top of the pickles. It is served in lightly waxed wrapping paper to keep it hot, and it tastes quite different from the traditional hamburger, with a fine bouquet of flavor from meat, bun, pickle, and onion. It was and is a culinary sensation. If you happen to be passing through Wichita, don't miss the experience of a Nu Way. Tom McEvoy also served chili, keg root beer (homemade fresh each day) in ice cold mugs, root beer floats (with floating scoops of vanilla ice cream), and root beer frosties (with the ice cream churned in). There were no French fries on the menu, and no catsup was ever available on the counters or tables—none, absolutely none. Tom believed it ruined the Nu Way, and he was dead right. There were also home-baked desserts available: apple pie and sour cherry pie.

In the spirit of Ben Franklin, who refused to patent the Franklin stove, Tom McEvoy refused repeated offers to franchise his product. He believed strongly that it could not be mass-produced under the quality control he made famous. His restaurant often had a waiting line, with people also standing around the walls behind occupied stools. After Tom died, his wife, Helen, managed the business in the same tradition, finally selling it to its current (as of 2003) owner in 1976. There are now four other Nu Ways on the east side of town; all serve French fries, and the abominable catsup bottles are on every table. I can see and hear Tom screaming from his grave. But the original West Side address still serves a great Nu Way as part of an unforgettable slice of Wichita-style Americana, complete as of 2014 with catsup, which makes me want to cry. Rest in peace, Tom: Your innovation has survived unaltered, as served, and catsup is not the only generational quirk of the last eighty-eight and counting years.

My best grades in the ninth grade were in woodworking because it involved actually hand-manufacturing something—a red-gum (*Eucalyptus camaldulensis*, native to Australia) knee-hole desk that I still had with me from 1952 to 1955 at Harvard. I was working evenings and weekends, continuing the employment I had started during the previous summer, at age twelve. I had begun my first wage work for Mrs. Blackburn, who owned the West Side Drug Store. It was located next door west of the Sinclair Station at the northwest corner of Meridian and Douglas—one-half block south and a block west of my home. I delivered prescriptions and sundries on my bicycle to customers who called in orders. The most common delivery items were prescriptions, over-the-counter remedies like Bayer Aspirin and cough medicines, bottled Coca-Cola, Kansas City's Muehlebach beer, Steffan's Ice Cream, Trojan or Sheik brand condoms, and Kotex. To qualify for delivery, the minimum order was twenty-five cents. To give you some perspective, a pint of Steffan's was fifteen cents and a six-pack of the original bottled Coke was twenty-five cents plus a private, profit-motivated, two-cent deposit on each bottle to ensure its return to the bottling factory.

Incidentally, until recently, I avoided drinking Coke or Pepsi from a can, so accustomed was I to the bottles—I swear that it tastes different! But actually, except for fountain cokes, a different experience then than now, I preferred Pepsi because of its higher carbonation, and perhaps its clever ad: "Pepsi Cola hits the spot, twelve full ounces that's a lot, twice as much for a nickel toooo, Pepsi Cola is the drink for you." (The classic Coke bottle was six ounces.) All that has changed. I now avoid all sugar and refined carbs having discovered the growing new as well as old evidence that these are sources of damage to health.

I must insert something in this chapter about movie houses in the 1930s. They were an experience lost in an unrecoverable past. I remember them being noisy, though not objectionable, because an intense audience participation was part of the visual and emotional experience. I often attended the Saturday afternoon matinée, West Side Theater, admission 10 cents, and it was always crowded. Occasionally, we still saw silent comedies—Charlie Chaplin was still making "silents," *The Great Dictator*, his first "talkie," was not made until 1940. The Chaplin classic, and in my view the greatest film of all times, was *City Lights*. While still powerful in the privacy of your TV room at home, it was a movie without comparison in a 1930s movie house. The audience made the difference. Similar legendary silent films were those of Buster Keaton, *The General*, or Harold Lloyd, *The Kid Brother.* We also had "shorts" like *The Keystone Cops*, but Chaplin, Keaton, and Lloyd were the great stars. They produced a bedlam, even convulsions, of laughter that came from the contagion induced by the extent of audience participation. You could not stop laughing. Chaplin was a cinematics master, as he produced, directed, wrote, edited, choreographed, and was the star actor in his movies—"Who'll Buy my Violets," the movie's theme song written by Charlie, was unforgettably blended with the pathos of the final scene.

Like so many in his time, Chaplin was a victim of the McCarthy era. On September 19, 1952, Chaplin was en route to the UK when the US Attorney-General ordered the Immigration Service to hold him for hearings if he returned to the USA, although he had been already been issued a re-entry permit. Upon arriving in the UK, Charlie Chaplin concluded that it would not be possible to return to the USA. His immediate reaction was that he would never return, "even if Jesus Christ was the president." Following the London premiere of his film "Limelight," judged highly successful, he lived in Vevey, Switzerland, where he died in 1977. Public opinion in the USA turned against him, and his European film "A King in New York," was not released in the USA until 16 years later. In 1972, he returned to the USA one last time to receive a Special Academy Award for lifetime contributions to film—a memorable occasion for me. In 1975, the Queen conferred knighthood on this icon of American films.[4]

This epic end to a great career will surely be captured, someday, in a tragic Chaplin-style film absent the comedy.

Recall the history of coal oil and shale oil, which shows that if the conditions are right, price, and cost, etc., you may get an environmentally friendly economic response that is otherwise not sustainable. Here, it is again with the spontaneous emergence of the cost-based deposit for the return of bottles. The California and other state redemption deposits that consumers have become accustomed to paying did not originate as a government-imposed policy to prevent littering, although governments would later codify the practice after wage regulation and manufacturing innovation had driven out recycling as an efficient market economic response. In the 1930s extending into the post-World War II period, glass bottles were valuable and more

---

[4]http://news.bbc.co.uk/onthisday/hi/dates/stories/september/19/newsid_3102000/3102179.stm.

costly to produce than the two-cent deposit inducement to get people to return them. Thus, container deposits became common because recycling was cost-effective. Container litter control was a problem solved by market incentives: The benefit to the bottler of providing deposit incentives for bottle return was greater than the cost of manufacturing a new bottle. This was before minimum-wage laws were binding—more on this topic will appear below. Cheap unskilled labor was profitably employed in a huge return movement of bottles to the factories. I must have returned hundreds of empty bottles, perhaps as many as a thousand, to the West Side Drug Store after delivering Coke or Muehlebach Beer. (This was Kansas City's entry into the local brewery tradition well before the 1930s.) My playmates and I regularly scoured the back alleys and trash cans for discarded pop and beer bottles to earn pocket money. One man's litter was another man's, or boy's income. We also collected papers, worth a half-cent a pound, and rags, especially rags, because they had a very high return on scavenging at seven cents per pound. We were in the waste sorting business—a profitable business when wage work was scarce. We were all poor but happy rag, paper, and bottle collectors.

All this experience provided the motivating background for four papers I wrote on the economics of the environment: "Dynamics of Waste Accumulation: Disposal Versus Recycling," *Quarterly Journal of Economics,* November 1972; "An Optimistic Theory of Exhaustible Resources," *Journal of Economic Theory,* December 1974; "Economics of Wilderness Resources," *Intermountain Economic Review,* Fall 1976. The last paper was inspired and written by a Grand Canyon white-water rafting trip, so I deducted all expenses for the trip from my taxable income. As it happened, the IRS audited me for that year, and, after I showed the auditor a copy of the research paper, my deduction stood unchallenged! Finally, there was "Littering, Derelicts, and the Pricing System," chapter 22 in *Economics of Natural and Environmental Resources,* ed. V. L. Smith (New York: Gordon and Breach, 1977; reissued by Routledge, 2013).

Incidentally, I still have my original Social Security card, which I signed when I was twelve or thirteen. To my mother, Social Security was an unrivaled social invention. Not understanding that it was just a tax, and that it was not vested, she wanted me to enroll early. Here, I sit eighty-odd years later, receiving Social Security payments of $4000 and some change each month. What would the payments have been if Social Security had been vested? Let me give you my off-the-cuff estimate: $40,000.

Between deliveries at the West Side Drug, I waited on customers and learned to "soda jerk" at an old-fashioned drug store fountain (cokes, milk and malt shakes, ice cream sundaes, ice cream sodas, etc.). To my delight, when Candace and I moved into a neighborhood near Old Towne Orange, California, in January 2008, I discovered Watson's Drug Store, founded in 1899 and located just off the Old Towne circle. It has the same kind of old-fashioned soda fountain that I learned to manage in Wichita. (I heartily recommend Watson's to you, both for quality and reasonable prices. Enjoy! However, a recent remodeling has largely converted that Americana tradition into a booze and food bar.) I can still make a great fresh lime soda with vanilla ice cream, but that delicacy is no longer part of my regular diet.

At the West Side Drug, I was paid fifty cents for a six-hour shift from 6:00 p.m. to midnight, plus rare tips. Let's see now, fifty cents per six-hour shift is the equivalent of about four empty coke bottles returned per hour—call it economics in one, easy lesson. You can see why there would hardly have been a bottle anywhere that was not found and returned. Minimum-wage laws, not yet such an important part of the national political do-good movement, would have helped to destroy the economic incentive for private firms to recycle bottles. More certainly, the good intentions from trying to force the payment of higher wages would have compromised Mrs. Blackburn's ability to hire me; later, that outcome was guaranteed in the form of the enforcement of prohibitions on child labor. I was fortunate *not* to have been protected by such laws, and perforce, I learned something about being responsible to an employer, and to her customers, at an early age. As for the recycling equilibrium, technology alone might have eventually lowered the cost of manufacturing new containers enough to justify a government deposit fee sufficient to induce recycling, and thereby save the public costs of waste handling (Figs. 5.1, 5.2, 5.3, 5.4, and 5.5).

Fig. 5.1 Vernon at Martinson School 80 years after second grade

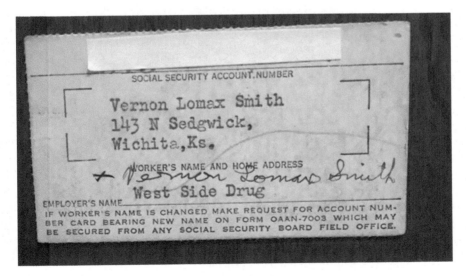

Fig. 5.2 Social security registration in 1940. Mom insists I register

Fig. 5.3 Nu Way 1957 stop-off on way to Santa Monica. My 1942 Cadillac on left, mom on left

Fig. 5.4 Nu Way history. Catsup invasion by 2014

Fig. 5.5   Vernon, Marlene Wichita 2014

6

High School, Boeing, and the War Years

For the first time in the history of the world, your young men are dying in a war that - despite all its horrors - is for them an experience of love. Do not betray them. Let them dictate their peace when the time comes! Let that peace reassemble them! This war is honorable; may their spiritual faith make peace as honorable.

I am happy among my french and american comrades. After my first missions in the P-38s Lightnings, they discovered my age. 43 years! What a scandal! Your American rules are inhuman. At 43 years of age one does not fly a fast plane like the Lightnings. The long white beards might get entangled with the controls and cause accidents. I was therefore unemployed for a few months.

—Antoine de St. Exupéry (1900–1944), *Letter to an American*

In January 1941, I finished at Allison Intermediate School and enrolled at North High School, commuting by bicycle three to four miles from home to school. On the way, one mile from my house at the northeast corner of Second Street and Seneca, was a restaurant and fountain called the OK Drive-In, owned and operated by Don Eaton, who had moved and greatly enlarged and extended the reach of his operation from its location at Meridian and Douglas. Keep in mind that I was an integral part of a community of family, extended family, and neighbors. Consequently, at age fourteen, on the strength of my soda fountain and other work experience, Don offered me a job at $1 per day, summers and weekends. That seemed like a very good wage to me—$6 per week with one day off. I remember in the early 1930s, after my father was laid off at Bridgeport, he was paid $1 a day

© The Author(s) 2018
V. L. Smith, *A Life of Experimental Economics, Volume I*,
https://doi.org/10.1007/978-3-319-98404-9_6

working as a temporary construction carpenter making and installing windows. At the OK Drive-In, I operated the fountain, also learned to "fry cook," and Don later gave me a raise to $8 per six-day week. But from Don Eaton, I received a much larger benefit than wage earnings of $8 per week.

From Don, I learned how to make really great hamburgers, and to this day people rave about them, yet the procedure is simplicity itself, spiced with a little loving attention to detail. You take a fresh large hamburger bun and slice it into two open-faced halves. The meat patty should be about the same size as the bun, and *not too thick*—one-quarter to no more than three-eighths of an inch is plenty. The idea is to avoid the meat flavor dominating everything. You nurture the subtle blend of meat, bun, dill pickle, onion, tomato, and mustard. If you are hungry for steak, go to Kansas City and order a rare KC strip steak, but don't obliterate the other important flavors in a good hamburger. Place the hamburger patty on the hot solid iron griddle (*not* a barbecue grill with iron slats that dry out the meat patties and change their flavor for the worse) to fry. Immediately, place the bottom half of the bun on the griddle near the hamburger after scraping any excess grease off the metal under the bun. Place the top half of the bun on the frying meat patty. When the meat is half cooked to order, turn the meat over and interchange the top half of the bun on the meat with the bottom half on the griddle. The griddle toasts the buns, while the frying meat steams each bun-half through and through with rich beef flavor. Take it off the griddle when done to order and wrap in sandwich form with a large paper napkin or hand towel to hold in the heat and marinate the flavor. Do *not* dump it unwrapped on a cold plate. Finally, you serve it with *very thin*-sliced fresh, vine-ripened tomatoes (Ponderosa tomatoes, if available), thin-sliced whole dill pickle (slice your own from whole bulk dill pickles; the sliced pickles in the canned jars are too thick), and thin-sliced onion, all prepared in advance so that the hamburger can be served hot. The onions can be fried if the customer prefers. Why must these three items all be sliced very thin? It's because taste buds respond to the surface area, not volume, and you want to maximize the surface area for a given bulk volume. (Recall the Nu Way principle.) You also can serve the hamburger with a little mustard spread thinly and evenly on the meat or bun. Above all, if you are preparing them to order at your party, *discourage any person from dumping catsup all over the meat*. In fact, hide the bloody catsup and if some yahoo asks for it, tell him that you don't have any. Catsup on a finely crafted hamburger is an outrage. Catsup destroys the subtle blend of fresh-sliced tomato flavor with the beef, pickle, onion, mustard, and the steamed and toasted bun. We are talking about an art form here, and it really must be respected.

Since the advent of the fast food hamburger, the art of fine handcrafted hamburger cuisine has largely disappeared.

I fried hamburgers for Don Eaton in 1941 for $1 a day, long before the minimum-wage laws were binding, even though the federal minimum wage law dates from 1938. The minimum wage then was 25 cents per hour, but in the world I am describing there was no universal coverage by the law. The Fair Labor Standards Act of 1938 (FLSA) applied to industries whose combined employment represented only about one-fifth of the labor force. In these industries, it banned oppressive child labor and set the minimum hourly wage at 25 cents and the maximum workweek at 44 hours.[1] These were union-inspired moves to keep young adults, blacks and Hispanics, and other minorities out of the labor force where formerly they had long had easy access.

Subsequent amendments to the FLSA extended coverage to additional employees and raised the minimum wage—in 1949, from 40 to 75 cents an hour for all workers. Further amendments greatly expanded the scope of coverage in the retail trade sector and increased the minimum to $1.15 per hour, effective September 1961, and to $1.25 an hour in September 1963. Throughout these changes, small businesses had been exempt, but by 1967 the sales volume cutoff for exemption had been lowered to $250,000 per year. In 1989, all employees of small retail businesses became subject to minimum wages and overtime pay, but provision was made for "training wages" at 85% of the minimum. Consequently, by this time the retail food industry was well-subjected to the effects of a minimum wage. Nowhere, it seems, was the "loophole" covered that enabled foreign imports of manufactured goods to escape these laws by shifting production overseas![2] An enormous social cost of this legislation was to undercut the on-the-job training that I had personally experienced and enabled me to advance to better jobs, pay, and increased skill. Teenagers and young adults, who commonly get their first jobs while still living at home, are among those most hurt by minimum wages.

The fast-food industry has been an extended study in how to save labor cost through mechanization, achieved by substituting machine capital for labor. This process would have been accelerated by minimum wage legislation, causing unemployment in the entry-level unskilled labor market for young adults. However, fast food retailing was invented long before the 1938 wage legislation. The first and most prominent fast food hamburger was produced by the White Castle System in Wichita. The chain had expanded to 123 establishments in 16 cities by 1934, including New York, when it moved to Columbus, Ohio. Reported in *Wichita Beacon*, July 16, 1934. The White Castle System preserved the custom-made hamburger far more faithfully than did the Post World War II chains. Tom McAvoy of Nu Way fame would have witnessed this process and deliberately sought to avoid it, convinced that no part of his quality Nu Way operation could be automated.

---

[1]http://www.dol.gov/dol/aboutdol/history/flsa1938.htm.
[2]See, http://www.dol.gov/whd/minwage/coverage.htm.

Don served the best chili you can buy anywhere. It was Dye's Chili, also served at the Nu Way. Dye's was ready-made in Wichita, distributed to local restaurants in solid five-pound blocks, and could be bought in one-pound bricks for home consumption in the local grocery stores. It was cholesterol-rich, a solid brick at room temperature, and a cholesterol nightmare for later generations of Americans taught to believe that it was not heart-friendly. But you cannot beat it for good taste. If you worry about fat intake, which I do not, then avoid fat for a day or two on either side of the day you want to eat a couple of bowls of Dye's Chili. At the OK Drive-In, we would put a five-pound block in a deep steam table pan with some water and gradually dissolve it. A separate steam table pan held cooked pinto beans. Chili straight was fifteen cents per bowl; chili with beans cost ten cents per bowl.

Can you make your own homemade chili that compares with Dye's? Yes, you can—without the cholesterol binge if you want—but it takes a day, a night, a second day, and some patience and tender loving care. To begin with, I don't work from a recipe. I have probably made it a couple hundred or more times, and I judge proportions depending on how many people I am cooking it for, and how I feel at the time. I will write out a recipe as I think through the sequence of making a batch, based on five pounds of beef. So I am only giving you estimates.

Read it through in advanced so that you can list the ingredients and have them ready, and also so that you understand the sequence. Some of the ingredients are for cooking the beans, while some are for the chili. Each is cooked separately and combined when served or consumed separately, depending on individual preferences.

You will need about an eight-quart pot for the chili and a four-quart pot for the beans. You cook the chili and beans separately because the cooking time is different, and when served, those who are prone to flatulence, or otherwise want to avoid beans in their diet, can enjoy the chili separately. The beans I cook have a moderately high yield of intestinal gas—about .38-caliber farts, on a scale up to .50-caliber. Also, some like lots of beans and some very little—more beans, more gas. It's the "musical fruit," as we used to say.

Begin making the chili sometime in the morning, on the day before you are going to serve it. This is because you are going to keep that chili pot hot for the entire day, let it marinate cold all night, and then reheat it ever so slowly and keep it hot the next day until it is served.

Start with very lean beef (this is the low-cholesterol compromise; if you don't want to compromise, use regular beef). Tell your butcher you want a chili grind; if he does not know what you mean, you need to replace your butcher. If he is otherwise a good butcher, tell him to set his grinder on "coarse" and run the meat through once and only once. Better yet, this is what I do: Buy a lean five-pound top round roast. Cut it in chunks about one inch square and dust with flour. The meat is going to cook long enough to crumble anyway, so it does not have to be ground. Next, you should coarsely chop four three-inch-diameter onions. Peel all the cloves contained in a full head of garlic; sometimes, if I am in a garlic mood, I use two heads. Notice that I said "heads," not "bulbs" of garlic—a head is maybe fifteen bulbs. They can be skinned and chopped, but they will cook to mush anyway and can be squeezed out of their skins, so why bother skinning?

Pour half to three-quarters of a cup of good extra-virgin olive oil in your big pot and heat it thoroughly. Put in the beef, and set the heat high enough to brown the meat. Now add the onions and garlic and stir it with a wooden spoon while it sautés. If you have fresh basil, by all means put in a big handful of leaves. Add several cans of Swanson's, or your favorite brand of beef broth, enough to cover the meat and onions an inch or two, and stir. This will give the chili a rich, undiluted beef flavor. Now add one or two large cans of whole tomatoes with basil (my favorite, Hunt's brand, cans it with basil—when I have a garden I sometimes use fresh vine-ripe tomatoes, but don't use store-bought fresh tomatoes unless you have a trusted source). Stir some more, and add about two heaping tablespoons of either ground or whole cumin seeds. Once it is thoroughly heated, turn the heat down under the pot. At this point cover it with a lid, and let it just barely simmer.

Never, never, never boil it.

Now there comes a crucial procedure. Listen up! Put fifteen to eighteen whole red, dry New Mexico or Anaheim red chili peppers in your sink—you may want to do this at the time you start sautéing the beef. Plug the sink and run in a few inches of water. Cut off and discard the stem tops and let the decapitated peppers soak long enough so that you can easily slit them up the side with a knife. Open them up. Take out all the seeds, and use your fingers to remove the long vertical membranes on the inside of each pepper. Why is this important? You are looking to produce a deep rich chili flavor, without corresponding firepower. Firepower is not even for Mexicans; it's for macho gringos. Most of the hotness in a pepper is in the seeds and membranes. The flavor is in the thin layer of chili flesh just below the tough skin. When you get them all well castrated, place ten to twelve of them whole on the top of the chili mixture (don't stir them in or you will find it more difficult to fish them out later). Keep the heat on low, and covered with a lid. The other five or six peppers can be laid aside for the beans that you will be cooking on the next day. Let the pot simmer for one to two hours. Check now and then to be sure that the heat is low enough to keep it from bubbling too much. All you really have to do is keep the pot hot—please, no boiling.

Also, check after a half hour to see if the whole pepper skins are very soft, but not cooking apart—take the lid off and fish the whole pepper skins out of the brew. I just turn the lid upside down on the table alongside the pot and put the skins on the inside of the lid. When they are cool, drain the juice in the lid back into the pot, place one of the peppers on a big cutting board, and use an ordinary table knife to scrape the chili paste off the inside of the tough, waxy skin. Throw the skin away and repeat with the next pepper. When you have scraped them all free of the chili paste, put the chili paste back into the chili pot. Stir it all together. Place the lid on the pot and keep it hot all day at the back of the stove.

Thinking ahead, you need to start soaking a pound of pinto (or red) dried beans in water about 24 hours before you cook them.

After simmering the chili for the rest of the day, let it cool. Put the entire covered pot in your refrigerator overnight, or if it is a cold night put it in your garage, but cover it with a tight lid to keep the varmints out.

The next day, put the pot on the stove again with the burner on low and let it gradually heat up. Keep it hot until you serve it.

About three hours before you intend to serve the chili, finish preparing the beans. Pour the water-soaked beans into a colander to drain. Finely chop one or two yellow onions and plenty of garlic, and sauté them in olive oil in the bean pot. Add a can of tomatoes, followed by a heaping tablespoon of ground cumin. Stir, then add the soaked and rinsed beans. Substitute at least two or more cans of beef broth for some of the fresh water for cooking the beans. The bean bag will have cooking instructions, except that you are going to cook the beans in mostly (if not all) beef broth. After the beans have started cooking, add the remaining cleaned, seeded, and de-membraned peppers to the bean pot, but don't stir them in. When they are soft, fish them out, scrape off the paste and return the paste to the bean pot. Beans should also be cooked very gently, never boiled. You need only to keep the bean pot hot checking now and then to make sure they are going to be ready at serving time. You do not want to overcook the beans. They should be firm and soft, not cooked until the starch is thickening up the broth.

Serve the chili and the beans with buttermilk biscuits, or sourdough bread, and/or Nabisco chili crackers. Enjoy.

In the summer of 1943, at age sixteen, I applied for an entry-level job at Boeing Aircraft. My three-plus years of work experience made all the difference. I was hired and went to work at an incredible—to me—starting wage of 60 cents per hour, with a 10-cent premium for working the graveyard shift from midnight to 8:00 a.m. I was earning $5.60 per day! My savings started to skyrocket. I also attended summer school at North High so that when the fall term started I could graduate on schedule in January 1944 by taking only two courses. In that way, I could finish at North High School and continue at Boeing. It was very demanding, but it did not become burdensome until the following December when Boeing converted from three eight-hour shifts to two ten-hour shifts per day. I made it through the change, and after about six weeks, on January 28, I graduated. In her diary, on January 29, 1945, my mother noted, "Vernon off [work] today, graduated yesterday. Are we all glad [!]? Past 6 weeks have been tough, trying to work 10 h and go to school. Thank God, another year [before he] is 18 [and draft eligible]."

All my experience, learning, and wage earning at the low end of the labor market, starting with the West Side Drug would have been precluded by effective minimum wage laws—to say nothing of child labor laws. That there can be abuse in labor markets is not an issue, but the minimum wage is a blunderbuss whose abuse is to block all sorts of opportunities and means whereby individuals better themselves and their families. I lived at home, one of three who brought money into the family; both are important characteristics that are insensitive to calls for an individual "living wage." My father was already earning a living wage. Why refuse the opportunity to work for someone willing to accept less than a stand-alone living wage?

All employment involves on-the-job training. Your first job is of primary importance because it provides generic training in the protocol of working for another person, or a business—skills like punctuality in starting on time, coordinating with others, avoiding absences, committing to the satisfaction of the employers' customers. These are ubiquitous workplace skills that are transferable and benefit the individual in all future jobs. Here is a quote from an important Brookings Institution study:

"Teens and young adults with work experience in the previous year were more likely to be employed, lending support to the idea that employment is path-dependent among young people, with recent employment history acting as a strong predictor of current employment."[3]

Because these intangible benefits are subtle and not transparent, people are not aware of the good being done by not having a minimum wage. Knowing not the consequences, otherwise compassionate people quite naturally think minimum wages "sound and feel good" and such laws are therefore popular among people with no understanding of the immense harm they make possible. Politicians periodically make it a big issue, wanting to project an image of compassion for the underprivileged, get a warm response and ultimately find it a path to being elected. A currently popular bill to raise the minimum wage has just been defeated only because of a Republican-led filibuster—sometimes the Republicans get something right. In this case, it was a move in support of entry-level job opportunities for young blacks, Hispanics, high school and college dropouts, in that order.[4]

I recently had occasion to visit these issues again in a Facebook post responding to media commentary, some of which I reproduce below:

The print media had a feeding frenzy for a couple of days on the let's-you-and-him-fight theme. You may have noticed the fuss over the National Restaurant Association's (NRA) opposition to the minimum wage circulated under my name. I did not know that it was originated by the NRA—a fact not mentioned in the first report by the LA Times. The original version projected the usual political "gotcha" attitude and was full of errors. After I pointed out all the errors in the original article, it was corrected pretty accurately in the spirit of truth.[5]

---

[3]https://www.slideshare.net/RockefellerFound/the-plummeting-labor-market-fortunes-of-teens-and-young-adults.

[4]See http://online.wsj.com/news/articles/SB10001424052702304178104579533801387470492.

[5]http://www.latimes.com/business/hiltzik/la-fi-mh-nobel-laureates-for-suckers-20140317,0,3786129.story#axzz2wVqS1HNr.

However, I have to say that even after some redaction and correction in the update, the article incorrectly refers to me as a "conservative." Let the record stand that—as I understand what is popularly considered to be a conservative by writers like this one in the LA Times—I am not now and never have been a conservative. (I am better described as a "classical liberal" in the sense of the Scottish Enlightenment, but such labels are a slippery means of classification.)

My views on immigration and my largely peacenik stance, with exceptions, on US involvement in foreign conflict (have you noticed what a great job we do funding foreign Stalinist-style dictators?) disqualify me for this distinction, and would certainly outrage Laura Ingraham, whose show I love to listen to and learn the "conservative" point of view, although I do cringe when she rails against all the illegal immigrants she would deport. I must tell her some time that my favorite refrigerator sticker is: "Who would Jesus deport?" Whatever happened to the compassionate American?

Regrettably, the NRA did not disclose their role in all this to the signatories; consequently, it backfired. The not-liberal "Liberal" media focused on the NRA as a self-interested source, rather than the substance of our opposition to the minimum wage. When the self-interest of a private organization is also in the public interest I am happy to support them.

My involvement in opposing that particular bill began when Jim Carter, then at Treasury in the Bush administration, sent me an email; here is the exchange:

Dear Dr. Smith,

As I'm sure you have heard, the Congressional Budget Office recently found that increasing the minimum wage would reduce U.S. employment by 500,000 or more jobs. Would you be interested in signing onto a statement in opposition to an increase in the minimum wage? I'm still drafting it, but I intend to circulate it among economists—my database has grown to 13,000 economists nationwide—and I hope very much that you'll be willing to sign it once you see it. In fact, I would appreciate your guidance about what exactly you think the statement should say. That said, are you willing in theory to sign such a statement? Do you have any language that you recommend I use? Thank you.

Regards,
Jim Carter

From: Vernon Smith
To: J. Carter
Sent: Tuesday, February 25, 2014 11:38 AM
Subject: Re: Minimum wage

Jim:
Yes, I am. I believe the minimum wage has greatly reduced our ability to compete effectively with imported products, and has reduced the domestic demand for young entry level workers—particularly blacks, high school dropouts and college dropouts in that order who need to acquire habits of work, earning and building their future.

I also suggest that it be linked with an incomes proportional supplement at the lower wages for those below the poverty line. This counters those who say we are not compassionate.

Finally, this should substitute for other welfare programs, and lowers their public cost.

Vernon...

I should explain that I got to know Jim Carter after moving to Arlington-GMU in 2001. Earlier, I had supported an economic statement that Jim circulated for candidate Bush when I was at Arizona, but I have always respectfully declined to support his candidates. (Since the 1936 campaign of Norman Thomas, the only presidential candidacy I have ever publicly and actively supported was that of Ed Clark in the 1980 race against Reagan and Jimmy Carter—we lost of course, but remarkably we assembled a panel of 50 distinguished economists, including the editors of the two leading economics journals, who joined to support the Libertarian candidate, Ed Clark!)

At Boeing, largely due to the hands-on training in electricity principles and practice I received during high school, my specific work assignment was to the Functional Testing Department, where I studied the training manuals for the Central Fire Control (gun turret operating) System on the B-29. This was the first high-altitude bomber with a pressurized cabin for the nine-person crew—pilot, co-pilot, engineer, bombardier, nose gunner, two side gunners, an upper gunner, and a tail gunner. The gun turrets were remotely controlled by gun sights with electro-mechanical Selsyn (self-synchronous) "motors" located in the heated and pressurized cabin areas and on the gun turrets outside the pressurized areas. The Selsyn output generators were on the gunsight controls in the cabins, the receiver drive motors on the exposed gun turrets. This fire control system was the most advanced technology in aviation history, enabling long-range, high-altitude bombers to bring devastating firepower to bear on local interceptor attack fighter planes. Innovative, but enormously challenging to go so fast from development to application in a real time monitoring-feedback environment linking production and modification to the air battlefield.

At the West Side Drug, my customers to be served were the patrons of that little neighborhood store. At Boeing, my customers were ultimately the men being shot down over enemy territory. My fellow workers were women from the city and surrounding farms. Their husbands, fathers, brothers, and sons were fighting in the war in North Africa, the UK, or the Pacific theater. Also, my co-workers included veterans who had been in one of these theaters, wounded, discharged but able to work. By the war's end, some 1000 B-29s had been built in Wichita by a huge influx of women from the farms and city, discharged veterans, and 16–17 year olds.

My division had responsibility for troubleshooting this fire control system and aligning the gun sights with the firing trajectories. We learned about compensating for windage jump as the spinning bullets emerged from the barrels into the high-velocity air; and about "leading the target" to account for differential airspeed between source and target. This was the first "Buck Rogers" armament system; it was fascinating and important to master your part of it to avoid error.

Sometime after I got up to speed on the technology, I requested and was granted transfer to the third-shift flight crew. On this assignment, I would be part of the crew that did the final alignment checks on the system and fire-tested all the guns of each aircraft on the ground. There was a large abutment of stacked wood beams backed by an earth fill into which all the guns were fired. Each plane was set parallel to the firing range. The lower aft, lower forward, and upper aft turrets (two .50-caliber machine guns in each of these four turrets) and the upper forward turret (four fifties in a later-model B-29) were aligned on the target range, and we fired twenty-five rounds simultaneously through the guns of each of the turret in sequence. The bird was then turned 90 degrees and the tail turret, consisting of two fifties and a 20-millimeter cannon, was fire-tested, except that the Air Force required fifty rounds to be fired through the cannon; I never quite understood why it was called a cannon, as it spit out rounds like a machine gun. In later wars, this turret model would be escalated to batteries of ground-based assemblies consisting of four or more 40-millimeter machine-gun cannons. Having seen what the B-29 guns were capable of, I shudder at such firepower. Boeing's AH-64D Apache Longbow (helicopter) can be equipped with a 40 mm cannon as well as rocket firing guns.

After firing a bird's guns, we pulled all the barrels and the repeat-action loading bolts and cleaned and reinstalled them. Then the Air Force bought the plane, and it was flown to its base. The "base" actually was a modification center, where the plane was upgraded via additions and changes that had not yet gotten into the final assembly lines—gives you an idea of how big the rush was to get B-29 s from the design stage into operation, 1941–1944. Essentially, they were built, tested, and modified along the way.

About every fiftieth B-29 off the assembly line was flown by the Air Force out to Salina (they filmed *Picnic* in Salina), where there was a hillside gunnery range for in-flight firing. When the bird was returned to the Boeing airfield, we replaced the barrels, cleaned and reinstalled the bolts, and inspected everything. The barrels sometimes had no rifling grooves left in them; it was like looking down the barrel of my dad's (and his dad's) old smoothbore, lever-action 12-gage Winchester shotgun. This meant that the Air Force clowns had been firing the .50-caliber guns in excess of fifty rounds in sustained bursts, and our first thought was to check the props and fuselage for damage caused by cooked-off rounds. In fact, one plane came back from Salina with several bullet holes through the wings and a prop.

When you fire sustained bursts, the barrels get reddish hot, which quickly ruins the rifling grooves. When so heated, the guns start "cooking off" rounds on their own. When the spring-loaded bolt returns from discharging a round, it pumps a new round into the barrel. A very hot barrel will cause the new round to fire without the firing pin striking the firing cap at the base of the round. Hence, the round is "cooked off." Bear in mind that these were air-cooled fifties moving through stratospheric air—cold as a witch's teat—at 300 miles per hour, and you will get an idea of the tremendous heat buildup by .50-caliber-round explosions.

Normally, you fire the gun by depressing the firing switch with your thumb on the back of the remote control sight, causing an electrical circuit to actuate the solenoid that operates the firing pin on each machine gun. Release the switch and the gun stops firing. But if the barrel is at cook-off temperature she fires anyway. It is very dangerous to have a gaggle of fifties cooking off rounds, and it's a potential source of "friendly fire" disasters, as they are euphemistically called, while the gunner thinks he has stopped firing.

Of course, the friendliest fire of all is that which erupts from firing your own guns into your own plane, and that expresses the timeless truth that you can indeed shoot yourself in the foot. The B-29 had safeguards against raking off your own tail, wing, or engine in bursts of twenty-five rounds or fewer—well below the "cook-off" threshold for .50-caliber machine gun fire. The friendliest-of-all-fire problem was alleviated by an automatic fire-interruption mechanism triggered by a silhouette of the airframe as viewed by each gun barrel. Each turret had a large cylinder roughly ten to twelve inches in diameter at center bottom, underneath the inside access cowling. This cylinder had a raised sheet of metal wrapped around part of it, the top edge of which had a profile that replicated the turret-gun's-eye view of the airplane fuselage.

It was sort of a relief map of the plane as viewed from the perspective of each pointed gun. This raised metal sheet served as a cam that lifted the roller on a switch that tracked both the azimuth and elevation of the gun direction. The switch was normally on, but it turned off when it rode up onto the cam. So, when the upper aft turret was pointing at your tail or an engine propeller arc, the roller was on the cam profile and the switch, in series with the sight-firing switch, shut down the circuit and you could not fire into your own tail or props via the firing button. But, of course, it was not completely idiot-proof (or, "Air Force-proof"). If some yahoo releases a burst of fifty or so rounds and then swings the turret in line with the propellers, he will cook off lots of rounds into his own props before the barrels cool enough to stop firing.

This fire-interruption mechanism was later identified as the source of a faulty design that my crew uncovered on the first of a new series of modified B-29 s in 1944.

Modifications were being made all the time on the B-29, as experience in flying and testing it accumulated. Experience was used to feedback design changes and new rules for maintenance and adjustment of the whole airborne operating system. This is one reason why, decades later, I would find it natural to think of market and other socioeconomic institutions as subject to the continuous feedback of experience with consequent modification of rules and procedures, which is illustrated by the mutual voluntary recognition of property rights. This thought process always reminds me of the Chicago Mercantile Exchange, with its Constitution and Rules published as a three-ring loose-leaf notebook—a prominent clue to the dynamics of a changing institution.

I believe that studying how and why things work leads to generic principles that have validity across the spectrum of human creativity.

The new series was to carry a much heavier upper forward turret, consisting of four .50-caliber machine guns, replacing the two-gun turret. This was a monster turret by the aviation standards of 1944. It had to accommodate twice the weight of guns and the supporting structure and drive motors. Each gun had a conveyor tray that fed the clip-chain belt of bullets, each about six inches long, into the magazine for repeat firing. The tray carrying the belt of bullets circled back from the side of the fifty to a large metal box in which the belt was snake wound back and forth like Christmas hard candy until it filled the inventory box to the top.

With this first plane armed with the new turret, we rolled the modified bird into firing position, and cut loose firing each turret in order. We came to the upper forward; it fired a few rounds, stopped, fired a few more, and stopped again, and so on, just hiccupping away. Eventually, we set the turret at various elevation positions, firing again each time, and learned that the hiccups occurred when the guns were near their lowest elevation limit. The malfunction was due to the extreme vibration of the turret and the cylinder cam, which caused the fire-interrupt switch to open the firing circuit. When the firing ceased, the vibration ceased, the switch closed again, and when firing was resumed, the new vibration opened the switch, and so on. The solution was for Sperry Corporation, which supplied Boeing with the turrets, to design a heavier switch-roller mechanism. The design that had worked for a two-gun turret failed with a four-gun turret.

Another of the more memorable events on the flight line was the belly crash landing of a B-29 returning from an in-flight Air Force test. The crew could not get the nose landing gear down. It was impossible to land a B-29 with wing gears only, and there was no manual option for cranking down the nose gear. You press the activation switch and the relays close or they do not. This must have been pretty frustrating to the crew, as the landing gear and control mechanism was immediately below and aft of the bombardier and nose gunner. But there was no trap door access allowing you to kick or crank the nose gear down manually. As I recall, this led to a new modification, allowing manual operation. In this case, we heard much later that the gear's malfunction had been caused by a loose screw that had been left to rattle around in the gear-relay box. Such cases reminded you that it was critically important to carefully monitor your actions and to develop fail-safe procedures.

After circling, trying everything ground control could suggest, and running down the fuel level on board—you want it low before a crash landing—the crew prepared to bring the plane in on its belly. But first, the ground emergency crews brought out the emergency fire trucks and hosed down the ground parallel to the paved runway, making it smooth and soupy with mud and water. As we all watched, with emergency vehicles standing by, the crew approached the lane, feathered the props, cut the engines, and landed in a huge shower of mud. When the bird came to rest, it was amazing how fast the crew came popping out of that airframe.

The next several days were spent digging down far enough to place screw jacks under the wings, chaining a Caterpillar tractor to the tail to anchor it, then jacking up the frame far enough to get access to the nose gear, lock it down, lower the wing gears, and lock them down. The wrinkled bomb-bay doors were baling-wired shut, and the props—bent around the cowling of each engine—were removed and replaced. The engines were tested and worked fine, so a pilot and co-pilot took off and flew the plane to Tulsa, we were told, for base repair. It was remarkable that it was expected to fly, and did. I developed a high regard for Boeing engineering and manufacturing skill. Of course, the B-29 was founded on a lot of experience with the sub stratospheric B-17 which, according to legend, truly was capable of coming in "on a wing and a prayer," as one of the briefly popular Hit Parade songs of that era put it.

I am reminded of a recent story I heard that brings back those war years. British Airways Flight 600 is cleared and lands at the Frankfurt airport. The radar tower control officer says in his crisp German accent, "Attention, BA Flight 600. Captain, welcome to Frankfurt; please proceed promptly to gate 8."

The BA captain proceeds to taxi off the runway but makes the wrong turn in approaching his assigned gate. "Captain, you turned incorrectly; have you never been to Frankfurt before?" The reply: "Yes, in 1944, but I didn't stay."

I was now just seventeen years old and actually being paid by Boeing to do what they called work! It ended in September 1944, after I had worked steadily for fifteen months with hardly a sick day. You did not get paid for sick days, and there was no time for vacation, paid or not. I resigned and began taking classes at Friends University on September 14, 1944, using my accumulated savings to pay tuition, and living at home. I turned eighteen on January 1, 1945, and became eligible for the draft. While I was still seventeen, I had taken a test to enter the Merchant Marine as a radar technician, which was a much more attractive proposition than the draft. Mother recorded in her diary on December 14, 1944, "Vernon received word that he passed Radar test—one of 12 out of 500. Office here has to have authorization to pass his eyes." December 18: "Vernon left for Kansas City for physical." December 19: "Vernon returned; feels that they will not grant waiver for his eyes. What a pity if they don't. He is very discouraged." In fact, they did not grant the waiver, so I would soon be eligible for the draft.

The Merchant Marine was far preferable to the draft at the time because you could enlist in a specialty like radar, feel assured that you would be so trained, and make a contribution you thought would be meaningful. Although, failing to get the waiver for the Merchant Marine did not mean that I would be automatically classified 4F in the draft and be ineligible. That was right at the time of the Battle of the Bulge, which lasted from December 16, 1944, to January 25, 1945. Hitler had counterattacked with a great many divisions, including his crack Panzer Divisions and tanks, and local draft boards were reclassifying many 4Fs, preparing to take them if needed. A 4F classification meant that you were a liability to your fighting mates. But in that ferocious battle of the Bulge, everyone was a liability to everyone else. Both sides were using all the men available—Hitler was reportedly using underage boys. The Allied strategy worked, and the German divisions were badly beaten at great human cost on both sides of the Front. The battle was over in forty days before there was even time to train and deploy the many new recruits.

My draft number came up, and on March 10, 1945, I went to Leavenworth, Kansas, for the Army physical. The army bused the potential recruits to Leavenworth and back. Someone had dice, and I recall a continuous crap game in the aisle. With my glasses, I tested 20/20; without them, I was 20/800. I can hardly read the biggest letters on the wall chart; in fact, both the chart and wall are blurred. To test your hearing the guy across the room softly whispers, "Did you ever shit in your grandma's hat?" and looks for you to smile. They classified me 1A, but for "limited service" (1AL) because of my poor uncorrected vision. That meant that I was available if troops were badly needed. The local draft board, however, exercised its own discretion based on local conditions: According to my mother's diary entry of March 18, the board "classified Vernon 4F. We are all very happy."

By March, the war in Europe was going very well. The Battle of the Bulge was turning out to be Hitler's last desperate gasp. Victory in Europe, VE Day, came on May 8. The country erupted into celebration and was much more relaxed. I was not scheduled to return to Leavenworth for another physical until the following August. My mother's diary contains only two minor entries in July and August and none thereafter.

I probably left for Leavenworth on August 5 because I was there on August 6 taking my physical when a B-29, which I mistakenly felt certain I must have helped to build, dropped the atomic bomb on Hiroshima and caused unimaginable destruction. I remember at the time that everyone had a hushed sense that we had just been thrust into a completely new world, one totally without precedent. The destructions of war are, however, relative to your past experience. The Roman poet Lucretius, referring to earlier times, noted that "thousands of men led by the battle-standard were not wiped out in a single day," as in his own day with the invention of "horrible weapons for humanity, increasing day by day the terror of war."

I was shocked by Hiroshima. Why had we not given a warning that we had such a weapon and proved it by a test on some uninhabited or evacuated island in the Pacific? I was back in Wichita three days later on the ninth when the second bomb was dropped on Nagasaki. Those events soured me on a war that I had felt was fully and completely justified. It was already over in Europe, Hitler and his formidable war machine was dead, and Japan was retreating and losing badly. But two cities destroyed, the first without a threat and test, the second before there was a chance for the political consequences of the first to be determined? Franklin Roosevelt got his victorious unconditional surrender, in response to Pearl Harbor, but I have never felt that the arguments that led to the bombing decision were compelling. It was much more than a measured eye for an eye, a tooth for a tooth, and the "much more" maxim continues to be applied by all sides in Iraq, Palestine, Israel—on and on, without end.

I write the following lines in Tokyo; it's 10:26 a.m., May 25, 2005. I have just read the above lines and had pain of memory from nearly sixty years ago. It's all so different on this day: I had a wonderful dinner last night attended by two score friendly, lovable, bowing Japanese dignitaries, scholars, and businessmen, hosted by Dr. Yukiyasu Sezai, President of Nihon University, in celebration of the opening of the university's Advanced Research Institute for the Sciences and Humanities. Today at 2:00 p.m. I speak at a conference that I am informed will be attended by five hundred people. Three men in attendance at last night's dinner will comment on my talk "Experimental Economics and Electricity Restructuring." They are T. Masumoto (Tokyo Electric Power), J. Nemoto (Honorary Chairman, Japan Business Federation, also the NYK Shipping Line), and C. Minotani (Professor, Nihon University). I have read their thoughtful and incisive comments, which range well beyond my specific topic to deal with scientific method, freedom, moral sentiments, poverty, religion, globalization, and so on. I hope I serve well both Japan and America at these events and help in a tiny way to make amends for a past that was less than stellar, although my countrymen sincerely believed it was justified at the time.

I am unable to pinpoint exact dates, but while still living in Wichita sometime in the 1940s, along with my mother, I became active in CORE (originally founded by James Farmer and Chicago divinity student George Houser, as Committee of Racial Equality, later changing its name to Congress of Racial Equality). CORE pioneered the use of nonviolent confrontation of racial discrimination, and many of its early members were also active in the pacifist Fellowship of Reconciliation. This was a decade before the Supreme Court case, *Brown v. Board of Education of Topeka* (1954), and two decades before the Civil Rights Act of 1964. (I was still active 1949–1952, living in the interracial coop houses at KU, but more later on that unique and game-changing private institution that thrived locally against all odds, private and public, arrayed against it)

Our Wichita strategy was to confront segregation against blacks ("negroes" or "colored" please remember, in polite 1940s company; today, with some liberals who are not, the new doublespeak is "people of color"— may it crash and burn) by forming a mixed group of three to five people and attempting to buy tickets for the main auditorium of a movie theater. In those days, there was no way that blacks could sit anywhere except in the balcony of a theater, which for that reason was known as "n----- heaven." Ralph Bunche, long active as a United Nations special representative, Palestine negotiator and winner of the 1950 Nobel Peace Prize, could not have been seated downstairs in the Orpheum Theater, nor could he buy a sandwich in a downtown restaurant. Moreover, this was in direct violation of the Kansas State Constitution, which prohibited discrimination based on race, color, religion, creed, national origin, etc.

It was quite different in Oklahoma, a "Jim Crow" state, with no such constitutional protections. In Oklahoma, there was a small all-black town, Boley, east of Oklahoma City and southwest of Tulsa. Boley had the distinction of keeping a sign on the highway, next to the standard City Limits sign, which read, "White man, don't let the sun set on your head in Boley." Although there may have been nothing like that in Kansas, you can be sure that there were those Kansans who thought and felt the same way.

As CORE members, my mother and I, and a few locals were out to challenge a practice that was in wholesale violation of the state constitution. But we had a serious organizational problem from which I would learn a great deal: Black people were not comfortable in joining the effort. In fact, we had friends, a black couple who happened to be surnamed Smith, who exhausted the set of black people we could identify who were willing to take a public stand. We challenged at least two theaters, as I recall, which caved in, offering to settle out of court. CORE did not have the resources to make it a test case, without which we could not force any theater to be first in removing the targeted barrier, and the movement failed to effect meaningful change, however righteous we might have thought that we were.

> In the shoebox containing my mother's diary, my correspondence with Dr. Hertzler, and my dad's lyric prompts, and other treasures, I found a sheet of paper on which my mother had listed all the theaters in Wichita. Alongside each was a policy status notation: Southern, "no admittance"; Miller, "must sit in back"; Plainview, "separate section"; Wichita, "balcony"; Roxy, "seated in front"; State, "separate section." Two are checked off with a pencil and have the word *Reaction* written next to them. These were the Orpheum and the Boulevard. They may be the two that CORE acted on, but I thought that the Miller was one of them.

Eventually, of course, such practices were "eliminated"—at least in their most blatant and undisguised form—but out of that experience, and subsequent historical developments, I learned the futility of trying to change the social mistreatment of a group without the group's willingness to make it abundantly clear that they will no longer tolerate the abuse and will actively participate in changing it. It was the Watts Riot in 1965, I believe, that symbolized and effected change in America, not primarily Lyndon Johnson's Civil Rights Act of 1964. The Act may have been a consequence of some attitude change, but it would not change practice any more than had the Kansas Constitution, which had been in force far longer. Change came when the Uncle Toms were replaced by defiant blacks willing to commit violence in return for the violence they felt inside, who were willing to express it openly, and not just in a sign at the city limits of an obscure and unknown country town in Oklahoma. That violence is immoral, just as are the practices that incite it. I am not championing violence, but I believe we have to fess up to its capacity to produce change where voluntary mechanisms simply were not working.

The issues, if not the violence, hold true for women's rights. Women have changed their stand—we have fewer "Aunt Toms." The language has changed—it's now "blacks," not "negroes," and "women," rather than "girls," although there are plenty who have not got the latter message yet, and that is a barometric measure of the slower progress. What is difficult for women is to live a "no more crap life," without sacrificing their femininity, and I am on the side of the women who resist sacrificing that in return for some outward male prerogatives that may be more symbolic than game-changing, and who believe you do not have to sacrifice it in order to achieve needed change.

Why did "Negroes" transform into "Blacks"? The reason was made clear to me from earlier experience. I remember bumping into my friend and Harvard classmate Andy Brimmer at the American Economic Association meetings, at the height of the transformation, sometime in the late 1960s. Andy was lamenting that he had always worked to help "his people" by speaking out, forthrightly, at various public engagements and functions. He was now encountering resistance, cool receptions, and heckling in his addresses to "negro" audiences, as he put it. In particular, there was an objection to his use of "negro." I replied, "Andy, it's simple. Why has it always been 'negroes' in polite company, but 'whites' rather than Caucasians in the same company? For young blacks, this is flat-out condescending. It projects a verbal (but fake) image of respect while based in a grossly disrespectful double standard hypocrisy in the extreme. Your black brothers want to be recognized as unabashedly black, through and through, without shame, in fact with pride." Young blacks were identifying Andy with too easily going along with this dominant white culture theme; others like Louis

Armstrong and Duke Ellington were likewise being marginalized by the new movement.

Andy was the son of a southern black sharecropper and had won big swimming in the stream of white society. He was Lyndon Johnson's appointment to the Federal Reserve Board, where Andy served with distinction. He was gentile, a gentleman, in the mold of Duke Ellington, and like the Duke made it work. Yet it took a honky like me to explain why the language had suddenly taken on such significance, why the old distinctions rankled, why honky noses were being rubbed in it, and why blacks could use the n-word routinely and defiantly among themselves, but there was no way any honky could. It was a powerful symbol of black self-actualization, social change, and pride to have the exclusive nose-thumbing privilege of routinely calling each other n------. I believe it still is. Truth-based forms of outrage can be constructive, false-based never are (Figs. 6.1, 6.2, 6.3, 6.4, and 6.5).

Fig. 6.1 High school graduation 1944

Fig. 6.2 OK Drive-In 77 years later

Fig. 6.3 B-29 with 4-50s upper turret. Wikimedia Commons

Fig. 6.4 North high wisdom after 77 years

Fig. 6.5 Grandpa Lomax's MOP Engine 1478 at work in 1942 near Pueblo CO

7

Friends University, Caltech and University of Kansas

Great teachers are valuable not only for what they teach but more so for the pattern they put on one's life.
—Arthur E. Hertzler, MD; letter to me dated November 23, 1945

Inflation occurs when prices rise.
—Dwight Eisenhower in a news conference I heard

My family's sole "intellectual" was my mother's uncle, Sullivan Lomax, who, according to family lore, was left "crippled" by a leg injury caused by a farm accident.

Sullivan's older brother, Quintin Lomax (who had a twin sister, Nancy Matilda), provided more detail about the incident in a manuscript he wrote on the Lomax family in the mid-1940s when he was about seventy-eight. I obtained a copy of the manuscript from his granddaughter, Jane Beekman, of Muncie, Indiana. At about the age of three, Sullivan caught his left knee in the crack of a wooden gate. He was held there for several minutes until his older brother William released him. No one knew how to properly treat such an injury. It led to a "white swelling," and the joint became so stiff "that he had to carry that leg at almost a right angle." He was handicapped for life. Being ill-suited for anything "useful," like arduous farm work, Sullivan was passed around among various relatives who could ill afford to support him, but somehow "he got a fairly good education, and taught district schools in Kansas." Naturally, this gives me an image of a Mr. Hemberger, but more specialized and educated as a teacher. In 1905, he "entered Kansas University and graduated in the law in 1907. He took up practice

© The Author(s) 2018
V. L. Smith, *A Life of Experimental Economics, Volume I*,
https://doi.org/10.1007/978-3-319-98404-9_7

in Cherryvale [Kansas]." I remember Sullivan, and also his son, Otho, who graduated in law from Washburn College and stayed in Topeka to practice.

The story I always heard from my mother was that Sullivan had studied law by correspondence. Consequently, neither I, nor my parents, nor anyone in my family outside Cherryvale, nor any neighbor or friend had any idea how to go about choosing a college. In any case, my mother and, indeed, all of us were proud of him! With that inspiration, I went to the Wichita City Library, found a book on choosing a college, and learned among other things that the "best" college in the USA was Caltech. Being naïve and impetuous, I decided that I should prepare myself to enter Caltech, as, without further preparation, my C average in high school would not even qualify me to take the entrance examination. However, a small but very serious Quaker college, Friends University, was located near my home in West Wichita. I enrolled in physics, chemistry, calculus, astronomy, and literature courses for one year, earned top grades, and at eighteen sat for the entrance examinations for the spring 1945 term at Caltech.

My attitude at Friends University had been 180 degrees opposite my attitude in high school. I was a very serious and highly motivated student. I knew what I wanted, and had confidence in Friends' faculty: Reagan in mathematics, Greenfield in English, Kenneth Andrews in physics, etc. I did not take biology, but Earnest Crow, a fine biologist, was also at Friends. I was there to make up for my high school failure to learn, and to enter Caltech.

I would very likely have benefited had I been able to drop out of high school in the tenth or eleventh grade and gone directly to Friends for two years. Aaron, my wife Candace's youngest son, dropped out of high school in Pueblo, Colorado, with two years remaining, and managed to deal with a state catch-22. Normally, you need a high school diploma to get into a community college, but if you do gain admittance and perform, it makes no difference whether you had a diploma. Aaron went to Denver, appealed to the state commissioner of education to take a qualifying examination, passed, and entered Pueblo Community College (PCC) without a high school diploma. Two years later (2000), he received the degree of Associate in Science from PCC and was admitted to Colorado College. He finished there in 2003 and went on to graduate school.

It's not widely known—why should the public school bureaucracy advertise it?—but with a little entrepreneurial spirit you can just drop out of high school in the last two years, without prejudice, and go on to college. If you finish an Associate Degree, or just get college credits and show a good record, no one will care or ask whether you graduated from high school, and you will be plugged into the academic credentials system. Academic credentials are just one example of what is called "signaling" in the economics profession, and mathematical models of market signaling account for many learned papers that earned three Nobel Prizes in 2001. If you are careful, and work at it, you not only can emit the required signals, you can even get an education, in part by wasting less time and learning less that has to be unlearned later. Insofar as the public schools are evaluated by means of test scores, they would show up as seriously deficient if their most enterprising students bypassed their junior and senior years to enroll and earn associate degrees in community colleges. Public schools are not set up to produce achievement in their students' lifetime performance; they are set up to yield achievement on tests by students who do not drop out and produce good scores.

While at PCC, Aaron earned his keep by serving two paper routes, treating each of his clients as a personally treasured customer. One woman wanted the paper laid on the sill of the window by the front door so that she could open the screen door, reach around the frame, and pick it off the waist-high sill *without* going out on the porch. She got it positioned on that sill every morning about 5:00! It is no exaggeration to say that he pampered his clients, and they loved it. All customers received their papers delivered to the porch, not thrown randomly in the general direction of the front yard and winding up in mud puddles, bushes, or trees. Other newspapers, left elsewhere by competitors, were picked up and delivered to the porch along with Aaron's paper. Needless to say, Aaron developed an enviable reputation, as do most successful business people who are conscientious in serving their customers. And it was profitable, too. He collected the monthly bill personally and received tips of up to $30.

Candace and I substituted two mornings for him. It was our Christmas present to him so that he could go skiing in New Mexico. Each of his customers received a letter of explanation from him to the effect that his mother and her boyfriend from Tucson will take over his route for two days so that he can go skiing, adding, "and please be forgiving." Candace and I had detailed instructions, and we did pretty well. I think we made only about three mistakes.

Candace's and now my daughter Annie honored us by graduating from St. John's College in Santa Fe last year (2002). As an admirer of the Great Books basis for education, I was very pleased by that event. It felt good to be a part of an unusual experiment in serious education.

At Friends University, I did a lot of reading beyond that related to my courses. From my mother's diary entry for October 27, 1944: "Vernon is doing fine in College—reading lots outside his school work." I developed an interest in philosophy, science, and in the history and methodology of science, which has continued sporadically to the present. I read A. N. Whitehead (*Process and Reality*) and Bertrand Russell (*History of Western Philosophy*; later, at Caltech, I read *Human Knowledge*), Sir Arthur Eddington (*The Nature of the Physical World*), Sir James Jeans (*Physics and Philosophy*), Albert Einstein's popular and philosophical writings, and so on.

I lost track of my high school friends—Bob Patterson and Ray Reyes—until much later at North High reunions. I saw Bob at the twentieth reunion in 1964, but not Raymond, who did not attend. While in attendance there, I came to realize why Ray was not: our Hispanic and black classmates were not welcome—so much for the impact of the Civil Rights Act, passed the same year as our reunion.

I also went back for my fiftieth North High School reunion in 1994. As noted, my twentieth reunion in 1964 was not attended by any of the Hispanics I had known because they, and my black classmates, were flat out not invited. The same crowd that had run the social life of North High in the 1940s was back behind the driver's wheel in the 1960s. But there had been a modicum of change by 1994, and Ray Reyes was there. Of course, after fifty years the crowd was much smaller; judging from the people in attendance, obesity, booze, nicotine, and age had each taken their toll. I found it strange to be surrounded by so many people I recognized, but who seemed so much more than one or two years my senior. I felt as though I had skipped a lot more than the second grade back in Mr. Hemberger's one-room schoolhouse. But I stayed through the reception and dinner because they had a live big band. Moreover, the band was *good*, having warmed up at the dinner with old Glenn Miller favorites like "Little Brown Jug" "Tuxedo Junction," and "American Patrol," and I was looking forward to more. But after the dinner came all the credits, speakers, and reminiscing; the class valedictorian was probably lurking on the sidelines, and it was going on 10:15 p.m.

Nuts! I got up, left the dinner, and went out to the Marriott desk and asked if there was a country-western bar on the east side of town. Damned if there wasn't: *In Cahoots* was a couple of blocks east. I was out of there. The place had a big Texas racetrack-style dance floor (not my favorite, but better than line dancing, of which they had none), a good C&W band, and a big crowd of all ages, as is typical of C&W. My fiftieth anniversary was saved by local entrepreneurship and the cultural diversity of C&W.

At Friends University, I became very good friends with a classmate, Lamont Marsh. He was a premed major in biology and an outstanding student. Sometime that year, I learned that he had Bright's disease, which affects kidney function. The outlook was dim. I was quite concerned and got him into see Dr. Arthur E. Hertzler, who headed a famous clinic in Halstead, Kansas, where he also did medical research. Hertzler commuted part of the time to Kansas City, where he taught at the University Medical College.

Initially, I got to know Hertzler through correspondence about his books, from June 1945 to September 12, 1946. On several occasions, I had driven up to Halstead to see him. He was a mentor to me, and I greatly admired this forthright, wise, and humorous surgeon. In response to my first letter, he wrote on an old Underwood typewriter: "I was glad to send you the book requested. On second thought I am sending two more—all my nonprofessional books. I [am] glad to know that you are interested in facts." A religious skeptic, he said he wanted to collect transcripts or summaries of some of the sermons he had been listening to on KFH Radio at 6:15 a.m., every Sunday. He wanted me to collect them. "It seems to me to be a worth while thing to collect these sermons and print them in pamphlet form. If this turns out to be a satire of the character of these sermons it is not my fault." He hired me at $5 per sermon, to collect them and send them to him for selection. In due time, they were published, along with his written introduction. This was the beginning of a short but very meaningful friendship.

The hospital he founded in an old house in Halstead developed into a full square block of facilities that he eventually transferred to the Catholic Society for $1. It had some fame and reputation as a goiter clinic, but it housed a range of medical skills, and Hertzler was one of the most widely known general practitioners and surgeons anywhere in the 1930s. He had written a best-selling non-fiction book, *The Horse and Buggy Doctor*, which he followed with a less-popular but still well-known work, *The Doctor and His Patients*. His next book, much less well known, was *Grounds of an Old Surgeon's Faith*. I read the other books, and soon after our meeting he published the latter. *Grounds* was privately published, and not exactly a best seller—Hertzler gave it away—in the Bible Belt, since its message was essentially parallel to that of H. L. Mencken, but it is much less spicily written than were Mencken's works. Hertzler, however, had an unmistakable compassion for humanity, and for healing the flesh and spirits of the many that he had nursed, treated, and cared for. (Mencken is famously believed to have had no such sympathies, but that may well be an injustice.)

I still have a one-inch plus stack of letters from Hertzler. He was impressed with the human capacity to know death, and in the end—always, according to Hertzler—to know and face it without fear, regardless of religious convictions. He claimed that of the hundreds of individuals whose deaths he knew intimately, and in spite of any earlier trepidation, all in the end experienced a peace, an acceptance, a welcoming that made death as natural as birth. Hertzler died of uremia on September 12, 1946, at age seventy-six—my age at this writing. One of only two letters I have from his secretary—he typed his own—Ruth Rose, dated the same day, reads as follows: "The Grim Reaper took our beloved Chief today at 12:25 p.m. I'm sorry you were unable to make that trip [the planned trip would have been my return to Wichita from Caltech, over Christmas] to see him before he left us. I am sure he would like for you to have a copy of his newest book, *Always the Child*, so will mail you a copy in a few days." This book was inspired by his daughter, Agnes, a physician whose death much distressed him; he had performed surgery on her in a desperate but unsuccessful attempt to save her life, and this weighed heavily upon him. Standard protocol in medicine prohibits a surgeon from performing on his own kin in life-threatening procedures. Hertzler was never one to follow standard protocol, and his surgical record was better than any other that was available.

I was privileged to know such a kind, affectionate, accomplished, remarkable, and adventurous man for a short sixteen months before his death. All such deaths seem untimely to those who are indelibly marked by the person. I am reminded of what Kahlil Gibran said in my favorite of his books—a book better even than *The Prophet*—"If you can tell me *what is death*, then I will tell you *what is life*" (*Jesus, the Son of Man*).

Hertzler traversed the Kansas backcountry roads making farmhouse calls to treat the ill, tend spirits, counsel families, and perform surgery. He did what he deemed necessary on the spot, often in emergencies with family, neighbors, and friends present and eager to help. They also helped prepare and bury the body of the loved one if Dr. Hertzler failed to deliver the miracle he would try so hard to make happen. Today, instead of inpatient treatment in hospitals, many people are treated as outpatients in doctors' offices, but the cantankerous, unconventional, and committed Dr. Hertzler treated people out-of-office, in their remote farm homes, or even outdoors on the farm.

He reports the commonplace problem that the farmhouses were always dimly lit, and he could not see well enough to perform surgery. His solution was to do the surgery outdoors, in broad daylight, in the shade of a tree. He reports that the best surgical table is not the dining room table, which is too wide, but rather one of the narrow interior farmhouse doors, removed from its sash and swung across two sawhorses from the barn. After he finished, he went to the next farm, staying over in small-town hotels or, where there were no towns, he slept in the buggy on route. The horse knew to stay on the road, and even to return home, if he was on his way home. On the long treks between calls he relieved his boredom by shooting at startled jackrabbits with his .45-caliber revolver.

He also reports that he once removed a kidney whose condition was puzzling and unfamiliar to him. Curious, he decided that he had to take it back to his Halstead laboratory for examination and study. He cleaned it up a bit, wrapped it in a few layers of newspapers, and made room for it in his handbag. After staying overnight in a small hotel he continued his journey, only to discover soon that he had taken the wrong handbag. Returning to the hotel, he found a visibly shaken traveling businessman who had opened his handbag to discover that he surely must have picked up the wrong one.

But these events are from my imperfect memory. Read the 1938 masterpiece by the doctor himself, and enjoy. You will love this man, this scientist, this surgeon, this family physician so much a part of a long-vanished breed.

I wrote to Hertzler, told him what I knew of Lamont's problem, and asked if he might be able to help. He replied, "Bring him to Halstead, we will run a bunch of lab tests, and it will not cost him anything but his time." I discovered that Hertzler was famous for treating people who could not pay—he just absorbed the cost. The upshot was that Lamont got confirmation of much of what he had already been told. Hertzler said he might last quite some time with a careful diet. Knowing that, Lamont would never drink booze, but he died in the autumn of 1945 after I had departed for Caltech.

What was strange was that Lamont had hidden lives. For starters, he was married and had two children, and that was never once mentioned to me, or to anyone that I knew at Friends. He and I had taken a trout-fishing trip to Colorado, staying at the Antler's Hotel in Colorado Springs, so we were not exactly casual acquaintances. Curious about him, I went to see the machine-shop foreman for whom he had last worked. I knew that Lamont had worked as a machinist, because he had once told me how he learned the trade. Lamont had applied for a machinist's position at Boeing, completely ignorant of the skill. Before his first day he visited another machine shop to get a better idea of what machinists did for a living, the names of the tools, and what they were for. He reported for work, asked questions, observed others and sought help when given a job, and he learned the trade. His last foreman informed me that he had never known a machinist as good as Lamont. His verbal agreement with Lamont was that Lamont was to come to the shop anytime, night or day—there would always be work—leaving finished work along with an accounting of hours worked, and the foreman would mail Lamont his check. He said that he had known Lamont to arrive very late at night in a suit and white shirt, take off his coat, don an apron, fold the sleeve twice to below the elbow, perform his work, and get not a spot of oil or grease on that shirt. You get to know some remarkable people passing through this life.

Returning to my preparations for Caltech, the one hurdle was the entrance examination, embracing physics, chemistry, and mathematics. This examination was a unique creation of the Caltech faculty, and the entry decision was famously dependent on how well you performed on that examination, and not upon prior grades. The examination consisted of problems: How fast is a snowball thrown against a wall if the snowball melts on impact? Let's see now, if the mass of the snowball is m, and its velocity is v, then its kinetic energy is $(1/2)mv^2$. If it takes C calories of heat energy to convert each gram of snowball (ice) into water, you had only to equate Cm with the kinetic energy and solve for v with suitable account taken of the units of measurement. The examination went to the heart of basic principles, and although a working knowledge of mathematics was essential, it required no special mathematical virtuosity. It was a test of basic scientific principles requiring a developed intuition. Many Caltech faculty were like that, emphasizing the basics, but the most famous example is Richard Feyneman who became part of the fixtures at Caltch after I had graduated.

I passed the examinations, took the Santa Fe's California Limited (the Chief and Super Chief were out of my ticket class) passenger train west out of Newton and through La Junta, Colorado (where my wife Candace was born and lived as a child), Tucumcari, Clovis, Gallup, and Albuquerque, New Mexico; Winslow, Flagstaff, and Kingman, Arizona; then Barstow, California, arriving in Los Angeles in September 1945. It was "all the way to L.A. on the Santa Fe," as the concessionaire announced in each car as he went through with peanuts, gum, candy, pop, and cigarettes. This route became familiar in the next four years, whether I was traveling by train or driving on the parallel famous Route 66. Forty-six years later, curious about a bar in Wellington, New Zealand named Route 66, I walked in and asked the small coterie of late afternoon customers and service persons clustered in the rear, "Anyone here who knows where Route 66 is?" The friendly reply: "Where is it, Yank?"

I wrote Dr. Hertzler about passing the Caltech examination and he replied, on September 14, 1945, "Delighted to know that you passed the examination—didn't expect anything else. Nothing like getting a good start. I have always said to get anywhere one must have at least one great teacher." Two months later, I wrote him my impressions at Caltech, and he responded, on November 23, 1945, "I am delighted to know that you are in such an important institution. Great teachers are valuable not only for what they teach but more so for the pattern they put on one's life.... I am having heaps of fun out of the Sermons.... I will be very glad to hear from you from time to time as something comes up." I had not realized it at the time, or until rereading this old correspondence, that maybe he and I in some measure actually mentored each other. I can see him as if it were yesterday: tall, gangling like a teenager, sporting a big, ugly, protruding, rough red nose, but gentle, eager, curious, and intensely lovable.

Caltech was a meat grinder like I could never have imagined. The first thing to which one has to adapt is the fact that no matter how high people might sample in the right tail of the "intelligence" distribution, or whatever it is that measures college performance, that sample is still normally distributed in performing on the Caltech curriculum. The second thing you learn, if you were reared with my naïve background, is the incredible arrogance that develops with the acquisition of what you ultimately come to realize is a really very, very small bit of knowledge compared with our vast human ignorance. My new awareness was captured, years later, in the story I heard about the difference between Harvard and Caltech: "At Harvard they believe they are the best in the world; at Caltech they know they are the best in the world."

I studied night, day, and weekends and survived hundreds of problems, but what a joy it was to take freshman chemistry from the inspired and inspiring Linus Pauling. A tradition at Caltech was to applaud your professor on the last day of the quarter, but Pauling was occasionally given standing ovations throughout the quarter (Bohnenblust, the differential geometer whom we called "Bony," also received such ovations in freshman calculus!). I would also hear guest lectures in physics class by J. Robert Oppenheimer on his frequent visits to Caltech; attend a public lecture by Bertrand Russell; and regularly see von Karman, Anderson, Zwicky, Tolman, Millikan, and other legendary figures of that time on campus. In those classes, I discovered that one kind of great teacher is the one that simply thinks out loud, in commonsensical terms of basic principles, and you easily can read his thought processes.

At Caltech I was majoring in physics, but switched to electrical engineering (EE), then in the same division (Mathematics, Physics and Electrical Engineering), just prior to my senior year. In this way, I was able to avoid the dreaded "Smyth's course." It was rumored that Carl Anderson, awarded the Nobel Prize in physics for discovering the positron, had flunked Smyth's course. The course was required for physics majors, but not EE majors, so I received my BSEE on schedule in 1949, unmoved by those for whom it was a big bloody ego trip to take Smyth and pass. But it was Carl Anderson's contribution that people came to know, not those of the egocentric smart alecks. I'm sure as hell glad I learned that lesson then, early enough to save my soul later on. I sometimes wonder whether lasting knowledge is inversely proportional to pretensions of knowledge.

Early at Caltech, I came to relish the seemingly unbending rigor of mathematics, physics, and engineering, but then, as a senior, I took an economics course and found it intriguing—you could actually learn something about the economic principles underlying the claims of socialism, capitalism, and other such "isms"? Curious about professional economics, I went to the Caltech library, stumbled upon Samuelson's *Foundations of Economic Analysis*, and later that year, von Mises's *Human Action*. From the former, it was clear that economics could be examined just like physics, but from the latter there seemed to be much in the way of reasoning that was not like physics. I also subscribed to the *Quarterly Journal of Economics*, and one of the first issues had a paper by Hollis Chenery on engineering production functions. So economics was also like engineering! I had not a clue then how much those first impressions would be changed in my thinking over the decades to come. But in 1961, my *Investment and Production* would have a chapter on engineering production functions. Later, teaching the concept as part of the Graduate Theory course at Purdue, the students would call the subject "engine-omics."

An important distinction of the Caltech program of the 1940s was that 25% of the curriculum was in the humanities and social sciences. This requirement, plus electives, plus overload, enabled me to get thirty undergraduate units in history, the equivalent of a major. Looking back, I really do not understand how I pulled it off; during one-quarter I was enrolled in seven courses. History was good at Caltech. I particularly remember John Schutz, who was also the debate coach, and who taught American history, including the diplomatic history of the USA—a stretch of the word *diplomatic* for this upstart new democracy. There were also many distinguished history scholars visiting Caltech, attracted by the Huntington Library, who taught seminars and one-quarter courses in their areas of specialty. One British visitor, Davies, taught Anglo-American relations (leaving out the Irish, but then my ancestors from Ireland were not Anglos). It was an intensely interesting course with about five of us enrolled in it.

I was an antiwar protester in those years, along with a handful of other Caltech undergraduates. I was registered for the draft as a pacifist for limited service (4AL was the class, I believe). I have already mentioned the antiwar stance of Norman Thomas, for whom I would vote in 1948. Two leading national pacifist organizations were represented on campus: The War Resistors League and the Fellowship of Reconciliation, the latter having a more Christian orientation, but that made little difference to me although the strong nonviolent roots of Christianity are evident in the life of Jesus. I participated in various protests during my four years in residence at Caltech. One was in opposition to the first peacetime draft in the history of the USA. As I recall, the wartime draft was expiring and President Truman proposed to extend it. A group of us demonstrated against the draft bill in downtown Los Angeles. Some of us mailed our draft cards to the president, while others burned them with much fanfare. There were many non-pacifist types at that demonstration, most notably the local Communists, who cared not a whit for the principles we had tried to articulate. But I knew the history of the alleged Communist attempts to infiltrate the Socialist Party, so I was very wary of them spoiling our day.

Later, in 1957, as a young assistant professor at Purdue, I was invited to work as a summer consultant at the Rand Corporation. This required me to file a background history registration form, in which I articulated all my earlier activist racial and political history. Normally, a summer consultant was given a low-level "confidential clearance" after a routine credit check, provided there was nothing incriminating on your application. Of course, my application had red flags all over it dating back to age 16 and earlier. Consequently, the clearance process required a complete background investigation by the FBI. This turned out to have some of the flavor of a Keystone Cops comedy. It is worth a briefing, because it is a truth-is-stranger-than-fiction story that characterized the times, and I would guess it still does, as we read of the security cases that have erupted in the wake of the Hillary Clinton vs Donald Trump election campaigns.

The Rand Corporation always had several hires who were awaiting clearance. So Rand leased office space in downtown Santa Monica for employees who were not yet security-clean. I waited the entire summer, working on non-classified problems. Space in the building where I was sequestered was also leased to other users. Next to my office, on the other side of the wall next to my desk, was located the Santa Monica office of the FBI. Moreover, the walls were not very thick, and immediately on the other side was someone frequently on the telephone, and I could hear everything he said. So here I am, age 30, able to eavesdrop on the FBI in Santa Monica, while other FBI agents were back in Wichita checking to see how subversive I had been at age 16. I didn't bother eavesdropping for the simple reason that none of the conversation was the least bit interesting, and I had work to do to earn my summer salary.

At the end of the summer, I returned to Purdue. It was a clear, mild, autumn day with the office windows open. I heard my colleague in the next office greet a visitor, who introduced himself. He identified himself as an FBI agent, and he wanted to ask my colleague what he knew about Vernon Smith! And there I sat within earshot of the interview. So much for the government's security investigation of me in my only direct experience of any such grave and serious matters. It's not the sort of narrative you get from watching British or American spy-catcher thrillers. I hope the British are a little more circumspect.

That investigational process ultimately ended and resulted in me receiving not a mere confidential, but a Secret clearance. By that time, I was no longer active at Rand. I wonder how many countries so easily enable citizens to overcome their earlier politically unpopular stances. What a fortunate advantage I had to be born in this country, with all its warts, fumbles, and foibles, but free to think, live, choose, and speak; to learn and to correct my own misguided early socialist beliefs without subsequent prejudice.

You are not marked forever by your beginnings.

After graduating in engineering, I went to the University of Kansas to get an M.A. in economics, useful in its own right, but principally as a vehicle to continue in economics, should I decide. I still think of myself as having two homes in Kansas: one in Wichita where I grew up; the other in Lawrence. At KU I took classes from Dick Howey: price theory, where I came to know the wonderful little book by E. H. P. Brown, *Framework of the Pricing System,* which would lay the foundation for the first two-commodity exchange experiments at Purdue in 1964; mathematical economics, using works by R. G. D. Allen, Jacob Marschak, and J. R. Hicks; imperfect competition, Joan Robinson and Edward Chamberlin; but much more significantly for my deeper scholarly development, a full-year course in the Development of Economic Thought.

Howey was a surviving member of an endangered species, a scholar in the history of economic thought, but it was from him that I learned the deeper meaning of scholarly commitment. He was one of the "great teachers" to whom Arthur Hertzler so wisely alerted me. To be good at whatever you did, you needed to acquire knowledge of all the supporting structure, tools, and primary sources of inspiration. If you were Dick Howey, and dedicated to economic thought scholarship, that meant knowing mathematics and being fluent in French, German, and Italian, as well as English. Since I was a country boy who barely knew English, he made a lasting impression on me. His teaching model seemed just right and easily generalized to accommodate the interest of his students in other fields of economics. He also taught a thorough course in imperfect competition, in which we studied Chamberlin and Robinson without getting caught up in their professional feuding. With Dick as a mentor, I soon decided economics was for me and continued by pursuing an economics Ph.D. at Harvard beginning in 1952.

At KU I lived in the Rock Chalk Co-op House. KU was unusual, I believe, in having many student co-op houses for both undergraduates and graduates. They were inexpensive ($35 per month for room, board, utilities, and laundry facilities) and attracted blue-collar students with little means, no love for the Greek fraternity crowd, and a taste for radical politics. These were postwar inflation years, and as instructed by President Eisenhower, that meant prices were rising. We were all trying to get the most out of the dwindling purchasing power of any savings. The co-ops also provided me with the social life I had little time for at Caltech.

The co-op house movement originated in the 1920s, when Leonora Ricker Hollingbery bequeathed her residence to the local Lawrence Unitarian Church to be dedicated as "a place where a woman with money may hire a room at a fair price, one with little money for less, and one with none may get a cot or place to sleep for nothing, with the use of the kitchen and laundry for nothing."[1] The house was not specifically dedicated to use by KU women students. By the

---

[1]For perspective on my KU days, here is a brief account of the KU co-op house movement, based on the following source: http://kuhistory.com/articles/unitarian-utilitarianism/.

late 1920s, Ricker Hall (or Ricker Club Co-op) became recognized by the KU housing system: "During the years 1942-47, Ricker residents annually had their names and group photos published in the Jayhawker yearbook." But it was never University property and remained in the possession of a trust administered by the Unitarian Church. Admission to Ricker was considered a form of scholarship. Indeed, as the Ricker rules put it, "those who can afford to join a sorority do not need the help which the Cooperative house affords."

In 1946, a controversy involved Ricker Hall. The Hollingbery trusteeship had passed to the American Unitarian Association in Boston, which sought to formalize the ad hoc student housing relationship with the University by naming the KU Endowment Association (KUEA) as Ricker trustee. But the proposal encountered opposition: KUEA was reluctant to administer activities outside of its defined purview and remained concerned about the potential of renewed demand for the use of the property by women not connected with the University; and the Unitarians balked at the University's policy that Ricker was to be occupied solely by members "of the Caucasian race." The Unitarians were unwilling to agree to this stipulation since "This Association has taken the position that we will not discriminate against either Negroes or Orientals, [and] would be subjected to severe criticism if we put any such clause into an agreement made by the Association."

From this beginning, the KU coops evolved into a separate off-campus multiple-housing facility that was incompatible with the Caucasian-only discrimination policies at KU. Those policies were still in full effect when I arrive in 1949.

The Rock Chalk was typical of Co-op House organization. Seventeen house members were assigned to meal preparation and to clean-up crews in teams that, through secondary trade, individuals were able to adapt to their class schedules, tastes, and temperaments. The initial schedule and allocation of tasks were posted each week by a committee whose membership rotated. Individuals then traded assignments to eliminate conflicts with classes and external work obligations; the system actually worked—central initial assignment followed by decentralized free exchange. In addition to ideals and principles, there were built-in team and community pressures that controlled the shirking of one's duties. Freeloaders got in line or would suffer the consequences, but I do not recall any such problems, so well did the work ethic norm perform in these communities. Also, it was a temporary lifestyle; we were all self-supporting, and the cash savings were a boon toward survival. We were good at saving money, but I could have done with less mackerel loaf and certainly without scrambled brains (they sold for cents per pound) with eggs, but that is what the menu team had decreed, and others had to wait for their turn!

At the Rock Chalk, I learned to make home brew—beer, if you don't know what that means. At any of the grocery stores in Lawrence, you could buy Pabst Blue Ribbon Barley Malt, light or dark, in one-quart cans. We used a twenty-gallon stone crock, so we procured two cans of Pabst malt, ten pounds plus four cups of sugar, a couple of cakes (or packages, if dry) of yeast, and about 16 gallons of water.

You cover the crock with a tea towel to keep out the bugs and varmints and let it brew for four days, checking each day with a flashlight for bubble activity. Yeast consumes the sugars and starches and produces alcohol and carbon dioxide gas as by-products. At first, the yeast has a great abundance of food to convert and is very active. The surface of the brew will build up a three- to four-inch head of tiny bubbles. The activity rate slows down (exponential decay) as the food supply is reduced, and the alcohol builds up in the solution, which in turn will kill the yeast. That is why, we believed, you can't ferment anything to an alcohol concentration above 12% (wine), with beer normally running no more than about 8%. Our beer was not that strong. When the rate of bubble formation has slowed substantially—which takes about four and one-half days—you bottle it in quarts and cap them. We used a three-eighths-of-an-inch red rubber hose to siphon the yeast-muddied beer from the big crock and into the bottles.

Now store the bottled beer in the basement. You have to bottle at just the right time for good beer with a natural, carbonated head, but you get a lot of practice when you are doing a crock a week. I developed a foolproof method. The day after bottling, open a test bottle. If it goes "fffttt," recap it, and it will be ready to drink as soon as the yeast settles to the bottom. If it only goes "fftt," you bottled it a little too late, and it will be flat. The beer has to ferment in the bottle just enough to provide frothy bubbles and a "head." But I learned how to fix it: open every bottle and add one-quarter of a teaspoon of sugar, then recap. This is the low-cost way to recover inadequate "head." Alternatively, if you open one the next day and it goes "fffftttt," then open them all for an hour or so and recap them. This gives you the right head and avoids a chain reaction of explosions, machine gun-like, that we used to hear all the way to the third floor.

We were usually drinking the beer two to three weeks after bottling, with incessant arguments over whether to allow the brew to "age," but we never wanted to wait. Waiting meant the possibility of forfeiture under the rule-of-capture governing common property resources, and it was so good that it was hard to imagine it getting any better.

The only other Lawrence producer of home brew was the Illinois Street Lithuanian Club, one of the radical centers in KU life that was not among the co-op houses, but housed a ragtag assortment of Bohemian types known to many co-op members. They were not fussy about technique, and occasionally they had big explosions.

I made many good friends and met my lovely wife, Joyce, at KU. Bob Campbell, my roommate, left for Harvard ahead of me to enter the Russian

Studies master's program, staying on for a Ph.D. in economics. At the Rock Chalk, it seemed that he was always studying Russian and Japanese. After completing his Ph.D. at Harvard, he became a member of the faculty at Indiana University, where he had a long and very distinguished career as one of the leading Russian research economists in the USA. Bob was quiet, task oriented, competent, and very thoughtful.

The co-ops were interracial because it was a routine belief in the lives of all of us as individuals, and in the principles with which we infused these organizations. (As I recall there was one exception, and we called it the poor girl's Phi Chi.) The co-ops had several Mexican and black members. We had no quotas and no special acceptance criteria. Basically, everyone who applied was accepted. Blacks and Hispanics were hardly part of the social mainstream at KU, where we had a lily-white championship basketball team. The star of the team was "Cumulus Clyde" Lovellette, one of the last of the basketball greats when only whites were allowed to play. Clyde went on to play with the Minneapolis Lakers. Of course, there were plenty of great black players in those days and had been for years, but they played for the Harlem Globetrotters. It had been the same in baseball until Jackie Robinson broke that racial barrier. Although, for years black baseball greats had played for the Kansas City Monarchs, who did exhibition games all over the country. I had seen them in Wichita when they played the House of David, another exhibition team whose members all sported long bushy beards; they loved to do hidden-ball tricks, using their beards, to catch runners off base.

Satchel Paige, arguably the best pitcher who ever lived, also played for the Kansas City Monarchs and other teams in the Negro National League and later the Negro American League. He played for a short time for Cleveland before finally retiring. Even then, he did pretty well for a supposed over-the-hill guy and held his own against far younger players. If you want an enjoyable read get a copy of *Maybe I'll Pitch Forever* by Leroy Satchel Paige. He was a store of quotes that surely must have been an inspiration for Yogi Berra: "Don't look back. Something might be gaining on you." "My pitching philosophy is simple - keep the ball way from the bat." "Ain't no man can avoid being born average, but there ain't no man got to be common."

In fact, racial discrimination was everywhere in Lawrence, at the University, in housing, and in ways that I am sure only blacks could really speak to from experience. That was the autumn of 1949 and the spring of 1950, four years before *Brown vs Topeka* and 14–15 years before the Civil Rights Act (1964) and the Watts Riot (1965). I used to go to a black bar, the Green Lantern in North Lawrence, with my black housemate. What made it interesting was that I felt very welcome there, and it was a joyful place that literally rocked in cadence with the jukebox music. But I tried to go in once, unaccompanied by my friend, and the owner politely said that he could not allow me entrance unless Andy was with me. I accepted his decision, but felt the arbitrariness of discrimination. I wanted what could never be: to feel at home and accepted—without a chaperone—in the Green Lantern. So I walked about three blocks northeast to the Tampico, a Hispanic bar where my black friend would never have been able to enter with anyone, even Benny Sanchez, another housemate. I was accepted alone, with whites, or with Benny at the Tampico. Hispanics and blacks simply were denied the opportunity to mix and did not mix in public places, although each could mix with whites and get away with it, in spite of discomfort in the community. I never understood this phenomenon, although there is no shortage of attempts to explain it. As a honky, I was critically positioned to bridge the racial divide between Hispanic and black, by moving back and forth across the weaker white/black and white/Hispanic barriers. And I enjoyed being in that position and doing it. If you wanted to learn about life, circa from 1949 to 1952, in Lawrence, Kansas, you developed a taste for beer and hit the off-beat segregated bars. My mother gave me the values and my father gave me the personal characteristics that made that possible, but the experience could never be as complete as I would have wished.

I met Joyce Harkleroad at KU in September 1949. We were married in June of the following year. She sat in front of me in John Ise's economic systems course and had lovely long black hair. She was a political science major. We were married for a wonderful and adventurous twenty-five years. Joyce was in Henley House, an interracial women's co-op. We decided to see about starting the first Couples' Co-op at KU. Joined by two other newlyweds, we located a big three-story house with a full basement at 1334 Ohio Street, just off the "hill" (the KU campus), which we rented for $180 per month. We were in business. We had Ralph Ross and Joanne Michner, Bill and Mary Brown, but we needed more people to keep the per capita bills down. So we placed an advertisement in the local newspaper, and Bruce Miller and family showed—one young child. Why not take on kids? A fifth couple was Harry and Norma Kirchner. The "families" divided up the first and second floors, doing some rebuilding to create five sleeping apartments. The landlord was Dave Park, a fine gentleman of about eighty years, who encouraged us to build partitions with our labor and his lumber, and had a penchant for saving rubber bands that he stored on doorknobs all over the house. The basement was converted to a very large kitchen and dining area, and the small Graduate Women's Co-op moved into the unoccupied third floor. We were up and running at $35 per month per person, children free.

University housing had a problem and called us for help. Beulah, a young, blind, black undergraduate, needed assistance, and there was of course no on-campus place for her to live. Would we provide space for her? We voted unanimously to take her in and decided to offer her a room-and-board "scholarship." We simply absorbed her cost by, in effect, sharing it equally. We delighted in providing the means whereby university housing could avoid any discomfort. The scholarship consciously defied and one-upped the university's stance in racial matters.

The next-door neighbor, disturbed that we were harboring "Negroes" (Beulah was our second!), told us that he could see that we wanted to provide charity for the "blind one," but what was our "excuse for the other one?" You had to hold back your anger. As mentioned, this took place in Kansas, a border state with an excellent constitution prohibiting discrimination. The neighbor, a fourteen-carat asshole who, as you might have guessed, was also anti-Semitic, eventually took one of us (Harry Kirchner) to court for violating the Lawrence City Ordinance against "harboring a barking dog." Never mind that it was blatant harassment, since it is in the nature of dogs to bark. The judge took testimony on the question of whether the dog barked "excessively." I testified for Harry, arguing that my newborn twins slept in the bedroom directly above where the dog was "harbored," and were never once disturbed.

Harry lost the case in spite of the fact that the entire city police force was rooting for us, so much did the police hate our vigilante neighbor who was constantly reporting people—and cars with out-of-state license plates parked longer than thirty days—to the police for trivial alleged violations. When the police ignored his reports, he reported to the commissioner that the police were not enforcing the law. Of course, we ignored his perpetual window peeping around our house, no doubt calculated to find us running a white slave operation. The judge found Harry guilty, but levied no fines or penalties.

That would have ended the matter, but one day Harry was walking past the neighbor's house, after a hard day at the Lawrence gunpowder plant in which he'd spoiled a titration. The guy was on the front porch and mumbled some "obscenity" too quietly for Harry to hear for certain, but he had no difficulty imagining what anti-Semitic epithet the old Scrooge must have uttered. Harry bounded up those porch stairs swinging and restrained himself too late to prevent some minor damages. We tried to explain to Harry that he should merely have feigned an attack in hopes that the old pest would wet his pants, but Harry was not in a mood to be that restrained. As you can imagine, the old fart pressed assault and battery charges, and he had a good case. Harry brilliantly defended himself, arguing cumulative provocation, and we all testified that the neighbor was always spying outside our windows, professing that we had some sort of "white slave" operation going, etc.—you had to admit that the guy was imaginative. There were lots of laughs in and out of court, with a few city folk sitting in on the entertainment. Of course, in the sober eyes of the law it is your responsibility to not allow provocation to accumulate—make your formal charges when the insults occur, and then leave the action up to the authorities. So the judge—delighted, we were sure, from his poorly disguised smirks, that the old racist geezer had gotten punched—did what he had to do and found Harry guilty as charged, but he suspended the sentence and put Harry on probation for a few months.

I was really impressed with the tremendous nuisance cost of having all sorts of minor prohibitory ordinances on the city law books. It gives arbitrary power and control to local citizens or authorities to apply them discretionarily to whomever they happen to choose. The process is easily described: some unusual event occurs—such as a dog barking hysterically—a complaint is lodged with a law-making body, and a law is passed. None of the unintended costs of the law, which are borne by everyone, are part of the decision as to whether the law is efficacious. Or consider the sexual mores of the day that outlaw certain bedroom activities. The culture changes, but the law remains on the books. The result is a collection of obsolete or minor prohibitions that set the stage for harassment by police or by citizens against other citizens. It's the laws against victimless crimes—prostitution, alcohol, marijuana, etc.—that are the primary source of police corruption, not police efforts to stop crimes against people, including the theft of their belongings. I remember well the Fourth of July during the 1940s, in prohibitionist Kansas, where two Wichita police officers were caught bootlegging whiskey out of the trunk of their city police cruiser while on duty.

Bruce Miller and I shared the job of the house purchasing agent for the Couples Co-op. We were good at scouting out bargains, like shoulder hams for 25 cents a pound, beef hindquarters at 60 cents per pound, New York Herkimer cheddar for 60 cents a pound—Harry loved that cheese, but we refused to buy the barrel of kosher dill pickles he was always lobbying for. These purchases were all at bulk wholesale prices, and we rented a frozen food locker for the meat.

Bruce and I also bought a 1930 Model A Ford panel truck, advertised by a local rural postman. The postman had bought it new and employed it for his deliveries until 1939, when he replaced it with a station wagon. He had cared for it lovingly, but now needed to sell it. The price was $60. Bruce and I each put up $30. Later, for $20, the automotive engine repair class at the famous Native American Haskell Institute in Lawrence overhauled the engine with new piston rings. When my family and I left for

Harvard, Bruce and family left for northern California. Bruce bought out my one-half share for $30, bought a four-wheel trailer, loaded it down with his family belongings, and drove the rig across the Rockies with hardly a whimper.

Bruce had been a conscientious objector in World War II, whose stand on war made no exceptions (as had I, Bertrand Russell, and many others, for World War II). Since the grounds for his pacifism were not religious, he did not qualify for alternative service, and was interred for a couple of years in McNeil Island Federal prison, known euphemistically as a correction center—Bruce did not feel that he needed correction so much as did the human race! The Cato Institute would later have a similar stand, opposing Desert Storm (and all such adventures), and would suffer a temporary dearth in contributions.

I received a letter from Bruce dated January 3, 2004, 52 years after I knew him in Lawrence. He was still supporting peace causes: "I just returned from the 30th anniversary of the Heart Mountain Fair Play Committee at the Japanese American National Museum in L.A. I was in McNeil Island Federal Prison when they brought in 33 of the young men who refused to change from 4C enemy aliens to 1A draft until (the) government restored their civil rights and allowed their families to leave Concentration Camp."

On May 5, 1951, Joyce gave birth to twins, Deborah and Eric, in that order, and I was part of a rapidly growing family. When they were born, two months premature, the iconoclastic John Ise, KU professor of economics, said, "Yeah, these kids just can't wait to get out and find what a hell of a fine world this is." John was the author of many other choice impromptu wisecracks. My favorite was occasioned by the resignation of the local KU Business School dean to accept the presidency of Washburn University Law School in Topeka, Kansas. John said: "Both institutions gained."

After receiving the Nobel, I was invited back to the University of Kansas to receive its Distinguished Service Award in the spring of 2003. While in Kansas I visited Wichita and gave a talk to Koch Industries' management. I also gave a talk at North High, where the Koch Foundation supports a student entrepreneurial program. When I arrived at North High, the band, honor guard, and cheerleaders were out in full force to greet me. The cheerleaders—all sweethearts in school red and white—showed me around the building, which had hardly changed. It's a beautiful sandstone structure, finished in 1932. It still has the same convenient stair landings at the extreme ends of the halls where you could pitch pennies to the wall and easily stake out the approaches so that you did not get caught gambling your lunch money. And we visited the cafeteria that doubled as a study hall, where we would surreptitiously release birds and engaged in other diversionary pranks. In the gym, I mentioned the fact that that was where I learned to jitterbug, 1940s style, as every Friday was coeducation day. One of the cheerleaders asked if I would show them how we danced.

I did, with her, and the *Wichita Eagle* snapped a picture for the article they ran on my visit.

In my talk in the auditorium, I spoke of sitting in that very room, at a special assembly called on Monday, December 8, 1941, to hear a radio address by President Franklin Delano Roosevelt concerning the previous day's attack on Pearl Harbor, "a day that would live in infamy." We were at war, and many of my classmates sitting in that auditorium with me were destined to die in battle or be lost on bombing raids over Italy or Frankfurt. It was very quiet in that auditorium full of young faces as I reminisced about those days, those war years, and the sacrifices that were endured. I also told them the truth: that I had not been a good student at North, strictly C average, and that they should understand that it was never too late to get your act together. "Don't let anyone tell you that you are marked, that you cannot overcome a past that failed to shine. You can."

In 2014, I was invited again to the University of Kansas to receive an honorary Doctor of Science degree (For Notable Contributions to Experimental Economics). I had been invited earlier, but I was pre-committed on the award day and not able to accept. If I had gone, I would have been joined by Sheila Bair, Chairwoman of the Federal Deposit Insurance Corporation, one of the two heroines of the housing bubble and crash that you will learn about in Chapter 19. She also had been a KU graduate, born in Independence, KS.

In 2014, I was joined by Joyce Didonato, who received a Doctor of Arts, For Notable Contributions to Opera and Vocal Performance. Joyce has an incredible voice; a combination of power and lyric depth that is just marvelous (Figs. 7.1, 7.2, 7.3, 7.4, 7.5, and 7.6).

Fig. 7.1 Friends U selfy in 2014

Fig. 7.2   Best friends at Caltech Irving and Belle Krumholz

Fig. 7.3   Ford model A like Scott Maynes' Juggernaut

Fig. 7.4 Joyce, Dad, Deborah, Mom, Eric Couples Coop Porch

Fig. 7.5 Couples Coop house 2014

Fig. 7.6 Bruce Miller left, Torrie, Pat Miller next to Vernon 1971

8

Harvard, 1952–1955

While at KU in the spring of 1952, I applied to the graduate economics programs at Stanford, Chicago, Carnegie Institute of Technology, MIT and Harvard. I was accepted at all of them, though Harvard and MIT both offered badly needed scholarship money. The award from MIT ($1800) exceeded that of Harvard ($1200), but net of tuition, Harvard was a better offer, so that became my choice. In my Duke archived correspondence "Vernon L. Smith Papers, 1938–2007 and undated,"[1] I found a copy of my performance scores on THE GENERAL PROFICIENCY TEST, SEPTEMBER 1952, HARVARD. Enumerated below, my scores were hardly spectacular—in fact pretty average. The one-page report included a description of the scoring, and I quote directly:

G   V   S   M

Name: Smith, Vernon L. Scores: 545   476   404   556

What the scores mean

G-score. This is supposed to be a measure of general aptitude for academic work… not ordinarily related to any particular field of study.

V-score. This is supposed to be a measure of verbal aptitude. It tends to be predictive of success in fields like History, English, Literature, and Government.

---

[1]Duke University Libraries (http://library.duke.edu/rubenstein/findingaids/smithvernon/).

© The Author(s) 2018
V. L. Smith, *A Life of Experimental Economics, Volume I*,
https://doi.org/10.1007/978-3-319-98404-9_8

S-score. This is supposed to be a measure of aptitude for scientific work in those fields where mathematical ability is of secondary importance, e.g., certain branches of Biology and Geology.

M-Score. This is supposed to be a measure of mathematical ability. It tends to be predictive of success in fields where mathematics is of major importance, e.g., mathematics, physics and engineering...

For first year Harvard graduate students as a whole, the average score on any of these tests is normalized at 500. Compared with the total group, scores above 600 are HIGH, and those above 650 are VERY HIGH. Similarly, scores below 400 are LOW, and those below 350 are VERY LOW.

So much for test scores, performance, schooling and life experience. You can see why I am not a fan of testing, of "leaving no child behind," or of new standards of "achievement" in the public schools. I sense that whoever wrote the above report—"This is supposed to be..."—was also a skeptic. My fear is that testing motivates the bad habit of teach-and-study-to-the-score, and the educational process becomes of secondary importance to test outcomes.

We already had two children, Deborah and Eric, so I was determined to get my degree at Harvard, get a job, get out of there, and avoid the professional graduate student syndrome. When Torrie was born in April 1955, I would be on schedule to finish in May 1955.

Joyce and I moved to Cambridge in 1952. My parents used the occasion to take their vacation, helping us by driving Joyce and the twins to Massachusetts in August. I bought a used 1938 GMC pickup truck, had the engine overhauled, and personally rebuilt the truck bed with new two-by-eight planks. I stacked that truck high with all our worldly possessions, including the solid red-gum kneehole desk that I had built from scratch in my ninth grade woodworking class (which earned me my only A and was therefore fit furniture for Harvard), covered the truck bed with a tarp, and drove from Kansas to Massachusetts. It reminded me a lot of the Joad family move from Oklahoma to California in John Steinbeck's *The Grapes of Wrath*. The Joad family and I moved in similar poor-folk style, and of course in great anticipation of opportunity. The Joad family was soon disappointed, but I was certainly not; Harvard was for me a warm source of great opportunity, although I was never entirely certain that the warmth was reciprocated. Arriving in Cambridge, my very first and quite memorable experience was to go into the well-known Wursthaus, just off Harvard Square, for lunch. I sat on one of the high counter stools and viewed the menu. An item that caught my eye was "Chili, Mexican Style." Then, eyes right came the parenthetical translation: "(No potatoes or carrots)." Welcome to the New England culinary scene—I nearly fell off the stool in a fit of laughter. At Purdue a few years later, I would find that it was routine for the chili to include macaroni. These outrages are second only to ketchup on a finely crafted hamburger or dumped on a Nu-Way.

I was the "advance man" for Joyce and the twins, and soon found an apartment at 89 Rice Street, up the block from an Irish pub and the Irish Catholic Church on Mass Ave. (that's New England Yankee vernacular for Massachusetts Avenue). The pub was known for its custom of serving a jigger of whiskey together with a tall stein of beer. The customer dropped the jigger of whiskey into the stein, and it mixed thoroughly with the beer as it glugged slowly to the bottom, remaining there until the contents had been emptied. Ugghh, what a concoction—like a blend of wood alcohol and varnish remover! I would just have a beer and look sheepishly around to see if anyone noticed. I guess the Irish boozing syndrome got bred out of my genes by the English; if so, then I am grateful that my English ancestry was a source of such great value!

After my parents, Joyce, and the twins arrived and were settled into our apartment, some of us went for a drive in the New England countryside accompanied by a native New Englander. My dad pointed excitedly to one of the farms we passed, saying, "Oh. Look at the rock fence." And the native sternly replied, "That, sir, is a stone wall!" Yes, indeed, and I would also learn that farms posted "No Shooting" signs, which translated into the same stricture as the Midwestern version, "No Hunting." Both signs in their respective regions warn you against walking through the fields carrying a gun to shoot at rabbits, squirrels, birds, and less frequent favorites, such as pole-top telephone insulators. But there are no farm signs in New England referring to the prohibition of hunting, because "hunting" refers to donning black riding boots and a bright red jacket, mounting a horse, and chase wildly after a bunch of yapping dogs who have flushed out some hapless fox.

At Harvard, I took the macroeconomics course from Alvin Hansen—unchallenged as the foremost American Keynesian—who was also very eclectic. In his class, we read everything from Foster and Catchings to Hayek, and not only Keynes, but his interpreters and critics—Hicks, Samuelson, Metzler, Friedman, etc. Hansen's macro-inspired optimism, circa 1952, was unbounded. I remember well a lecture in which he used some macroeconomic growth and monetary statistics to show that we (or at least he) could foresee the day when taxes could be greatly reduced with no effective deficit: Government would be financed by the government's creation of money to meet the legitimate liquidity and transactions requirements of a large and growing economy. The Federal Reserve would simply buy bonds in the open market at the same rate that the Treasury was issuing them. The economy would be large, and its monetary growth needs alone would be equal to the government budget—a "free lunch." (What is the fallacy here? Alvin thought the economy would grow much faster than government; that'll be the day, as John Wayne would say.) Or as Gottfried Haberler said when a comparable macroeconomic bootstrapping point was made by a student in the Haberler/Leontief joint seminar, "So much for ze facts," after which he swept his great outstretched arm across the table, his long underwear protruding an inch below his shirt cuffs.

Alvin Hansen was much beloved by the students. Chicago had little (in stature, big in intellectual impact) Milton Friedman, but we had little Alvin. (George Stigler, at the University of Chicago, used to say that if you went to a cocktail party, and saw a group of economists standing around in an empty circle, that Milton Friedman would be down in the center of that circle). From Hansen, we also learned the important principle, passionately believed by most of us to be the truth, that when monetary policy was ineffective, as in the Depression, then the government had to invoke fiscal policy and engage in massive deficit spending. Sir Dennis Robertson, as I recall, had coined the phrase, "pushing on a string" to describe the impotence of monetary policy in economic slumps like the Depression. The evidence universally cited, and which continues to be cited, as to what extricated us from the Depression was the increase in government spending accompanying the US defense buildup from 1940 through the end of the World War II. I learned Hansen's views on this in his Money and Banking and Business Cycles classes in 1952–1953. Some 60 years later when I was researching the last 14 recessions for *Rethinking Housing Bubbles* (2014), with Steve Gjersatd, we would discover that severe economic slumps, like the Depression and Great Recession, could be understood as examples of what we called "balance sheet" recessions, with large numbers of households and their banks in low and even negative equity. This provided a causal explanation of why, in such circumstances, monetary policy was ineffective. But I also realized, harkening back to Alvin Hansen, that fiscal policy was ineffective for the same reason. Steve and I had an explanation, not just Keynesian words—"liquidity trap"—for the ineffectiveness of massive monetary ease, which, circa 2014, was still with us. And the same cause underlies the widespread disappointment of economists and policymakers with the Bush stimulus, and later with the much larger Obama stimulus. A full treatment of the myth that deficit spending by the government will extricate the nation from a balance sheet recession is contained in Chapter 19, Volume II of this book.

Henry Wallich, who we will encounter later with regard to the auctioning of Treasury debt, preceded me by a dozen years as a Harvard student. In the 1970s, Henry will champion a series of field experiments in auction market bidding behavior. He took classes from Alvin Hansen in 1940 and learned the same durable "lessons." However, to his everlasting credit, Wallich appears to have been a lifelong skeptic of Hansen's position on monetary and fiscal policy. In his essay in *Recollections of Eminent Economists*, Vol. 1 (1988, Edited by J. A. Kregel) he states dryly: "Hansen was sure that monetary policy had failed and that it had to be replaced with fiscal policy. He was sure also (Hansen was occasionally in error, but never in doubt) that the American economy had reached a phase of stagnation and that in the absence of growth generated by the private sector it was the government's job to maintain full employment, however unproductively, by sufficiently large deficits."

Keynesian economics at Harvard was much tempered by the dry wit of Gottfried Haberler; the sarcasm of Wassily Leontief; Guy Orcutt's deeply serious search for the messages hidden in all data; Alexander Gershenkron, who lectured on the topic, "ven Breetan vas ze voikshop of ze voild"; and a coterie of graduate students trying to make sense of it all for their own careers. When Fritz Machlup visited, you wondered how the two polite Austrians—he and Haberler—would determine which one would go through a door first. Schumpeter was no longer alive, but his ghost was lurking in the halls, with Haberler countering any macroeconomic claims that inflation ("ze monster" to Schumpeter, and Haberler would have agreed), if not too large, was good for the health, soul, and spirit of the economy.

Harvard graduate students were kept in good humor by a blizzard of memorable encounters, lectures, and imaginative introductions involving both visitors and Harvard faculty. Here are only a few:

- Wassily Leontief taught the graduate introductory theory course. At the end of a two-week lecture series on utility theory, a student asked what utility theory was good for. Wassily, hesitating for only an instant, replied, "It's good for teaching."
- In an opening lecture on time preference and interest theory, Leontief explained why Irving Fisher failed to generate a school of Fisherian thought: "Irving Fisher wrote so clearly that everyone understood what he was saying."

- When Jan Tinbergen arrived from Holland to give a lecture, Leontief chaired the meeting and introduced him to the audience. When Tinbergen began his lecture, without a trace of an accent, you had the impression that it was Leontief, not Tinbergen, who had just stepped off the boat in Boston Harbor.
- Gottfried Haberler was the masterful chairman whose hilarious introductions always guaranteed an audience, whether the speaker was local or a visitor like Jacob Marschak. Harvard's Seymour Harris was a prolific publisher who supervised many Ph.D students in applied policy, money, and macrotopics. If he needed a graduate student for a new book, he would post an advertisement on the first-floor bulletin board of Littauer Center, advertising for some erstwhile lucky student to be funded by Harris on some AID, bank, or government grant program. Introducing Harris, Gottfried rose, walked to the podium, tall, poker-faced as usual, and gave his shortest and most memorable introduction: "Our speaker today is Professor Seymour Harris. You all know who Professor Harris is. Those of you who are not busy reading his many books and papers are busy writing them."

For microeconomics, I supplemented with courses Paul Samuelson taught down the (Charles) River at MIT. These were very lively, interactive classes of eight or so students. Except for Ron Jones, I no longer remember any of the other students in that class. Paul, ever the consummate showman, loved to dash into the room, barehanded, note-less and empty pocketed, pick up a piece of chalk—in the good old days of blackboards—and ask what the students wanted him to lecture about. He would get a few responses and would start talking while writing notes on one or more of these topics. A joke that circulated—I have no idea whether it actually happened—was that once, in one of these classes the students had prepared for the upcoming ego trip by the professor. Paul waltzed in, asked his question and there was only one suggestion. Furthermore, the suggestion was esoteric enough to require a little more than an impromptu rendition from Paul's formidable memory. So Paul replied, "Well, I thought I would talk about ..."

MIT had a much different feel from that of Harvard. The halls were light and airy, and if you passed a faculty member in the hall, he (no she's; I understand from a recent issue of *Science* that MIT is among the last universities to be progressive in this area) would acknowledge or speak to you. Upriver, at Littauer Center, the halls were dark and dingy, and most of the faculty would walk past you as if you were a lamppost.

After Caltech, Harvard seemed easy, and I got virtually straight A's (I think I made a B+ in economic history; grade inflation was in early incubation at Harvard). My classmate Dick Quant and I often scored among the highest on examinations. At best, though, one of us would finish only second—the top score always seemed to go to Barbara Jay, who married an artist and dropped out before dissertation time (Barbara married Peter Talbot Westergaard, a composer with many compositions and performances to his credit). Graduate school is an endurance test coupled with the belief that it is worth enduring, but it was not that demanding for me, having survived Caltech's undergraduate meat grinder. And I seemed to have a fairly good natural entry-level intuition for the subject, though ultimately I would leave behind almost everything that was central to a graduate education in economics in the early 1950s.

Living in Cambridge, we graduate students were also treated with some good laughs from kibitzing on Massachusetts and Boston politics, and by reading the *Boston Traveler*, always alert to the exposé and the anomalous. I observed that some graduate students, who read only *The New York Times* and seemed to be practicing for life's cocktail parties, were almost totally humorless. Here are a few tidbits, straight out of my memory, and therefore almost certainly there are omissions, errors in detail, and perhaps some pure fiction. Please do your own research if you are curious.

- At that time, "Ted" (Theodore) Green was one of the FBI's ten most wanted criminals. He had been apprehended in Boston and was quartered in the Charles Street jail. The jail had been designed for the temporary internment of prisoners until its inmates could be properly sentenced or moved to a more secure facility.

  Local citizens were well aware of the jail's faults, having been reminded incessantly by the *Traveler* that the hated Democrats left them unprotected by failing to modernize the prisons. Ted Green, an escape artist *par excellence*, and therefore a local hero, had already busted out of the Charles Street facility during an earlier internment. In fact, that is what had made him a local hero. Like Willie "The Actor" Sutton, he robbed banks, and you got the impression that that was not an altogether disgraceful line of work on the Boston side of the Charles River, not where you lived if you were a Cabot or a Saltonstall. On that earlier occasion, Ted Green had gotten past the police guards in a laundry bag carried out in a delivery truck.

  We were not to be disappointed. The headlines shortly after his internment proclaimed that Ted Green had somehow managed to get under the hood of a truck and ride out on the hot engine without getting scorched. He was free, like the one who flew over the cuckoo's nest. However, he was subsequently apprehended.

Some fifteen years later, after Joyce, I, and the family had moved again to the Boston area, I would learn that Ted Green had served a prison term, paid his debt to society, and was out in the free world. A local journalist had interviewed him. He was working as a used car salesman in Brookline, and he had an enviable sales record. He had his customers spellbound, articulating the relative advantages of Fords, Chevrolets, and other cars as getaway vehicles after a bank robbery.

- The Democrats were always the party in power in Massachusetts. While I was at Harvard, however, Governor Dever was defeated miraculously by the Republican candidate, Christian Herter. The *Traveler*, in this rare political window, sought to make the most of it. Dever had just built a new state prison, and it was a good time for the *Traveler* to check it out for construction faults—a dependable and often-reported feature of Massachusetts construction companies—and blame it on the departed Democrats. Indeed, there were big cracks here and there, and the story carried pictures of these construction faults. But soon thereafter, an even bigger story hit the streets; poking around in the cracks, it was found that the prison had knives, saws, and weapons of various sorts hidden in walls and cellblocks. The Boston underworld had infiltrated the construction crews and planted the tools of the escape trade!

- Also about this time, the Great Brink's armored car robbery case came to trial. This had been a tough case to solve, but the authorities finally had their case together. The principal witness in the case was Specs O'Keefe, who, as I recall, had turned state's evidence. He would get off free if he told all he knew about the greatest robbery of the century (since exceeded!). The prosecution was under pressure to move the case along quickly because, as I recall, the three-year statute of limitations would soon tie its hands. Specs had been testifying regularly, and on weekends and evenings, he would go visit his girlfriend. The Boston underworld decided to rub him out, so they imported a garden-variety thug from New York, with trademark low IQ, to kill him. So the guest killer trapped Specs in a dead-end alley near his girlfriend's apartment. The gunman emptied his submachine gun on Specs, putting bullet holes all over the alley wall but failing to kill him. Specs, it seems, had fairly minor wounds.

I have heard many other such reports of gross incompetence by lawbreakers, such as those of the Pima County Public Defender in Tucson, who tended of course to get the worst of the lot to defend. One guy robbed a convenience store and went out to escape in his old car, but the car would not start. He went to a nearby phone booth and called a cab. The cab and the police cruiser arrived at the same time, and he was arrested.

• And then there was Officer Callahan on the Boston side of the river across from Cambridge. A sign on the Cottage Farm Bridge over the Charles clearly stated "Right Lane, Right Turn Only." Of course, if you knew Boston, drivers routinely ignored traffic, parking, and warning signs. On a drive to Fenway Park, for instance, I recall being hesitant to take the last parking place under a sign that read "No Parking," and being ordered by a policeman to "hurry and get that car paaarked!" But with Callahan in the center traffic box you bloody towed the line—no exceptions. Above all, you respected him, because this was the one place in the whole damn Boston area where a super congestion point flowed as smoothly as possible, and you had the rule of loudly advertised law firmly in place, and enforced by Boston's best-known Irishman since the days of Boss Curly. If you came to the crossroads in the right lane and tried to continue, Callahan stepped down from his traffic box and stood squarely in front of your car until you turned, backing up all the honking bridge traffic, windows rolled down for greater ease of cussing. One day, a high-ranking city official on important business tried to drive straight ahead from the right lane and was prevented from so doing in spite of loud, angry threats from the driver that he would "get Callahan." As expected, Callahan prevailed, but he was soon busted to a walking beat. The event was widely publicized, with front-page pictures of Callahan walking his beat. The citizenry was in open revolt, supporting Callahan with a deluge of protests to police and city officials. Shortly thereafter Callahan was back in his traffic box. Sometimes in Boston, the revolutionary spirit reemerges, and the people win one against the city's double-breasted Brooks Brothers suits.

I want to close with an in-context digression on Daniel Ellsberg, whom I met at this time through a classmate of mine, Floyd Gillis. Floyd was a resident Fellow attached to one of the student houses at Harvard and had occasion to know Ellsberg as a resident. Dan had finished as an economics undergraduate in 1952, where he achieved unusual distinction. He then spent the academic year 1952–1953 in Cambridge UK and returned to enter the Harvard graduate economics program in 1953–1954. His senior thesis, supervised by John Chipman, who taught graduate econometrics at Harvard, was entitled "Theories of Rational Choice," 1952. Two articles on distinct topics would be published in leading economics journals out of that senior exercise: (1) "Classic and Current Notions of Measurable Utility," *Economic Journal*, 1954; (2) "Theory of the Reluctant Duelist," *American Economic Review*, 1956.

When the second article was punished, Dan Ellsberg was on leave of absence from Harvard with the US Marine Corps, serving as a platoon commander. He would return, complete his graduate studies, and submit his doctoral dissertation, *Risk, Ambiguity and Decision* to the economics department in April 1962.

My impression of him, circa 1954, was that of a brilliant student, yet naïve in the ways of the use of military power by government. Dan was intense in his commitment to understanding the foundations of decision theory. He was equally intense in his personal patriotism, and his commitment to the Marine Corp and to the American military mission. He was and has remained a loyal American who loved his country. Some people, perhaps most, have a common theme throughout their career. In the above works, a single theme emerges from his pursuit of understanding. He thoroughly probes and masters a topic, and, inevitably, finds that it has fundamental flaws. In utility theory, in game theory, and in the theory of decision under uncertainty, he found flaws. His duty, through publication, was to expose the flaws and set right the record concerning the content of that theory.

The circumstances were hardly different, with far higher personal stakes, when he leaked *The Pentagon Papers* to the *New York Times* in 1971.[2] As an intimate insider with a top secret classification at the Rand Corporation, and in his many trips to Vietnam he came to see America's entire role there as a "quarter century of aggression, broken treaties, deceptions, stolen elections, lies and murder." As in his scientific papers, his was a mission of exposé—the essential first step (as I interpret Dan's view) if great and unspeakable wrongs were to be made right so great were the infractions of human decency. If anyone other than the paranoid Richard Nixon had been President, Dan surely would have been the first person in recent times to be convicted under the wartime Espionage Act of 1917. National Security Advisor Henry Kissinger was quoted as telling his staff that Ellsberg was "the most dangerous man in America who must be stopped at all costs."

Nixon incurred those costs in a personally authorized burglary of the offices of Ellsberg's psychiatrist in search of incriminating evidence. He attempted to conceal his actions and undercut the Government's case against Ellsberg, who went free. Nixon effectively certified Ellsberg's entire mission of exposure with the stamp of "truth." Never was there such a commitment to the principle that the end justifies the means, nor a better demon-

---

[2]For details and biography, see: http://www.ellsberg.net/bio.

stration of its inherent power to corrupt, than Nixon's intervention in the Ellsberg case.

My direct experience, over 60 years passed, is quite limited, though I do see Dan as a loyal American patriot, then as now. The only change is that he is no longer a naïve young idealist, but a mature, seasoned, and knowledgeable idealist! Here are some notes from his 2010 interview for the documentary film, *The Most Dangerous Man in America*:

One of the interviewers wondered how you talk to a seven years old, an inquisitive child, who is starting to ask questions about the war (this is the Obama administration's war), about the current situation, without sounding unpatriotic? Dan's answer:

It's easier than it may seem…to be patriotic is to be loyal to the principles of our Constitution, and the First Amendment. …the policies of the government are sometimes in conflict with that…Tell the 7 year old that presidents are very often wrong…And when they are, it's our…responsibility to do our best to set them right.

Fortunately for me, my mother never gave a damn, whether or not she sounded unpatriotic in what she said to anyone; moreover she always conversed in a completely constructive spirit. She was in fact an American loyalist.

As I write, many of the same issues have arisen concerning Edward Snowden. Unlike Ellsberg, Snowden ran from the charges, and for me that sends a far different, and more conflicted self-serving message. *The Guardian* journalist Glenn Greenwald reported (June 22, 2013) the following: Edward Snowden was charged with two felonies under the 1917 Espionage Act. Including the charges against Dan Ellsberg, there have been only three cases brought under the Act since its inception. "That's because the statute is so broad that even the US government has largely refrained from using it." Yet during the Obama Administration, there have been seven prosecutions. It seems remarkable that Obama would be a greater threat to First Amendment rights than Richard Nixon, who was oblivious to such rights in his attitude toward dissent. But what is to be considered "dangerous" to freedom in the light of terrorist attacks on the very existence of the idea of an open society? Hitler's Nazi onslaught was much the same, but one knew what and where to counterattack (Figs. 8.1, 8.2, and 8.3).

Fig. 8.1   Milton Friedman in the Circle

Fig. 8.2   Dan Ellsberg Harvard to 'Most Dangerous Man in America' Commons Wikimedia

Fig. 8.3   Deborah and Eric Happy Days

9

Thou Shalt Honor Thy Father and Mother

Give me courage and gaiety and the quiet mind.
—Lula Belle (Lomax) Smith; inscribed on the back of a wood
plaque for a therapeutic handicraft task, about 1956

Heap not on this mound
Roses that she loved so well:
Why bewilder her with roses,
That she cannot see or smell?

She is happy where she lies
With the dust upon her eyes.

—Edna St. Vincent Millay, "Epitaph"

It is terrible to find how little progress one's philosophy and charity have made
when they are brought to the test of domestic life.
—C. S. Lewis, Letters to Arthur Greeves. (pp. 362–363)

I have spoken often of each of my parents, and there is much more that
could be said. Now, I want to speak of their final years at a time in my life
when I was only just beginning to see them as adults rather than as parents.
This will lead me to tell you about my grandparents, particularly Grandpa
and Grandma Lomax, sisters Billye and Aileen, and to discuss some of my
personal insights and impressions concerning family relationships. Those

© The Author(s) 2018
V. L. Smith, *A Life of Experimental Economics, Volume I*,
https://doi.org/10.1007/978-3-319-98404-9_9

relationships were complex, sometimes adversarial and emotional, but somehow it was the good times that always seemed to surface in my memories and in theirs, and constitute that which lasts and inspires. The good times were the enduring times, but I am not sure why this is so. I was the only one to escape that nest, and I kept moving from one new challenge to another, rarely looking back. I think that it is the early values from home, family, neighborhood, and particularly parents that ultimately make the formative differences in a person. Other sources, however, must matter as well; otherwise, you cannot explain why there are so many whose earliest value experiences are so negative, yet they are able to overcome.

After I finished at Caltech, my father wondered why I did not actively pursue a career in engineering. His concerns stemmed largely, I think, from his own aspirations if such a dream had been possible for him. But I never recall his contesting that decision or any other that I made. He would listen to me, and maybe ask a question, but he would accept what I said and try to facilitate what I wanted to do. His was very much a live-and-let-live, can-do personality. My mother was much more proactive, and for her the world badly needed changing. My father agreed that it needed changing, but he had a less visibly confrontational approach to making change. Each of their approaches to the dynamics of living was valuable, and I was fortunate to experience and learn from both.

They always lived modestly and could never have lived otherwise, thanks to years of frugality. The frugality was made necessary by their circumstances, but the lifestyle became ingrained long after it became less necessary. After Caltech, I was entirely self-supporting, relying on scholarships and earnings from part-time or temporary work, so my parents were able to accumulate more savings. They soon bought an empty lot and built a new three-bedroom home at 324 South Gordon, just a few blocks south and west of their original home. This one had two bathrooms! They also bought a new 1949 Dodge, my father's first and last new car. Except for this modest splurge, their spending habits, born of years of financial hardship, changed very little as the end drew near for them, but they continued to provide in-kind support for Joyce and me. They deliberately timed their vacation to help us move to Cambridge.

Occasionally, I have been asked if I am related to Adam Smith, whom Kenneth Boulding correctly described as the first great post-Newtonian scientist—other obvious candidates, such as Michael Faraday and Charles Darwin (who was significantly influenced by Adam Smith and who records in his notes having read *The Theory of Moral Sentiments*), came too late and have to be classified, respectively, as the second and third of the post-Newton greats. In response to the question: Smith never married, and there were no direct descendants.

Of course, "Smith" is so common a name that people give up trying to trace it. My father's middle name comes from his paternal grandmother, who was a Chessman, and I do have a Chessman family book. Inserted in the family copy of the Chessman book are miscellaneous references on the history of the McCurdy family tree, but nothing specific about the lineage of Maggie Blanche (McCurdy) Smith, my father's mother. (The Chessman book reports the first oral tradition in the Chessman family. George Chessman lived in Glasgow, Scotland. At about age 19, he was captured by a press gang, put aboard a warship, where he served for two years. His ship was lying at anchor in Boston harbor near Nantasket Roads. He dropped into a boat at night and made his way up the Monatiquot River, landing in East Braintree. Taking to the woods, he followed a path until he saw a young woman, Jane Duran with a cow. The family cared for him, and he married her!)

Grandpa, Charles Alexander Smith (1865–1956), born just six years after oil was discovered in Titusville, Pennsylvania, was a tool dresser in the Pennsylvania oil fields. He traveled from rig to rig to rework, sharpen, and repair the worn drilling bits as a well shaft was being drilled. He talked to me at length a week or two before he died, in early 1956. He had a respiratory infection that evolved into pneumonia after our holiday visit to Wichita. We probably imported his fatal virus from Indiana. He died in a hospital, after being taken there unconscious. He was a Christian Scientist and would never have consented to being taken to a hospital. The man deserved to die at home, and his wish should not have been violated.

We had a good visit, unlike any other, in which my grandfather felt that he had conveyed to his descendant key features of oral family history as he had experienced it. There was no one else for him to talk with, and I was intensely interested in what he had to report. He had outlived all of his children, and Grandma had grown senile, perhaps with what later would be called Alzheimer's disease, and lived in a nursing home. At ninety-one, Grandpa was as sharp as ever. Uncle Norman once said to my father, "You know, Vern, he can remember the first three-cent stamp he ever bought."

Grandpa filled me in on several details. He had left Pennsylvania for Oklahoma in 1915, to work in the Tulsa oil fields. He then lived for a time in Riverton, Wyoming, where earlier oil discoveries were being developed. He finally settled in the Wichita area and bought a home there, following the oil strike in Eldorado, just east of the city. That was his last job as a tool dresser. Feeling financially secure from accumulated savings, he bought some rental property, retired sometime thereafter, working only occasionally as a night watchman or in some other part-time job. His roustabout days were over. He found religion, and he must have lived some thirty odd years after retiring.

Here is my take on the economics of oil-field development, which explains my grandfather's decision to leave Pennsylvania and ultimately settle in Kansas. At that time Kansas probably produced only wheat and cattle as significant net exports. Oil and aircraft were yet to become major parts of that export base. Tool dressers were in greatest demand during the resource development period after a strike. Once wells were producing, tool dressers moved on unless it was a big field that would be drilling many more wells. Also, wage offers would likely have been highest in that development period after a new strike. This, of course, was because there was no specialized local skilled labor pool of tool dressers. They had to be attracted to the area from other regions. The best money was made by those who were not based in one area and could move from strike to strike, scalping off the early and highest wages for several months in each location.

Oil strikes create new boomtowns. Jack Nicholson's early movie *Five Easy Pieces* was about the lives of roustabouts—drilling crew who hopped from one oil discovery to another. Oil strikes were exactly like the gold strikes whose prospects are what moved Wyatt Earp from Dodge City to Tombstone for a couple of years, then on to California, and eventually to Nome, Alaska. That was why Grandpa left the old, producing oil fields in Pennsylvania. By 1915, it had been fifty-six years since Colonel Edwin Drake dug his first well; initially, the oil was so close to the surface that it leaked into the creeks of northern Pennsylvania. Nature can do much environmental damage when left unchecked.

See the obscure movie *Waltz Across Texas*, filmed in Midland, Texas, if you want to see the "uureeal binnus" (oil business) accurately reported from the leasing side. Lease rights to drill were obtained by the "Land Man," who had to be a local who was well known in the community. Otherwise, there was no way to get a lease from a distrustful rancher such as the one played masterfully by the incomparable Richard Farnsworth in this sweet, offbeat movie.

Uncle Norman lived a comparable life as a wildcat driller, which did not even have the security of high initial wages after a new field was discovered. Wildcatters were looking to hit the really big one, and of course a few did, thanks to the great R. A. Fisher "folk theorem" that holds that "events of small probability happen at about the expected frequency." It was a crapshoot in which the payoff, if there was one, came at the end of the sacrifice, not at the beginning. But they dreamed rich, worked and lived hard, and never gave up hope.

Uncle Norman visited us only rarely—usually when he was flush with money after bringing in a well. Then, he would pay off loans on his drilling rigs, car, etc., and start living out of hotel rooms and "sliding my ass around on that slick leather in hotel lobbies," as he once put it. But, compulsively, he would drill some more dry holes, spend his stake drilling and living it up, and get back into debt before another modest strike. He never hit into an important new pool of oil; he just found a few little necks sticking out on the side of a known structure. That was enough, however, to fuel hopes that the next one would be a big hit. The big hit never came.

Dad opted for more stability, apprenticing as a machinist in Cleveland after serving as a sergeant in Company B of the 308th ammunition train in World War I. Of his siblings, dad was really the one you could call a "family man." He wanted marriage, children, and a family and chose a wife who gave him a running head start and was not averse to adding one more to the sample.

Grandpa Smith and Uncle Norman were always a delight to have around—lots of jokes, wisecracks, and laughs. If it was hot and humid, Grandpa would have some crack like, "It's not the humidity, it's the humanity." Broke, Uncle Norman finally quit the drilling business around 1944 and married a widow who owned a farm in eastern Kansas. We drove over to visit him, and I remember my dad asking him if he had gotten any oil out of that last well we had stopped to see him drilling in Iola, Kansas. He replied, "Yes, about a quart, and I got it all over my clothes." Norman died of a heart attack on September 7, 1946, less than two years after that visit.

Many families have a legendary figure in the three contiguous generations of children, parents, and four grandparents. Our legend was Grandma Ella (Moore) Lomax. (I know nothing of the Moore family. My sympathy and admiration for the Irish came through my father and those beautiful Irish ballads.) Grandma Lomax was *the* legend. The rest of us classified Grandma Lomax as—and I am quoting—a "hypochondriac, kleptomaniac, and pathological liar." Billye's husband Carl, in jest, would refer to her as "Kleppy," but that was a severely truncated, oversimplified characterization of the complex figure of my maternal grandmother.

Let me give you a collage of true events compressed into a single hypothetical sequence in which Aileen, Billye and Carl, and Grandpa and Grandma Lomax are at our house for dinner. One or two of whom might, in some actual instances, be living with my parents in the downstairs bedroom at the time.

In this instance, Grandma might be helping with the family dinner, but, in search of family sympathies and attention, might carry on with many heavy sighs and groans, signaling internal distress or illness. We would all sit down to eat, and Grandma would eat nothing or perhaps nibble on something. "Why?" "I have no appetite, and I feel sick in my stomach." "Why don't you lie down and rest?" "I want to be near at hand." More heavy sighs. "Why don't you go into the living room and lie on the couch?" Now, we have a little beacon-flash of truth: "I won't be able to hear you talk."

It's a nice evening, and after dinner, someone suggests that we all go outdoors and sit in the yard. We clear the table. Grandma dallies in rising from the table and then offers to clear the last few items. We go out, but my dad slips around on the south side of the dining room to peek through one of the windows. He comes back laughing as if he had been watching a Chaplin movie: "She's in there stuffing leftovers into her goddamn mouth with the fingers of both hands." We all erupt with laughter.

Later, she comes outdoors, still in feigned agony, and sits awhile as we talk—heavy sighs continuing. We ignore her, chatting. As it gets darker, Aileen suggests we go indoors for a card game. Grandma perks up, but then lapses back into her "misery." We talk some more and then rise and go into the house. In the interior light, Grandma's state appears much improved— no deep sighs and groans.

Aileen says, "Who wants to play Pitch?" I volunteer. Silence follows, and Grandma then announces that she is feeling better, and she will play so that there will be "enough players." We all knew that come starvation, tornadoes, drought, illness, hell, or high water, there is no way that Grandma is going to pass on a card game. Aileen who was probably setting her up now says "How come you feel better?" And Grandma would have some cock-and-bull story that she had taken some baking soda before leaving the kitchen and was now cleared of her pain. Now we have only three for Pitch, so Grandma, who ostensibly is only trying to accommodate the rest of us, simply volunteers Grandpa Lomax. He could not care less, but he knows better than to refuse.

Grandma and I are matched against Aileen and Grandpa. After several hands of Pitch, Grandma has just updated the cumulative score after a hand. She announces, "Vernon and I are ahead." Grandpa responds, "Well, you're keeping the score." And Grandma, now in great spirits and radiating energy, lets out a snort of disapproval. We all knew that she constantly cheated in card games—scoring, adding, peeking at cards, you name it. We sometimes caught her in the act, but to no avail did it bring any change. Aileen was once roped into a game. After playing awhile, just after a new hand was dealt, she laid her cards face down on the card table—these were the old folding card tables that were always ready to be exhumed from the closet for Grandma—and said, "I have to go to the toilet, but I will be right back." Feigning closing the door, she peeked back into the living room and saw that Grandma had picked up her cards. Grandma examined them and returned them to the table. Of course, Aileen returned and continued the game, saying nothing. When we confronted her, she'd say, "Well, I'm old."

If there was a church rummage sale, Grandma always volunteered to help sell donated clothes and sundry items. These were cash transactions, and we knew that she stole from the kitty, keeping some of the sales receipts while allowing some increase in her initial inventory of petty cash. She would have stolen from Jesus himself. It was all tolerated, though. We merely tried to maneuver her, for example, giving her inaccurate information about when a sale would start, so that when she showed up to help, the only job left was wrapping the purchases.

All this occurred in the 1930s and 1940s. Grandpa died in 1945. Soon thereafter, my mother, angry with Grandma over something—I have no idea what triggered the exchange—unburdened herself about how badly Grandma had treated her father. It was a very emotional outburst, and I don't recall anything comparable from my mother. It was known in the family that Grandma had had lovers while Grandpa was away on extended railroad runs up to Genesee, Kansas.

Mother once related to us that when she and her brother Denny were eleven or twelve years old, they followed their mother to a place where they suspected that she was visiting another man and "confirmed" the affair (or at least that some sort of hanky-panky seemed to be going on). Also, Grandma always seemed insistent on remodeling whatever home she was living in and always needing to manage the painters, carpenters, wallpaper hangers, yard workers, or other workmen connected with the project. My grandparents would sell their house, move into another, and the new one would need to be remodeled, as there was always something not quite right. Unlike so many in those days, Grandpa was employed all through the Depression and made a steady, adequate income. Grandma made sure the income was spent.

When she was in her sixties, and especially after Grandpa had died and her railroad pension had been reduced, she started working as a personal caretaker for "old people," as she called them. These were typically widows in their seventies and eighties. They were not much older than Grandma and certainly not as sharp. We never had any doubt that she took them to the cleaners. She would move on if their health or ambulatory ability deteriorated, as they then became too much trouble for her, and she would feign not being strong enough for their needs. Her clients were women who used elevators and needed domestic assistance with shopping, cooking, errands, and had to be driven here and there. They lived in nice east-side multiple-unit residential buildings.

Grandma managed all these chores, and it was a great opportunity for a little petty theft. In particular, she would shop for her clients at specialty grocery stores and appropriate for herself some of the food—expensive specialty hams and esoteric canned goods that were never part of our diet when we were growing up. We knew about it because she was always generous with friends and family—giving away much of the contraband to obtain praise and thanks. She would give an entire Smithfield ham, cans of fine Vienna sausage, a slab of bacon—things we would buy only on some very special occasions, or never—and always under the pretext of an unconvincing story that her client was overstocked and gave it to her. You can afford to be generous with other people's money (OPM).

Soon after our twins were born, Joyce and I took them to visit my parents in Wichita—the South Gordon street home. This was the summer of 1951, before the suburban shopping malls had decimated the downtown shopping area. Grandma was well known to most of the clerks in the major downtown department stores like Innes's and Rorabaugh Buck's. They also were aware that you had to keep an eye on her and nail down the valuables or she would lift them. Anyway, the twins were maybe two months old. Grandma was proud of them, but of course it was always better to lavish affection using OPM.

The second day we were there, Grandma came home with matching boy–girl light-yellow summer suits, shirt, and pants, for Eric, and a dress for Deborah. She had guessed at the proper sizes, they did not fit, and they needed to be exchanged for larger sizes. I suspected that she had stolen them, and volunteered to return them myself, as Grandma could not do it until the next day. Grandma said that she couldn't find the receipt. Of course, as I knew, there was no receipt to find. "Where did you buy them?" I asked. "Rorabaugh's," she replied, referring to the high-quality department store at the northeast corner of Broadway and Douglas, but she did not want me to return the merchandise.

I ignored her and went downtown to the children's wear department of Rorabaugh's. I identified myself to the clerk and showed her the clothes, explaining that my grandmother had said that she bought them there. Of course, the clerk knew Grandma—who didn't. But for most clerks, it was all OPM, and their loyalty to their employers did not include fingering Grandma. The clerk told me that Rorabaugh's did not carry those items, and that Grandma had not recently been in the store. The clerk looked at them carefully, and was pretty sure that they were from Kresge's, which was just across the street. Interestingly, it was Grandma's desire that all of us believed she had bought the clothes at one of Wichita's finest. This is pure conjecture, but I suspect that the basic problem for Grandma may have been that she was too well known in the better stores. They had a very slow turnover of employees, and there was a good oral tradition that would have spread the word about "Kleppy."

I crossed the street to Kresge's and went to the children's-wear counter on the first floor. Yes, they carried the brand, and the clerk showed me where they were arranged on the counter. I asked if she had sold any that morning to an older woman. "No." She had made no sale from that stock to anyone. I explained about my grandmother and returned the clothes. I had caught Grandma in a lie and a theft, and I was pissed. It was time to stop the family charade. I returned to mom's house and told her the story. Grandma was not there—she was out on an errand or just gallivanting around, as usual. I told mother that I had had my fill of it. Grandma was stealing to buy good-will for her generosity, and using my children, no less. Who needs this crap? I was going to confront her with the evidence—theft and lying—when she returned.

Mom did not want me to do it. She begged me not to do it. In tears, she said, "Vernon what good will it do, or difference will it make? That's my mother, and you and I and the rest of us are helpless to change it." My moral outrage evaporated instantly, as I came to my senses—or rather, my mom's good senses. "How right she is," I thought. But I also realized that mom and the whole damn community were in an unspoken pact to protect Grandma from herself, from getting caught, and from going through the emotional tension of it all. Our complicity meant there was more than enough of the OPM problem to go around; things usually did not get returned. There was no proof unless someone wasted an afternoon playing detective, as I did.

I relived all this, as well as my awareness of my mother's suppressed resentment at frequently having her parents living with her, in writing this memoir. I re-read Grover's letter to his brother George (see Chapter 1), in which he mentions his mother-in-law: "Well Dad & Ma Lomax are hear with us ... Ma she is going to work soon she has her a good job hear in one of the best stores." And in a note added by my mother, "Mother and Dad are going to stay with us all winter." I wondered if that good job in one of the best stores in Newton, circa 1918, is where the shoplifting began. Or had Grandma already become well-practiced at humankind's oldest form of involuntary income redistribution?

I accepted the resolution of the issue just as mom had intended it, but I can tell you for sure that there was a lingering sense of incompletion, of that which cannot be resolved, and I bloody well remember it as if it were yesterday. Above all, I remember my mother's pain, trying to reconcile "thou shalt not steal" with "thou shalt honor thy mother and father." None of us could honor Grandma, but, when the chips were down, mom honored her by defending her. Grandma had borne the brunt of 90% of the family's laughs. But it was never funny to mom, and I can't recall her ever laughing with the rest of us. Mother knew it was a sort of illness. Would we have laughed at a relative with Down's syndrome? Not on your life, but we made a perpetual joke of Grandma's antics. It was not funny, but we laughed, at least on the outside.

What do you make of all this, reader? You need to understand that the morality underpinning my outrage had been taught to me by my mother, but she tolerated her own mother's behavior. I remember coming home from Cole's grocery with a piece of candy when I was about four. Mom knew I had no money and that Merle Cole was not one to be passing out gifts to the local kids. "Where did you get it?" "Out of a basket at the store." "Did you buy it?" "No." So I was marched down to Cole's and returned it to Merle Cole, a mountain of a man. I told him I was sorry, and I will never forget it. Suppose someone with the same moral outrage that I felt had turned Grandma into the authorities. So she would have been fined, or whatever the hell they do with petty thieves. She was ill—a kind of sociopath, I suppose—and had been so all her life. Stealing seemed to be an autonomic disease of her social mind that went with lying and sympathy seeking. But suppose she were sent to a mental hospital, which then and now is a kind of mental and bodily prison. Would that have been a solution? Not then and not now. Yet I believe she should have been held accountable, somehow, as I was at age four.

Returning that candy to Merle Cole was indeed a memorable lesson, although it probably was only one of many and I had no need to remember the others. To this day, I find it abhorrent when someone tells me about packing up "souvenir" towels—or worse, fine bathrobes—when checking out of a hotel; it's seen as an entitlement, not a violation of the right of private property and of the imperative "thou shalt not steal." In retrospect, it fascinates me that mom had a really strong entitlement attitude toward legally sanctioned government programs of income redistribution, particularly "profits," but at no time did that slip over into any idea of cheating the government. It's wrong to steal from a government charged legally with the duty of taking from the haves and giving to those who have not. In later years, I would scrupulously pay all taxes, while taking full advantage of legal tax shelter programs—for example, putting the maximum allowable by law into supplemental retirement annuities. In my fifty-five years of paying income taxes, I have been routinely audited three times. Twice the government owed me money after the audit, having found I had erred in its favor—now *that* is unsettling!

I was reminded again, recently, of that seemingly trivial childhood candy episode in reading Paul Ormerod's 2005 book *Crime: Economic Incentives and Social Networks*. The study notes, among other important factors in crime among juvenile boys, the importance of social networks and, in particular, the important difference therein between boys who commit zero crimes and only one. Once the latter occurs, there is no typical number of crimes that an individual commits: "Policies of rehabilitating hard-core criminals have had little success, and ... are of very much second order importance compared with the need to deter individuals from committing their very first crime." (p. 88)

Well, in the end, Grandma would be severely punished, and it was as a result of my mother's actions, though no one will ever know in what sense it was intended.

I do not remember exactly when I became aware that my mother had been suffering from depression, nor do I know when the symptoms first appeared. I did, however, come to realize that she deliberately sheltered me from any detailed knowledge of it. Early in the summer of 1957, in a stopover in Wichita as we drove to the Rand Corporation, she told me that when she was ill, it was only with great difficulty that she could lift her arms to comb and prepare her hair. She also told me that she had not wanted me to see her that way. While I was a student at Caltech, she had been hospitalized for a short time, took medications, and sometime later was admitted, perhaps twice, for longer periods to private mental health institutions. I never knew the details, and Billye is no longer here to recount them. It is accurate, I think, to say that she was unipolar.

In preparing this memoir, I read the diary she kept from January 1944, to September of 1945. There were many days with no entries, particularly in 1945. I see her condition in many entries; my additions are in brackets:

February 17, 1944: "[Uncle] Denny, Mother and Dad drove down" [from Kansas City].

February 18, 1944: "Confusion with so many in the house."

February 19, 1944: "Tired—can't stand so many around. Mother and Dad make me nervous—I try not to be."

February 22, 1944: "Mother and Dad left this a.m. what a relief to be alone."

April 11, 1944: "I am worn out these days—don't know if I can take it. Meals alone are a job."

June 26–29, 1944: Each day she records simply, *"tired [or] not resting so well at night."*

My father died suddenly and unexpectedly—is death ever really expected?—in March 1954. Joyce and I were living in Cambridge. We flew home with the twins for the ceremony and to spend some time with my mother. She seemed to take it pretty well, but the next three years would be difficult for her. Her depression became worse. She was hospitalized and was given electroshock (Electroconvulsive) therapy—a routine treatment in those days. She was terrified by the treatment. It was pioneered in the 1940s and 50s, and apparently is still used today, but only in severe cases of depression, and with patients who do not respond to drug therapies.

Hospitalization was particularly difficult for my mother: She lost all control over her life, her decision-making, and her humanity. Thomas Szasz has written extensively, passionately, and knowledgably about the so-called modern treatment of "mental patients." Electroshock was called "therapy" by the psychiatrists who were using it on my mother. Their professional forerunners had treated masturbation as a disease as late (if I recall correctly) as the early twentieth century. This was reported in a paper by my friend Tris Engelhardt of the Baylor College of Medicine, a renegade professor of medical ethics. The oath of Hippocrates requires one to "abstain from all intentional wrong doing and harm." I wonder when in the history of medicine the tide turned, and the medical profession began to save more people than it killed.

The fear of electroshock weighed on my mother, and upon her release, she was determined to get better. She took piano lessons again and returned to the serious study and practice of music. Some of this I learned from her, but most of what I know about her return to the study of music I learned from Billye. My mother got better for a time, but then she began to slip seriously, in spite of her determination to improve.

In referring to difficult times or situations, my mother often used the phrase "this will pass." Folded and inserted into her diary, I found a faded yellowing clipping from a *Wichita Beacon* column by Harry Emerson Fosdick, a nationally known minister at Riverside Church in New York. Here is an excerpt from it that is also available online in a downloadable PDF "On Being a Real Person": One of the commonest causes of personal disorganization is despondency. Some despondency is physically caused, but the moody dejections most people suffer are not altogether beyond their control.

A first suggestion for dealing with this problem is: Take depression for granted. One who expects completely to escape low moods is asking the impossible. To take low moods too seriously, instead of saying "This also will pass," is to give them an obsessive power they need not have.

A second suggestion is of daily importance. "We can identify ourselves not with our worse, but with our better, moods. Deep within us all is that capacity. The ego, the central 'I,' can choose this and not that mood as representing the real self; it can identify itself with hopefulness rather than disheartenment, with good rather than rancor."

Billye had borne the brunt of care for mother; her sister Aileen was herself bipolar and of little help. Desperate, and knowing that her care was a serious burden on Billye, mother asked Billye to prepare the papers for her admission to the state hospital in Larned. After the papers were ready and Billye brought them to mother for her signature, she wouldn't sign them. She had changed her mind, telling my sister she did not want to go through with it, but offering no explanation or justification for the reversal. This was not without embarrassment for mom, as Billye had gone through much trouble to set it all up and run through considerable bureaucratic hurdles; the State of Kansas, naturally, did not want to give free meals and warm beds to all who applied. It was traumatic for mom because she worried about money, and had said that she did not want to return to a private hospital, without resources adequate to pay for it. She would accept no financial help within the family, and she had said that this time she wanted to go to Larned, where the Kansas State Mental Hospital was located.

Every family has its givers and its takers. Billye was a giver, like our parents. She was there to do the grunt work not just for mom, but also for Aileen and Grandma, and to do whatever needed to be done. But the needs of the others outweighed their gifts. If there were problems to be solved, they were not there to help, or, worse, they were at the center of the problem to be solved. Billye was so much like her mother, yet, as some might say, stable. Mom *wasn't* unstable; depression is not well described by the word *unstable*. Billye just took life as it came and did what was needed.

I am so very grateful that in her later years I got to know Billye as a sister, a confidante, and a dearly beloved friend. I miss her. On balance, within that family, I believe I was also more of a taker than a giver. Billye helped me learn to give more, or at least be more aware of gifts from others, and she did it by example. What a really great lady she was. She and Carl were divorced for a few years in midlife. Carl married again, was absolutely miserable, divorced, and wanted to remarry Billye. Eventually, she consented.

Years later, though, she confided to me that they never bothered to formally remarry; they just told everyone that they had done so.

Aileen, I should mention, had been married seven times to become the other behind-the-scenes family joke. She was still a distant second place to Grandma's legendary stature in the family jest and paled in terms of family conversation. But Aileen still got lots of local attention since she lived with us, in the downstairs bedroom, during each of her transitions. I will spare you the details of alcoholic husbands (two, one abusive); a jealous teetotaler (he was considered "progress" by mom) who prohibited delivery service drivers from stopping at his and Aileen's house; another big-time loser; three of these four were free riders who sponged off her (Aileen was smart, competent, and always had good jobs); and among the seven were three that passed through so fast that I never knew them by name or person, or even heard any detailed family gossip about them. I can remember only four of their names (Philippe, Ward, Cook, and White), and all together, I don't think she could have averaged much more than a year per husband. She finally got the message: Don't marry them.

In the summer of 1957, Grandma, Aileen, and Aileen's young son Denny, who was about fourteen, were living with mom. Grandma, Mother, and Aileen had a love–hate relationship, and here, they were living together. Denny was destined for schizophrenic oblivion, but that was not known at the time. That summer, my mom's home had to have been a monumental snake pit. At the time, I was a summer consultant for the Rand Corporation in Santa Monica. At Purdue, I had been working with Abe Charnes, Rubin Saposnik, and others on a research project for the Saint Louis and San Francisco Railroad—the Frisco, as it was known. (Here was another one of the many US railroads whose names expressed hopes that were never realized. The Frisco never got west of Dallas or north of Kansas City, let alone to San Francisco.) We were due to deliver our final report that August at the Frisco home office in St. Louis. My portion of the report was critically important, as it dealt with the railroad's leading policy issue: whether and how to enter the "piggybacking" (known today as the "intermodal container" business). The Frisco management was not sure—but I was sure— that they should enter this new transportation technology. No one else on the team could make my case, and I had planned to fly back to St. Louis in August. Since my fare was paid, under the regulatory rules of the day, it would cost nothing to stopover in Wichita and see my mother on my return from St. Louis. As the time approached, I was in touch with mom regarding the dates for my visit. I very much wanted to see her, as I told her on the phone, but she was hesitant about it. She had been deteriorating all summer, which was evident in the last two letters she had written just before my expected departure to St. Louis. She never dated her letters beyond "Sat. a.m.," for example, but I am pretty sure of the dates I use below:

Sat. a.m. (July 20, 1957)
Dear Vernon-Joyce-Children
Vernon's letter Friday.
So glad you are having an enjoyable time.
Wish I could write good news to you—guess it is no use to keep the bad news. I think you would be disgusted with me. I am worse each week, but surely there will come a change.
Sorry I can't write more.
Love,
Mother

Sat. a.m. (July 27, 1957)
Dear Vernon-Joyce-Children
Received Joyce's letter.
I am no better and that is all that I can write,
Love,
Mother

It was August 5, 1957, only a few days before I was to depart for St. Louis. I was writing in the library in Santa Monica, and happened to look up from my work and see Joyce at some distance across the room, walking toward me. She was normally at home with the twins and Torrie. Something had happened, and I had no clue what it might be.

I was puzzled as Joyce approached, concern writ deep in her expression. She went immediately to the point: "Vernon, your mother has committed suicide."

The details, as we came to know them, were not the least bit complicated. Aileen was at work. Grandma had gone out shopping and had returned to find Mother not in the house. Grandma went looking for her, but she was not in the garden. She looked in the garage. Mother had hanged herself from a garage rafter using a chain. Nearby was the kitchen butcher knife my father had made for her, years ago, from drop-forged carbon steel—I still have it and use it regularly in the kitchen. It was thought at first by the investigator that she had considered using the knife on herself, but apparently the knife was there because she considered cutting a length from a nearby piece of rope. Instead, she used a chain. It was so like my mother—a clean job with no mess. Everyone who knew her knew that she would never have used the butcher knife. Even the hanging could never have occurred in the house. No fuss, no mess; a clean job, with no room for error. Here is the newspaper report.

The Wichita Beacon

Tuesday, August 6, 1957
Woman Hangs Self with Chain
Services for Mrs. Belle L. Smith, 61, of 416 S. Gordon, whose body was found hanging from a garage rafter Monday afternoon, will be held at 10 a.m. at the Culbertson Mortuary.

Mrs. Smith was pronounced dead at 2:30 p.m. by Sedgwick Dean L. Bratt County Coroner. Cause of death was listed as strangulation.

The body of Mrs. Smith was discovered by her mother, Mrs. Ella R. Lomax, 79, in a garage at the South Gordon home shared by the two. Mrs. Lomax said she began a search for her daughter following a shopping trip.

Bratt said the dead woman, apparently despondent because of ill health, had used a ladder to tie a length of chain over a rafter. The chain used on a porch swing was then wrapped around her neck.

She surely knew that her mother, and not Aileen, would return first and find her. Billye came over immediately. She was living on West Douglas, not many blocks away. Billye said that after mother's body was removed she went through the house. Mother had systematically turned over, face down, every photograph in the house in which her own image appeared. Only pictures with Mother had been moved. She was, indeed, disgusted with herself. She had used these very words to me, in reference to her deepening depression, just a few days earlier on the telephone as well as in the letter above.

Mother believed that all people have the inner resources to overcome adversity, weakness, anything; that was her heritage, her life experience, and her teaching. It was what sustained her. But in the end she failed herself, and she was disgusted with her failure. No bitching, grousing, or carping about someone else failing her—it was her failure to live up to her own expectations. In life, she had always done what she had to do, and no exception would be made even in her last desperate act.

You could say her timing was perfect, I suppose. I changed my ticket to leave a few days earlier than originally planned. I went to Wichita for those days and for her funeral. Then, I departed for St. Louis, gave my report on the piggyback business for the railroad, and returned to Santa Monica. It was over, over, over, but it seemed strange. At the funeral, I was told by many attending, "Your mother did not know what she was doing."

Well, there was no consolation for me in those words, because I knew otherwise. More than once, years earlier, I had heard mother tell of a distant relative, or family acquaintance, who was diagnosed with cancer and, knowing that he would suffer slow deterioration, committed suicide without warning, but left a note of explanation. She admired his courage, which enabled his family to get past the inevitable quickly and conserve the family's limited resources. Over and over, she had said that she did not want to be a burden on her children—as I see it, a burden in the way my dad's parents and her parents had been a burden on her and on my father.

Mom knew exactly what she was doing. She also had a choice between death and the terror of being institutionalized. Knowing her, I believe it was a deliberate act intended to preserve the one thing she had left: her deep sense of personal control, integrity, and dignity. She was going to take charge and do what had to be done.

When I saw Jack Nicholson in *One Flew Over the Cuckoo's Nest*, I felt my mother's unbearable terror in the scene when he was subdued for the shock treatment and again in the surgical lobotomy scene. And did I ever feel good watching Chief as he prepared to escape and flew victoriously over the nest, free, free at last … thank God almighty, free at last.

That movie brilliantly captures an unpleasant but universal truth about mental illness. Citizens who exhibit social-behavioral abnormalities outside the normal range of socially accepted behavior are confined in mental institutions that interfere or intervene into the doctor–patient relationship. My longtime friend, Deirdre McCloskey (*Crossing*), has written of her decision to have a sex-change operation and of the consequent attempts by her sister to have her committed to a mental institution. This was only yesterday—1995.

The causes are found in laws with a narrow interpretation of the range of behaviors that are considered sane, but the ultimate responsibility rests with people, including medical professionals, who do not understand and cannot relate to deviant behavior. That behavior includes projecting a childlike persona, as well as anger over trivial matters, as I have seen among the homeless. My mother's depression and suicide were surely exacerbated by her uncontrollable and overwhelming fear of shock therapy treatments, a patient response that should be central to the medical decision of whether or not to proceed with such treatment. Lobotomy was the next step after shock therapy, once the patient's opinion no longer mattered. Since a lobotomy greatly increases an institution's ability to manage patients, the benefit to the provider contaminates the objective measurement of the institution's medical effectiveness. A ward full of lobotomies is a community that is relatively more manageable.

A gripping account of the history of lobotomy procedures, as it was applied to ex-soldiers in the Veterans Administration hospitals, has been written by

Michael Phillips for the Wall Street Journal. *The Lobotomy Files*, published in December 11, 2013, is worthy of attention.[1]

During World War II, some 1.2 million troops were sent to military hospitals for psychiatric/neurological conditions, or roughly double the 680,000 hospitalizations for injuries in battle. For about 3 1/2 years, 1947–1950, more than 2000 discharged veterans, each in US Veterans Administration Hospitals across the USA, were administered lobotomy treatments. These men had served in the European, North African, and Pacific theaters and had returned psychologically damaged. (They were diagnosed as psychotic, mostly depressives, or schizophrenics, and a few were alleged to be homosexuals.) Recall that in my 15 months employment at Boeing, I had many co-workers that were discharged veterans. Only one ever spoke of his military experience, and these were occasions for expressing his raging hatred for the "Japs" as he called them. Another co-worker was prone to fits of anger. And one was prone to an occasional epileptic seizure. Otherwise, there was a silent dedication to our bomber-building task.

Sixty years after his committal and lobotomy, at 90 years of age, a stubbornly outspoken veteran and lobotomy patient was interviewed by Phillips. Roman Tritz, considered delusional, remembers when orderlies tried to remove him from his room: *"They got the notion they were going to give me a lobotomy. To hell with them."* He fought so hard that the orderlies, who had pinned him to the floor, were forced to give up. But they returned and the bomber pilot was subdued and lobotomized shortly before his 30th birthday. 60 years later, while relating his experience, Tritz rubbed the two divots left on his forehead: "It isn't so good up here."

I often wonder if it all could have been different, and if she would have lived, if I had not insisted on visiting her on my trip east in August 1957. She had not wanted that, and I had dismissed her wishes, thinking that I could help and not really believing or understanding why she did not want me to see her. This desire on her part is a truth that I have accepted. Her action was her choice, not mine, but I do believe that my decision to come and see her nudged her in the direction she took. It eventually became clear: She was disgusted with herself, and more than anything, she did not want me to see in her what she saw in herself. Never mind that I would not have seen what she saw. And yes, of course, it could have been different and also much, much worse indeed. Imagine what it would have been like if she had signed the papers and gone to the hospital for the remainder of her life, living in fear, self-contempt, loneliness, and no longer in control of her life and thoughts.

---

[1] http://projects.wsj.com/lobotomyfiles/.

The wooden plaque she made in therapy hangs above my bedroom dresser (today, it is on the wall to the right of my bathroom sink): *Give me courage and gaiety and the quiet mind.*

I have been able to locate the text source my mother used for the plaque. Here is the stanza containing the quotation:

Give us grace and strength to forbear and to persevere.
Give us the grace to accept and to forgive offenders.
Forgetful ourselves, help us to bear cheerfully
the forgetfulness of others.
Give us courage and gaiety and the quiet mind.
Spare to us our friends, soften to us our enemies.
—Robert Louis Stevenson, *Prayers for Success*

Mother had astonishing courage and far, far more gaiety than you might think from what I have just written; I saw it radiating from her many times with my father, in her music, in his music, in their music—when they sang their duet, "Indian Love Call," at various public events—and in her love of gardening and tending of plants, animals, and people. In her diary, on March 30, 1944, she wrote, "Vernon worked 15 hours last night [Boeing]. Gosh he is a good boy. 9 months until he is 18. I just look and look at him." And as reported earlier, the following August 16, 1944, she wrote, "Our 23rd wedding (anniversary); thought of it Monday—forgot it today; Vern (Dad) remembered today. A wonderful 23 years. I love him." She had enough of the quiet mind to have yearned for more, or she would not have chosen that text for her plaque. I am just so sorry that she did not have more of that quiet mind. "Oh, God bless you and keep you."

Mom would have a Unitarian service, of course, in a funeral home on the west side of Wichita. None of us had much use for the pomp and ceremony of funerals in those secular-drenched times. There would be an open house on the day of the funeral, with friends, neighbors, and passersby bringing in mounds of food and oceans of drink for the gathered family. It was essentially an Irish wake without the open casket and the Catholic touch. A tremendous support network came out of the woodwork, as had occurred when my father died. Mother and dad had longtime contacts in church and community, and of course we lived in a real neighborhood—people don't so much anymore. People just came in and took over the daily routine of preparing food, washing, cleaning and so on, and of course that meant talking a lot, catching up on other peoples' lives. You talk an awful lot about life when there is a death on your minds. It was the same with John Hughes years later at Purdue. He had friends all over the world. We came together and talked about all the good times. Everybody seems to put on the equivalent of an Irish Wake—read *The Last Hurrah* for a great inside description.

We had to make the arrangements with the funeral parlor. Billye, Aileen, and I decided that the three of us would all go down to the west side funeral parlor and lay it all out with the managers, being certain that it would be exactly the modest affair that mom would have wanted. No one knew that better than the three of us, and together, we would be a unified mutually reinforcing front that was not going to be fragmented and conquered by a sales pitch. It would be, I am happy to say, our finest hour together—two sisters and a brother in defense of our mother.

We went into the parlor and were greeted by a salesman. Right away, we got our feathers ruffled by this guy. He said that one of the many ways that they serve "a family in their time of great grief is to arrange for all the flowers and manage all the contributions for flowers that will be offered by friends and loved ones: flowers at the parlor, flowers in the hearse, flowers at the grave site, and flowers at the reception." As it happened, we were not feeling any great grief in need of flower-bedecked halls at just that moment, but were there to do business. Billye said, "We want *no* flowers; all contributions will go to the First Unitarian Church, and we want this to be advertised." The clown says, "We understand, and are happy to do that, but most families, and others who are friends of the family, still want lots of flowers *for the loved one.*"

Aileen replied, "Well, we don't." That settled, we asked about the funeral itself, its cost, and our choices. He said, "The total cost of the funeral, including *some* flowers at no extra cost, is entirely expressed in the price of the casket." We realized that these guys were determined to sell flowers, whether we wanted them or not, so we didn't make a fuss over a few flowers to be proffered in a package deal, the absence of which might be blamed on the mortuary, not the customer. He said, "The casket choices are on display downstairs, and the price on each casket is the total cost to you of the funeral. There is a huge range of choice. You can pay as little as $90 and up to $10,000. We provide extra limousines and other services with the higher-priced caskets." He escorted us downstairs, jabbering all the way about grief, about the mortuary's task, and "satisfied customers." I resisted the temptation to ask whether they got lots of repeat business from such satisfied customers.

He started us out with the top of the line—a very elaborately tooled copper casket—and a long explanation about the indestructibility and preservation properties of a copper casket. Then, there were more copper jobs, which were less elaborately tooled and had thinner copper. "Definitely lower quality," he assured us. Next in line were two or three aluminum products. I thought, "Uh oh, copper in one grave and aluminum in the next. Wouldn't this produce a thermocouple effect or 'battery action' that would destroy the caskets?" But I said nothing. Then, we were shown two or three wooden ones with various degrees of plush upholstering. *None* of them had a $90 price tag. I said, "Where is the $90 casket," and Billye chimed in, "Yes, we didn't see it." He replied, showing a little surprise, as well as some consternation, at our single-minded dedication to the obvious, "Oh that one is in the back hallway." We went to the back hallway, past the array of display pieces and elaborate waist-high stands, and there it was, just a plain pine box in all of God's glory, covered with cloth, resting on a cheap stand and waiting for our dearly beloved mom.

I think it was Aileen who said something reflecting our common thoughts, "I like it. It's got Mom engraved on it. Let's buy it." Billye and I agreed, and we all stood there looking at the salesman. The crass guy just lost his gooey composure; he was pissed, really pissed. He said, "You know, we make no money at all, none, on a $90 funeral! But if that's all you want..." I resisted the urge to thank him for contributing his profit to our mother's memory. We shelled out ninety bucks cash to the jerk—a tidy sum in 1957—and hightailed it out of there.

So mom was buried in a $90 wood casket (with funeral thrown in), and the three of us were delighted and happy to have conspired to get only what mom could have tolerated, let alone wanted. This was the woman who, faced with a high bill from a physician, threatened him with socialized medicine and then negotiated a reduced bill. If all patients were like mom, there would be no problem for which the alleged solution was socialized medicine!

We had held out against the invasion of the body snatchers. It was our final gift to mom. She was laid to rest in the last available plot in a four-plot family gravesite in the Maple Grove Cemetery, just off Hillside Avenue on the east side of Wichita.

She had finally crossed the tracks to an east-side home—in a hearse.

She was buried next to Grover, because it was the only plot left. That was because Uncle Denny and Aunt Marjorie had a child, Dal Lomax, who was born in 1921 and died the same year. Since no one had applied the principle of backward induction to ascertain the endgame, dad was buried in a third plot in 1954, leaving just the one plot next to Grover. Billye once said that this seemed inappropriate, because it was dad who was the real father to us all, and we all knew how close mom and dad had been.

Yes, inappropriate as the subsequent history unfolded. But who cares, really? We didn't. And mom did not care. What we all knew and felt could never be expressed, stated, or captured by any unpoetic ordering of four burial plots. "She is happy where she lies, with the dust upon her eyes."

As I write sixty-one years later, my hope is that the casket, that $90 wood marvel, has rotted to nothing, and that mom's elements, essence, and love have been recycled back into the "prairy erth," where they are needed to honor that ultimate biblical truth: Dust unto dust, with life continuously and perpetually reformed and reborn from that dust. We are here to make our own luck before returning to that dust from which we came.

To the Hopi, it's "the mud from which they came," symbolized in the mud-head on my silver-on-black watchband—if your culture is rooted where there is little rainfall, as on three mesa villages in northern Arizona, you like your dreams to wet the dust enough to call it mud.

There is a postmortem, however, to the suicide narrative. Billye looked everywhere for a note, in the garage and throughout the house. There was none. Billye had been in close communication with mom on the issue of being committed and in discussions of how mom felt, and she was very surprised that there was no note. She strongly suspected that there *had* been a note, and that Grandma had destroyed it.

Here, as you can see, is the problem with having a reputation like Grandma's: People make assumptions about you that go well beyond the facts; they rationalize beliefs with "facts" that they cut out of whole cloth. It's fair to say that there was not one among us who did not believe that Grandma was capable of destroying the note, but of course that did not make it true, and it may have been a gross injustice to believe that she did.

Throughout the aftermath of the whole affair, Grandma was into sympathy seeking. She got lots of that from her son. Mom's brother, Uncle Denny, flew in from Missouri for a few days and for the funeral, and Grandma was glued to him like a postage stamp. True to her reputation, she helped herself to mother's things, some household items, a couple of fine blankets, and so on, neither telling nor asking the rest of us, giving them to Uncle Denny, as she reverted to the OPM problem. Billye could always call a spade a spade, and as she described it, Grandma stole from our mother in death. That was not entirely accurate, however, and Billye would agree with me. Grandma stole some things from the living who had inherited what mom had left; but the real gift that Mother left for us all was a heritage that could not be stolen: an example of how to live and how to die, whose value was immeasurably greater than any of the trinkets and blankets that her mother expropriated in death.

I never saw Grandma Lomax again, although she lived for many more years, to ninety and some change. True to form, she went to live with Uncle Denny and Aunt Marjorie, who had no use for her. Grandma must have had a field day: The local department store clerks would not have been onto her for a while! Later, there was a big falling out between Grandma and Aunt Marjorie, and Grandma moved to her own place; I did not learn the details, and I did not want to.

And finally, there was Aileen's son, Dennis Ward, whose father was an alcoholic woman abuser who was killed in a head-on collision, along with the woman in his car, somewhere near the Kansas–Colorado border. There was much conflict between Denny and Aileen, and when he was sixteen,

Aileen called to see if we would take him to live with us because she could not handle him. I knew that Aileen also had her own agenda, but refusing for that reason was not going to help Denny. In fact, no one could help him, but I did not know that yet.

We took him in. I do not recall the decision process. Joyce had every right to feel put upon, but she never complained and we decided to give it our best. Denny came by train, and I picked him up at the station. What Aileen had not mentioned to me was that she had told Denny she was sending him to my family because of his "bad behavior." He had not come voluntarily. He must have harbored the idea that I was an instrument of punishment. Essentially, Aileen had made the whole situation more difficult. I resolved to get on with it and ignore a history that could not be changed. Denny enrolled in the local school and made one "friend," and soon, the two of them put together a plan to run away and go to Wichita. Somehow, without train tickets, they got to Chicago on the New York Central, changed to the Santa Fe, and were heading for Wichita. They failed to elude the Santa Fe conductor and were turned over to the sheriff in Chillicothe, Illinois. The sheriff called me. I explained the circumstances, and he said that Denny could not be released, except to my custody.

I drove over to Illinois and signed the papers to spring him from the brig. I never read the documents, which no doubt held me liable for something or other, but it made no difference in terms of the action I was committed to take. When we returned, I repeated what I had told Denny earlier—that we would do our best to make a home for him. If he wanted to go to college, I would pay for it, and that was an opportunity for him that would not be available in Wichita.

After our return, my dear friend, colleague, and rock of support—the ultimate giver—John Hughes, said, "Let me talk to him. When I look at that nephew of yours, it's like looking in the mirror." John had often told me that he was saved—my inference was that it was from drinking, carousing, and whoring!—by the clarinet when he was fifteen. He was good at playing that clarinet. It had brought true self-confidence by proving that he could master something. John was expressing the wisdom of Kansas quarryman McClure Stilley, quoted in *PrairyErth* and the outset of this volume. John could speak to Denny as an insider. He did, and spoke with eloquence to the boy, but the message fell on deaf ears.

Denny said that John told him (in John's characteristic, no nonsense, this-is-how-it-is style) that he had the opportunity of a lifetime, saying, "Do you have any idea at all that your uncle is actually an honest man? You will someday learn there are precious goddamn few such people anywhere in this world." Denny had two comments: that John was sure a cynic, and that what I was offering him was a "good deal." Denny just didn't get any lasting lessons from it all, and that was why it was destined not to work. John told me that he had the urge to reach into Denny's brain, pick up all the scattered cards and sort them into one complete deck. But John could not do that and no one else who tried would be able to do it either.

What became clear was that Denny had no sense of himself in social relationships with others. Sometimes he seemed dangerous, but I was not able to put it all together at the time and understand it. He returned to Aileen, and episodes of mental illness kept surfacing. He was treated, eventually hospitalized, then released, and hospitalized again. I couldn't keep up with the bewildering details. What reliable information I got came from Billye. Aileen was like Grandma—she eventually took over that role and even came to look like her with age—and might tell me almost anything, which Billye would then have to correct. Aileen was bipolar with big-time ups and downs, but the medications were getting better, and she was able to function well enough to avoid the "mental health" hospital, a euphemism for the black hole that can strip patients of all their dignity, that is, life, liberty, and the pursuit of happiness.

Denny was discharged from the hospital, and after a while, he decided to join the Navy. Incredibly, they took him! Since then, I have been made to wonder about the Navy's ability to defend us. It was, however, a benefit to Aileen, who no longer had to pay for his hospitalization and treatment. Denny was in the Navy only a short time, but it was long enough to get socialized (veterans') health benefits. The mental health system was now into the world's deepest pocket: the US Treasury. It was not long, incentives working the way they do, before Denny was permanently committed. Denny was officially diagnosed as schizophrenic, as I recall, although the diagnosis seemed to drift around over time sometimes with a modifier, such as "paranoid." I saw him only once after he returned to Wichita, although he called me collect a few times to check my views on whether China was about to take over the world, or some other idea that would not loosen its grip on his mind. He died in the hospital an old man at about age fifty-seven. He became horribly addicted to nicotine. Billye said his fingers were stained yellow and his body reeked of tobacco. Such a waste, but what could have been done to prevent that waste? (Figs. 9.1, 9.2, 9.3, and 9.4).

Fig. 9.1 Mom in her garden

Fig. 9.2 Thanksgiving GPA Smith, Mom, GMA Smith, GMA Lomax, Aileen Billye, Dad, Carl

Fig. 9.3   Grandpa and grandma Smith on Edwards street

Fig. 9.4   Mom's therapeutic handicraft

10

Above All to Thine Own Self Be True

And it must follow, as night the day,
Thou canst not then be false to any man.
—Shakespeare (*Hamlet*)

There may sometimes be a fine line between what people call *madness* and what they call *genius*, and this theme (M/G) has been mined many times. Long ago, attention to the M/G mix was mentioned in the study of European royalty. Early in the last century, eugenics was perceptively criticized by those who had studied the genealogical reports on royalty and were at a loss to see how anyone could execute any kind of meaningful preselection for breeding. It is a wise man indeed who can separate the sane from the insane, although society maintains the pretense that it has this wisdom. Herein, I can only speculate based on what little is known.

Understanding the M/G nexus is not simply a matter of nature vs. nurture, although on both sides of this ridiculous and politicized argument there are people who want the default state to be the one they favor, unless the other is proved beyond all scientific doubt. If one of two identical twins, whether the twins are reared apart or not, is diagnosed as schizophrenic, the other has a much better than 50% chance of being schizophrenic, but it's still less than 100%. (Bear in mind that each identical twin is a genetic clone of the other.) That is consistent with the hypothesis that schizophrenia is shaped by both inheritance and environmental factors. Certain environmental "insults" in the latter are believed to be part of the picture that provides the interaction between inheritance and the environment. It is nature *and* nurture. Neuroscience is today on the trail of attempting to sort out some of these factors, but it has a long distance to travel.

What we do know is that there is great variation in how brains and minds work, even among closely related kin. I had a bipolar half-sister on lithium and other chemical treatments for the later decades of her life. Billye said that Aileen would often become confused about whether she had taken her medication, and take it twice; that she confused the dosages of different medications; that she was "lithium-ed" out. Denny, my half-nephew, was schizophrenic and once cut his wrists in an incompetent attempt at suicide. Several times in her later years, Billye, looking back, reported that she believed that Grandpa Lomax had suffered from depression as well. I certainly remembered him as withdrawn, aloof, and quiet, but always thought that was a conditioned response to Ella, who seemed to be giving him hell most of the time and wouldn't lay off. Then there was my mother, who became seriously depressed, and suicide was her escape. Furthermore, unlike Denny, when the time came she chose a method that left no room for error.

But Billye and my dad, so far as I know, were never depressed. And if I have ever been down more than a few minutes, I have no memory of it. I recover quickly from "irritation," "anger," "fear," and "traumatic experience," which are words used by others but to which I find it difficult to relate—my brain does not linger and dwell; concern about something is not disruptive, because my brain goes to work on a solution, finding a way out, and that process crowds out what I hear people describe as worry.

This is not something I consciously will or plan. It's my autonomic brain doing its thing, or God doing His thing. I have good cause in all things to feel grateful. I do not feel self-made, nor can I imagine what that means in a world where almost everything we know is due to others.

For example, my mother's death and its surrounding circumstances qualify—by anyone's definition—as traumatic. What was my reaction? I went to Wichita, a stopover on the way to St. Louis, heard the whole story, went to her funeral, and took the plane on to St. Louis. I gave my oral report on the piggyback issue, with my brain totally absorbed in that project and reporting out through my conscious mind what it had learned. Nothing else interfered with that focus on reporting out to the Frisco management—president, vice president of operations, vice president of marketing, and other people, each listening with intense interest because it was important to them. After the funeral, therefore, I returned immediately to life, thereby putting into play the most important lesson my parents had to teach me. I think this was neither callous nor heroic; it was simply my brain doing its thing. In his *Second Treasury*, Kahlil Gibran said, "Do not give up hope or yield to despair because of that which is past, for to bewail the irretrievable is the worst of human frailties," but I am skeptical that you can will yourself to do that. I don't naturally dwell upon and worry about things that I cannot change.

All this variation over three generations seems to go with the brain/mind development territory of the *Homo sapiens* line. Of course, there is huge cross-sectional variation in the particular characteristics that cluster in family lines. This nature/nurture diversity is the stuff of human change across space and time and is how we got out of Africa, sometime in excess of 60,000 years ago, to where we are in this snapshot of time—warts, Internet, computers, biotech, terrorists, nanotechnology, and all.

My references to *brain* and *mind* are deliberate. I will use both terms at various times in this narrative. The brain is of course a bodily organ, and it has been said that the mind is what the brain does for a living (Timothy Goldsmith), but that seems to ignore so much that the brain does unmindfully on its own. In my more restricted use of the term, *mind* will be a metaphor referring to the brain circuitry that operates with deliberate, conscious self-awareness. *Brain* will be the metaphor I use to refer to everything else we think or do. When you are driving your car your mind is not thinking about driving your car, unless you are in driver training. Mind or "attention" resources in the brain are scarce, and our brain has evolved mechanisms for conserving those resources for high-priority tasks. To quote F. A. Hayek, "If we stopped doing everything for which we do not know the reason, or for which we cannot provide a justification ... we would probably soon be dead" (*The Fatal Conceit*, 1988, p. 68).

Yet our brains trick us into believing that "we"—the mind—is in tight executive control of all that we think and do. A natural extension of that mental bias or egocentrism is the belief that all useful social systems, traditions, norms, and institutions must necessarily be the result of someone's or some group's deliberately constructed plan. For example, it was once believed that language had been invented by some great genius in unrecorded history, and the same beliefs can explain money and markets and the great "thou shalt nots." The origins and functional operating characteristics of social systems as forms of emergent order are visible neither to the conscious mind nor to society.

This is the perfect time to talk more about how *my* brain works. As I see it, faint, moderate, or strong shadows of the M/G nexus on one or more of thousands of possible dimensions are found in every normal brain. Brain science is about how *the* brain works, emphasizing, as is proper, what has been learned about the common features across the workings of all brains. But I believe that most of our learning about the brain will come from the study of the breadth of extreme variations in particular mental characteristics, across individuals in the population. It's the breadth of variation, not the average that is significant in humans, and perhaps all primates. I want therefore to say something about how I think *a*, not *the*, brain works.

In particular, I will focus on mental self-perceptions in only a few areas: defective switching, and overcoming it through mental hyper-concentration; sociality; oral presentations; and working offline and reporting out.

Defective Switching. I have always had what my mind has gradually come to recognize—by comparative observation of others—as a brain task-switching problem. When I am thinking, writing, or composing, I pass into another world of experience, a world that is isolated from my surroundings. (In writing this book I have used the wardrobe metaphor to describe the passage because it is a tunnel to the fantasyland of the past, where one relives the present.) I experience many chaotic but loosely connected thoughts. One, then another, rises and there emerges a hint of how they are to come together. I have a strong sense that underneath these conscious thoughts there is an iceberg of activity—trying, testing, and sorting—because of the coherence in what can pop to the top. When something rises, I store it in memory, or better yet write it down, and move to the next natural thought pattern in sequence. I used to drive from Sherborn to Amherst each week, lost in thought as I drove, and sometimes I would stop on the roadside to scribble down some resolved mental output.

If I am interrupted, I lose that state of complexity in which I am trying to identify and sort out some kind of order, test it against common sense, and relate it to what I remember from experience—experiments or other observations that may be relevant. Recovering that state of complexity and inquiry is difficult. In fact, once interrupted I usually have the sense that I never recover that state, but rather, at best, only something like it. My experience may be related to what Temple Grandin reports: "I have terrible working memory.... As a result I have a hard time doing things that involve multitasking, like trying to make change and talk at the same time." (*Animals in Translation.*) Whether simultaneous or in sequence short-term memory may be challenged. Consequently, interruptions tend to leave a residue that takes the form of a gnawing and disturbing sense of irretrievable loss. They impose switching costs out and back into that state of complex understanding, and it can take me ten or twenty minutes or longer of mind/brain wandering to pick up those threads again.

I believe that this mental deficiency, or weakness, has produced a conditioned response: My brain stays on course and refuses to be distracted by the mind's attempt to reprogram and redirect the brain's attention somewhere that it does not want to go. My brain has learned to ignore the mind's attempt to intervene and redirect cognitive effort.

The brain knows things that the mind does not understand, so why bother to retrain the mind? It's better to ignore its inefficacious protestations.

This minute, I am having the time of my life, writing in the Admiral's Club in Chicago with a wonderfully and gloriously welcome three-and-a-half-hour layover before proceeding to Anchorage. I went to the Philly airport early to standby on an earlier flight so that I could have a longer uninterrupted session here at this desk. I won't even divert long enough to check e-mail—a distraction into temporary oblivion.

Sociality. Defective switching creates a corollary social problem that I have always had difficulty managing. In ordinary social interaction, I can usually interact, keep up, and respond meaningfully in a dialogue, although even there it is possible for me to suffer fatigue, and my mind relaxes enough to let the brain take over. But add a third person and I soon get lost, left behind. My mind is still into the last follow-on thought when someone else responds or interjects something, and my scheduling algorithm stutters. I switch slowly and miss hearing or understanding the initial added information. I often can figure it out from context, but sometimes I get it wrong. (That gets harder as you get older, when "the torch has been passed" sounds more like "the porch has been gassed.") Then another thought is expressed, and soon my mind is lost to the complex whole from which my brain is attempting to extract some essence.

With several people interacting, I am likely to miss half of what is going on—afterward someone refers to a statement that was made, and I do not remember or even recognize it. "When did that happen?" "It happened while you were sitting right there between us." I am even surprised that it transpired. My contribution, if any, even if it is said to have depth and significance, is limited to some particular subspace of the entire exchange. While my brain is lagging behind, working on an earlier expression from someone, it is not connected to other aspects of the conversation.

In private mental constructions—modeling, studying, writing—I seek and import new information when I am *ready* for it, and I'm not ready on somebody else's timetable. My brain, on autopilot, controls the pace of idea development and interacts sporadically, *only as needed*, with others, the literature, new observations, and other imported information. My brain is not easily shaken from its track by my mind. In normal social situations, this process of interaction between mental representations and input acquisition becomes chaotic and confusing for me, except when the situation becomes focused on a particular topic of investigation in a common problem-solving context. Then I can keep up and may even set the pace.

Does this mean I have Asperger's Syndrome, believed to be a form of "high-functioning" autism? I am not sure that is a well-formulated question. What exist are infinite variations on the mental theme of being human. Among so-called Aspergians the variation will encompass a particular part of this whole set: It's called individuality, the most human feature of humanity.

Simon Baron-Cohen, who has long studied autism and its variant forms, writes of one of his cases (a professor of mathematics and winner of the Fields Medal, which is comparable to the Nobel Prize, but causes much less worldwide hoopla) in his *The Essential Difference*: Edit_April 10, 2018

> *In the presence of visiting colleagues, he would often just leave them chatting with his wife, and withdraw into a book. He said that he was able to be with one other person, one on one for short periods. If he was in a group, he would get confused and withdraw. He said it had always been this way … As for chatting on the telephone, he admitted that he avoided telephones. I raised an eyebrow. "Why?" I asked.… It was the social part that confused him. What were you supposed to say to the other person? When was it your turn to speak? When were you supposed to hang up? How were you to know how to finish or start a conversation?*

I can relate to the one-to-one versus group conversation problem, but to only some of the specifics of his reaction to telephone use. I have long disliked using the telephone, and I generally avoid using it except for professional conversations. I do not know why, but I do not normally feel comfortable chatting on the phone, and generally do it only for a short time. It's the "loose wheel" feeling I get at cocktails parties filled with people who are "strangers" even if I know them—talking heads talking about things that I do not follow closely. There are exceptions, occasions in which I feel a strong one-on-one connection with the topic and the person, and become completely absorbed in the telephone exchange. I regularly had long, meaningful, deeply thoughtful telephone conversations with John Hughes after we left Purdue. I always gave him a call, at local rates, when waiting between planes in Chicago. It was the same with Candace. The exceptions, like John and Candace, are always cases in which I and the other person have a commonly defined task, discussion, or exchange that we are equally engaged in pursuing. Then my shared attention circuits work at high energy levels. But those connections are unusual for me. I resist calling someone out of the blue, or someone I do not interact with regularly. As with Baron-Cohen's

Fields Medal case, I also am not sure I would know how to start or end the conversation.

Often—some might have said characteristically, but I am trying to tell it the way *I see it*—I have been known to just fade away and go to bed before guests leave. No offense is intended, but I feel exhausted trying to keep up with the overload of input, especially if there are a couple of voluble people in the living room and it's not a conversation likely to rivet my attention.

I am reminded of the joke about the woman who asks, "How can I tell you what I think until I have heard what I say?" That is emphatically *not* the way I come to find out what I am thinking. For me, it's the contrary— conversation can get in the way unless I am ready and eager for it.

Baron-Cohen's book, *The Essential Difference*, 2004 contains four appendixes, each of which includes a test. His book is mostly about male/female differences in the occurrence of autism and Asperger's Syndrome, which will not concern me here. I will say only that it has been known for some time that autism disproportionately affects males, which strongly hints that it has a genetic basis carried predominantly with the inheritance of sex. The tests, and my scores on them, are as follows:

1. "Reading the Mind in the Eyes." If you score more than 30 out of 36 maximum, you are very accurate at reading a person's expression around the eyes. This was a very easy test for me. Moreover, my sense of having gotten almost all of them right was a correct assessment. I scored 30, which suggests that I am good at interpreting facial language, but that may simply tell you what I already know: I should be able to handle one-on-one interactions, but not group social interactions where reading the eyes becomes much more difficult and I depend more on the auditory sense. It is perhaps relevant for me to add that unless I am face-to-face with someone with whom I am conversing, it is harder for me to stay focused on what we might be sharing.

2. "The Empathy Quotient." 0–32 out of 80 is low, and most of those with Asperger's or high-functioning autism score about 20. This battery tests the ability to feel an appropriate emotion in response to another's emotion, and to understand that emotion. I scored an abysmal 8/80! I could not believe it. The questions seemed straightforward to me, and the answers weren't obscure. I not only scored very low, but that fact was not even remotely part of my expectation and self-perception. I went back to reread all the questions, and there was not a one that I would have changed to make it more self-representative. That one stumps me!

3. "The Systemizing Quotient." Average is 20–39 out of 80. I scored 34, well below the Asperger's and high-functioning autism levels. Most men score around 30. Most of the questions, however, do not apply to the things concerning which I have learned to systematize later in life. Systematize here means and includes not being able to pass by something that "needs" attention. I should retake it from the perspective of my younger years.

For example, as a Harvard graduate student, circa 1953–1954, I once could not start my 1941 Cadillac. That weekend I unbolted the engine heads, ground and reseated the valves, installed a tune-up parts kit, and drove it many more years. It's "yes" on questions of having to stop and get things fixed that gets you a high Asperger's score. I no longer have time for such distractions. The opportunity cost is too high, so I use the market. I think, however, that this earlier behavioral characteristic has become more refocused (I keep learning) on my regular work, research, and writing. There are two exceptions: One is gardening. I lived in Arizona for twenty-six years without missing the planting season window for some treasured plant; likewise for twelve years in Indiana. Later, being too much away from Tucson to plant, it weighed on me a little that I have missed out on something so important. I am now relocated in Orange, California, and into planting, but I still return to Tucson often, where I am more dedicated to that task. The second exception is cooking. I still absolutely have to cook from time to time, if not regularly as in the past. I say to myself: "It's your mother, stupid!"

4. "The Autism Spectrum Quotient." Very high, 32–50 out of 50, is where the Asperger's and high-functioning autistics score. I came in at 34.

Most of the research on autism and Asperger's has appeared in the last fifteen or twenty years, so understanding, diagnosis, and evaluation are still very much under development and subject to reinterpretation, and no doubt prone to a great deal of misinterpretation and error.

Here is a thumbnail description of Asperger's Syndrome from a Web site on Asperger's information that is no longer available, but still represents what people say and believe about the phenomena:

The main characteristics of an Aspergian are said to be a deep focus on a specialist subject or area [or consecutive areas], a difficulty in understanding human interactions and human social codes [almost like being an alien trying to understand a strange species] and thus also a difficulty with changing environments which need to be learned and adjusted to…. Aspergians tend to have a normal to high intelligence, often coupled with a special skill or ability [e.g. extraordinary mathematical or linguistic abilities, or animal behavior as with temple Grandin].

The quote is typical of information that can be gleaned from other Asperger sites and from the growing literature on Asperger's Syndrome. I invite the reader to research it further.

I have plenty of deep focus, going back to the farm when I was intensely interested in how everything worked: the protocols for everything from harvesting a chicken to Mr. Hemberger's classroom. I have never seen myself as having a social problem, but in recent years others have differed with me on this, pointing out that my eye contact is poor, especially when meeting new people (and look at my dismal empathy quotient, only 8 out of 80). Others, including family, commonly report that they feel they have to fend for me as social interpreters.

I don't care for most cocktail party talk, and most gossip bores me to tears. What bothers me most is that people are less disciplined in their utterances about people who are not present. I automatically tend to judge people by the distance between their private and public positions; in extreme cases, their stance is a function of who is listening—the popular image of the politician. My trust for a person instinctively varies inversely with that revealed distance. But I too can get suckered into that syndrome, for short periods, and that is why I do not like participating in gossip of this type.

> There is a management style that I do not like and believe to be disastrous. The head, director, or other officer communicates bilaterally with all those relevant to decision making. He/she never goes to a meeting without knowing in advance what the outcome is likely to be. His/her modus operandi is to acquire lots of asymmetric information. Bullshit: Bilateralism begets bilateralism. Everybody is encouraged, even forced, to play the game. The consequence is productivity well below its potential, trust turns into distrust, and the old Italian proverb reigns supreme: "It's good to trust, but better not to." Managers who utilize this style have a hard time surviving, because people don't trust people who don't trust anybody. What made the economics department work at Purdue University was openness.

Compared with many I am no doubt less guarded or socially sensitive to what others might think are inappropriate topics of conversation. I don't find it natural to vary what I say about anything as a function of who might be listening. It is too damned complicated to remember to whom you told what, so just stick with the remembered truth! If I don't trust people whose positions vary with their audience, why should I trust myself in harboring this characteristic, and why should anyone trust me? My discussion above of my family, their interactions, and their expressed or supposed mental problems focuses on issues that I know are not normally discussed, but I find it natural to tell it the way I see it. When it comes to what people consider mental illness, conversations either stop or focus on abstract others, as embarrassment sets in. That is why such conversations are so shallow and utterly meaningless.

The "changing environments" part of the definition of Asperger's does apply to me, interpreted as what I call a "switching" problem in social interactions. But I have no trouble changing cities, places, audiences, and countries to give talks and attend other events in a hectic schedule. Those situations, however, are pretty formal, and I generally operate in them at arm's length.

My IQ, 130 (measured for the first time at age sixty-eight), is said to be high, but there are lots who are higher. I have always heavily discounted IQ, and I believed that mine was not high until I finally went through all the testing in 1995 when I was 68. I was wrong about my own IQ, but I still cannot shake the sense that my capacity to hyper-focus has been far more valuable to me than measured IQ, although the two are probably correlated.

This "mental deficiency" has given me a great advantage. I believe that being slow to achieve focus and having a switching problem led somehow to an adaptation in which I easily and happily developed a capacity for deep concentration that blocks out the external world and helps me to maintain thought continuity. Why do I say that being slow is an advantage? More than anything else, it keeps me from ever getting the idea that I fully understand something and am finished with an inquiry. My mind may think otherwise, but my brain has learned to ignore it—my brain would not give my mind the time of day in deciding when a program is finalized. It's the instincts of the brain that I trust, rather than my rationalizing mind.

All my life I have encountered smartasses who are quick to learn and catch on to something and do not shrink from letting this become known. It's self-deception for them all the way down. One of the greatest human social diseases is the belief that we have conquered some long-standing intellectual puzzle and can enshrine it in a teaching curriculum, or a law, or a textbook, as final truth. Yet it is clear that we live constantly in a world of revisionist scholarship—monetary history, economics of slavery, standards of proof in mathematics (the standards are sociological and keep changing in one-upmanship style), language development and learning, child development theories, love and sex, postmodernism, women's studies—and revisionist history, but such constant reminders fail to cure the social disease.

Postmodernism is the champion: *If one applies its own arguments to it, ipso facto it cannot be taken seriously.* And that, I believe, is because the mind-brain nexus does not consciously experience an evolving understanding, and indirect evidence, although it can adapt over long periods of time. Just think how long it took modern humans and their cultures to accept that the earth is not flat, as the brain experiences it, but round, as the reasoning mind reinterprets the external world in the light of non-local observations. Somehow, the round perception of the earth became integrated into the brain's autonomic mental construction of the world. How does that happen? How does the mind reprogram the brain to accept that the earth is not as it appears—that truth is in the representation, not the direct sensory experience?

That adaptation is very narrowly restricted to individuals' spatial orientation, not to the corresponding time implications. We all—at least I—still have autopilot trouble with time changes when traveling. The brain's folk physics of time is still back in the fifteenth century. My brain does not automatically sense that it is getting earlier, that my watch has to be set back one or more hours, as the jet flies west with the night. It's my mind that reasons that the earth is turning east into the sun and that the airplane is speeding west. From that reasoning, I deduce that the clock must be set to an earlier hour because the sun is now further (lower in the sky) to the east, relative to the plane's position. Worse is the brain-shocker that upon crossing the international dateline there is a discontinuous jump to the day ahead. In one of my many trips to New Zealand or Australia, I would leave Los Angeles on Qantas at 10:30 p.m. Sunday, fly west for some fourteen hours, and arrive in Sydney at 6:00 a.m., with the day breaking behind you, on Tuesday.

"Tuesday?" asks the brain. "I thought you claimed that it was getting earlier in the day." "Of course, stupid," says the mind. "Just imagine two tennis balls, one the sun, the other the earth. The earth rotates forward, clockwise, relative to the sun. It keeps getting earlier in that day, but there has to be an arbitrary north–south line on the earth where each new day begins as the earth rotates into the sun. When you cross it traveling west you are in the new day. When you return from Sydney, flying east, you get that day back (without even having to pay interest). It's easy!" And the brain says, "Easy! Well screw you, smartass."

Oral Presentations. With lots of experience and practice, it may be possible for people to become less self-consciously aware of how they are coming off in public speaking. The mind is hell-bent on preparation for everything, including any oral presentation, by outlining in advance what it should talk about when the time comes. The mind fears that the brain cannot be trusted to organize its knowledge in real time. This is because the mind mistakenly and egoistically thinks the brain works incoherently in fits and starts, and requires executive control by the mind to keep it on track. It would be more accurate, however, to say that the brain develops the order that emerges and then deceptively proceeds to fool the mind into thinking the mind is in control of that emergent order. (See Michael Gazzaniga's 1998 *The Mind's Past* for a fuller development of this important neuroscience finding.) Of course, there is no reason for the mind to understand the brain, much less itself, without the tools of neuroscience—if even then—any more than the mind can understand the quantum mechanical physics of elementary particles, or that the world is round, without the machines and thought processes that leverage the brain's input into a more abstract but coherent interpretation.

At some point, I became able to give talks in which my brain seemed to bypass my mind and do its thing directly with listeners. My mind casually listens to what comes out, but does not pay very close attention. Candace sometimes asks me what I said at some speaking event earlier in the day. First I draw a blank—"Let's see …"—and then something may come to mind, but without the stimulus it will take a while for it to come, and it may not come at all because my memory of it is not consciously accessible. Then, while I am working on a problem, or writing, I will use an idea and immediately recall that I actually developed it (that is, it emerged) in that talk. Somehow, brain to mind to natural language is a monitoring/translation process that entails high transaction costs and interferes with communication with other brains/minds. But one can learn to skip the middleman we call mind and let the brain do the talking. (Steve Pinker calls the brain's language *mentalese*, leading to huge translation problems.)

If you do not know what I am talking about, I think it's for precisely the same reason—although different circuitry is probably involved—that a concert pianist cannot tell you in words how he translates the notes in his brain into the finger execution that produces what you hear. Nor is the skill in the last discussion teachable, any more than you can teach me how to be a concert pianist. But we learn from neuroscience that "brain to mind to natural language" is not actually how it works. This is an instance of the egocentric mind's misinterpreting once again. The sequence is more accurately from brain to natural language, with the mind simply observing the output with a half-second delay. The mind is not even a middleman, although it can wreak havoc trying to intervene, which is why it is feasible for the mind to learn to trust the brain to organize and express itself in real time.

Today, if I give a talk planned ahead by my mind, say as an outline written on paper, my brain tends to intervene and edit, modify, even abandon the mind's work and fit the words into a real-time stream that it (the brain) likes better, and senses to be more appropriate for the audience it is experiencing at the moment. This is why I used to like overhead transparencies, which I had learned to use out of order better than I have learned to use PowerPoint. Think of it this way: The planning mind can operate only on the basis of memories of similar past experiences, then trying to anticipate a speech-delivery event in an imagined future. When that future arrives the brain is there. Nothing about the context and circumstances needs now to be imagined. All the mind has is this stuff it thought up earlier, on the basis of a forecast, and it has no current input unless it returns to the well. The brain can bypass all those stored prepared notes, go directly to the primary input memory sources, and redo it all by directly translating its *mentalese* into natural language.

When a presentation has a narrow time constraint and/or is relatively formal, I am more likely to read from text, but modified by margin notes or in real delivery time. This is because my brain is lousy at external timekeeping, being wont to get lost in its own *mentalese*; so I write it all out in advance and stick to the timetable to keep the chairperson from descending on me with the hook.

Offline Brain Functioning. Everyone, I think, has had the experience of retiring after the mind has been working on a problem, a concern, or a decision. You wake up with a fresh perspective that enables you to return to the thought stream and get to a resolution of the issue. In fact, you may even wake up with a full-blown solution and wonder why you did not see it before. I have that experience regularly, and especially if I return to a topic in my brain's inventory of ongoing projects that I have not been consciously focused on. My mind returns to a topic at midday in my office, after changing flights in the airport, or after finishing a talk. My brain reports out, and it's not in the same state it was in when I left the subject. I have a sense that the brain has been cranking away offline, and it has no intention of distracting me by reporting out what it has been doing with the information that went in, and may not even find it worthwhile to remember for me what went in.

Since the recent increased interest in the study of autism, there have appeared a few books written by authors who have been identified as autistics, Aspergians, etc. My favorite of these is Temple Grandin's *Thinking in Pictures*. It introduces readers to a remarkable window on the workings of a different mind: how she has learned to overcome her incapacity to function intuitively and naturally in social situations; her success as a professional in the designs of perhaps a third to half of the cattle-handling facilities in the USA; how she prepares and gives public addresses using a bullet outline of her main points, each of which triggers a "videotape" in a vast library of such tapes in her brain; her personal views about autism and her experiences with other autistics. I have met her and heard her speak from notes, and I could almost see the tapes being loaded and reloaded—absolutely and totally without eye contact either with the audience or with anybody in one-on-one interaction. It's wise to listen to her and well worth the concentration.

> The wonderful, and for me gripping, documentary movie "Temple Grandin" directed by Mick Jackson appeared in February 2010. Claire Danes plays a perfect Temple Grandin. If you have read her books you might be able to appreciate what an incredible job this work of art does in capturing a sense of what Temple Grandin has gone through in her childhood, as well as her adulthood. I think I have watched this movie six times—twice alone—with English subtitles that help me catch every word, every nuance, every feeling that is in her, but also her mother, her aunt, her associates. I find it exhausting. The tears well up in me over and over throughout the showing, and I really do not understand quite why. I experience the characters, but most particularly the character of Temple Grandin who is desperately trying to understand why others are reacting the way they do; why she is different; why others do not see what is utterly transparent to her; why no one can answer her question "Where do they go?" when her horse dies, and again when her science teacher dies. I could watch it again, now, and would have the same reaction.

There are also many reports of events in the lives of well-known public figures that suggest they may have been high-functioning autistics, but identifying them as such is a hazardous and speculative preoccupation. However, I have such a candidate in Adam Smith:

> *Adam Smith, though perhaps only second to David [Hume] in learning and ingenuity, was far inferior to him in conversational talent. In that of public speaking they were equal [not very good]—David never tried it, and I never heard Adam but once, which was at the first meeting of the* Select Society, *when he opened up the design of the meeting. His voice was harsh and enunciation thick, approaching to stammering. His conversation was not colloquial, but like lecturing, in which I have been told he was not deficient [an immense understatement; Smith was exceptionally popular], especially when he grew warm. He was the most absent man in company that I ever saw, moving his Lips and talking to himself, and smiling, in the midst of large companies. If you awaked him from his reverie, and made*

him attend to the subject of conversation, he immediately began a harangue and never stopped till he told you all he knew about it, with the utmost philosophical ingenuity.[1]

Good show, Adam. I can now see why you were eminently qualified to write *The Theory of Moral Sentiments* (1759), a work that established the foundations of human sociability, and requiring intensity of observation, mutual sympathetic fellow feeling, yet a certain detachment and great depth of thought! (Fig. 10.1).

Fig. 10.1 Temple grandin TED pic—each bullet point loads a mental "videotape" to be read. Wikimedia Commons

---

[1]Alexander Carlyle, *Autobiography*. Boston: Ticknor and Fields, 1860 in public domain.

Part II

The Purdue Years

These were the years in which I see my career identity as being defined. That identity may have been a consequence of my choices in the context of the learning that I was experiencing, but in retrospect, I saw it as a mission impossible without my colleagues. Intellectually, it was a nurturing land of milk and honey: Titles like "The Good Land" and "The People" serve as entranceways to the corridors of that experience, that are still fresh in the heart.

11

The Good Land

And I come down to deliver them
out of the hand of the Egyptians,
and to bring them up out of that land
unto a good land and a large,
unto a land flowing with milk and honey…

—Exodus 3:8

In April of 1955, as I was finishing my Ph.D. dissertation, and Joyce—a bedrock of support—was typing it to conserve our cash, our second daughter, Torrie, was born, beautifully red-haired for life. The twins were soon to have their fourth birthday, and we were looking forward to my first authentic full-time employment as a university professor. In August of that year, we moved to my first professorial teaching research post, at Purdue University, nestled in comfortably familiar Midwestern plains.

Em Weiler was my department head at Purdue. He had interviewed me sometime in early 1955. Actually, this was the second time, as I had been interviewed by him in the prior year. In 1955, he said that he was interested in having me come to Purdue, and that if any other university gave me an offer before he got back in touch with me, he wanted me to be sure to call him before I accepted it. Later, those of us ending up at Purdue would learn from each other that Em left the same message with all of us! This was a strategy for obtaining and using the dispersed information in the new Ph.D. market to confirm his evaluation and implement his decision. Em understood markets and knew how well they reflected information far beyond

© The Author(s) 2018
V. L. Smith, *A Life of Experimental Economics, Volume I*,
https://doi.org/10.1007/978-3-319-98404-9_11

what any one participant could assemble on his own. He was tapping those wellsprings of dispersed private information.

After Em's visit, I would be interviewed across the Charles River by the Harvard Business School and receive an offer of an offer (Harvard does not make an offer until you indicate that you will accept it, and I had no interest in bluffing either then or in subsequent dealings). I was also approached by Hofstra College in that spirit; I received a firm offer from Princeton ($3750 for a family of five—they had to be kidding), and, after a fly-out, one from Carnegie Institute of Technology (later Carnegie Mellon University). I declined all of them except the last one. I called Em and informed him of my offer from Carnegie Tech; he made me a competitive offer on the phone, and I accepted it. Purdue seemed just right—unstructured, full of opportunity, with a department head that I liked. Em offered me $5200 for a nine-month contract; Carnegie offered $6000 for an eleven-month contract with summers devoted to working on a funded project unrelated to my planned research program. I no longer remember what the funded project was, but I recall that I had no interest in it. In retrospect, I think—perhaps incorrectly—that they needed someone to do whatever work they had proposed in order to get the grant. I had not yet learned how the grants economy worked.

The key consideration: I was hungry for an opportunity to follow through on an agenda brimming with excitement for me. At Purdue, I would control my own summertime and receive no additional summer pay, which would enable me to write *Investment and Production*. I already had in mind the manuscript for that book, based on research I had done for my thesis. I had deliberately narrowed the content of my thesis so that Joyce, I, and the children could get out of Cambridge one year after my prelims. Most graduate students at Harvard seem to stay on interminably, and it's hard to see the value added.

I had a single-minded commitment to finish that book. The next test of my resolve was in late 1959 or early 1960. John F. Kennedy had been elected president and was putting together his administration. My Harvard classmate, Otto Eckstein, called to invite me to Washington to be on the staff of the Council of Economic Advisers. It was tempting. Jack Kennedy was a very charismatic and popular figure, whom I liked. That promise was not idle; his tax cut was destined to fuel a 1960s growth spurt. But I told Otto it was essential that I not be diverted from finishing my manuscript, which was then nearing completion. Also, I said that I was not a macro person, but he said that was a good reason for them to recruit me. I suggested that he try me in another year. He did, but I still did not go. The fact is that I had my own agenda, and following somebody else's was not my cup of tea. As I think about it, that had never been my cup of tea. You cannot believe the number of people who thought I was crazy, passing up such an "incredible opportunity," but I felt that it would have deflected me from the opportunities that I was already pursuing, and I had plenty of support for that agenda from my close Purdue colleagues. If I am ever reborn, I hope to be a madman yet again. One of those opportunities was experimental economics. In 1960, I was working on my first publication in a field that did not yet exist, but unaccountably, unexpectedly, would come to exist.

At Purdue, I would gradually come to learn that, circa 1955, I could not have gone anywhere in the world and found better colleagues or a more nurturing and supporting environment. I felt that this had been the right decision although I had no idea yet how incredibly right it would turn out to be. I wrote John Ise at the University of Kansas and told him of my decision. In his answer, on June 10, 1955, he wrote, "Purdue should be a good place for you. Like you, I wouldn't be too enthusiastic about a job at the Harvard Business School, or indeed in any school in Massachusetts. The general environment there always depressed me a bit."

We moved to West Lafayette, pronounced *Law-fayette* at the University, *Laaa-fayette* by the townies, and *Lay-fayette* in the countryside. The conductor on the New York Central called out all three versions as the train approached the Lafayette station: "Next stop, for *Lay-fayette, Laaa-fayette, Law-fayette.*"

In our first year at Purdue, we lived in temporary housing that the University had created—a cluster of small two-story houses, called the "black and whites" that were very plain, and cheap enough to enable the five of us to better accumulate the upfront payment to buy a home sometime in the future. Purdue, West Lafayette, and Indiana had the feeling of "home." I knew that my mother's family had come from Paoli in Orange County Indiana. At Purdue, I would have some of that history brought home to me rather by accident. I was home, and the radio was tuned into WBAA, a local Purdue station that often played classical music. As it happened, the station was broadcasting a regular weekly program, entitled "Know Your Indiana" that recorded radio skits based on Indiana historical narratives. The theme song was, naturally, Paul Dresser's "On the Banks of the Wabash, Far Away." This week's program was about an early settler, named Abel Lomax. That caught my attention at once as I knew that Lomax was not a common name, and here it was being mentioned in Indiana history.

Afterward, I wrote to my mother on February 19, 1956.

Since I last wrote we accidentally tuned in one evening to a program called "Know Your Indiana" and learned the story of an early Indiana settler by the name of Lomax. I jotted down the facts to see if any of them were familiar to you and Grandma.

It seems that Abel Lomax married Elizabeth Ladd in South [sic, North]
Carolina, where they and their families lived at that time (around 1815). They
were Quakers and were opposed to slavery. Their opposition to slavery caused
them to move to the "free state" of Indiana. They settled in Wayne County,
Indiana. Eventually they saved enough money [by setting aside "wage" earn-
ings of the slave] to buy the freedom of their two former slaves "Jake" and
"Delsy" who joined them in Indiana. The Lomax's had several children, one a
daughter Sarah Lomax. Abel served in the Indiana legislature, 1823–1832. I pre-
sume that they farmed in Wayne County.
    The story was interesting and we thought since Lomax is none too common
there may be some relation. Could Abel be a grandfather or great uncle of
Grandpa Lomax?
    Let us know what you think?

From my mother's response and other sources, I have determined how I am
related to the Abel Lomax who moved to Wayne County, Indiana. My mother's grandfather was also named Abel Lomax (1840–1879) and married Tanner
White. He was a southern sympathizer, and she was northern, which caused
much pain and dissension in the family. Abel's father's name was Quintin
(1806–1861), whose father was one Jonathan Lomax (1779–1846) whose
brother was the Abel Lomax (1782–1857) who moved to Wayne County in 1816
amidst a great migration of Quakers from North Carolina. Earlham College,
one of the most famous Quaker colleges, is in the city of Richmond, in Wayne
County. Straight North of West Lafayette (58 miles) is a town called Lomax in
Stark County, Indiana. So there were several Lomax settlers scattered around in
Indiana.

I have recently discovered a digitalized and searchable registry of all land
grants in the State of North Carolina from 1663 to 1960:

Access at http://www.nclandgrants.com/home.htm.

Abel Lomax received a grant of 109 acres in 1809 and in 1816. There were
several other grants to members of the Lomax family during that period. Abel's
father was William Pemlott Lomax (02/14/1745—07/02/1813).

There are also digital records of all Federal land grants from sometime in
1776 for military service from the Revolutionary War through the railroad and
Homestead Act grants. I searched the records from the Revolutionary War
Bounty Land Grants at:

https://search.ancestry.com/search/db.aspx?dbid=49315.

They show that William was a private in the revolutionary war and in
1784 was awarded 274 acres in North Carolina for his service. My first
Lomax ancestor born in this country helped to gain our glorious independence; as a consequence, and even more important, that helped to turn the
tide of privilege in Mother England to freedom. That freedom swept west
eventually gaining strength over much of the globe. Of course, pockets of
totalitarian privilege remain: North Vietnam and Venezuela—unable to feed
themselves—Cuba and portions of Africa. But China has liberalized its foreign
trade to its great economic betterment, with strong forces supporting more
domestic economic freedom—ultimately their people will demand more
political choice.

In the autumn semester of 1955, I taught Principles of Economics and found it a challenge to convey the basic microeconomic theory of markets to students. I could bend the curves, as Ed Ames used to say, and manipulate the equations as well as anyone, but how does any market actually approximate a competitive equilibrium, if it ever could or does? What was the connection between the economist's theory of supply and demand and what real people did on the ground in markets? I and nobody else, and none of the pretty books, could answer these questions. Some students, finding no answers to these questions, leave or never enter economics; those of us who stay perhaps forget that we ever wondered—theirs not to reason why, theirs only to do and lie. Not having any answers bugged me in teaching what I had been taught.

One night I was unable to sleep; the topic was on my mind. I went through a thought process after which I resolved that on the first day of class the following semester I would try running a market experiment. The experiment would give the students an opportunity to experience an actual market, and me the opportunity to observe one in which I knew the alleged driving conditions of supply and demand, but they did not.

Let me backtrack to 1952, I was 25 years old, and my fall classes were beginning at Harvard. The tradition at Harvard for anyone who had already received any graduate instruction was to attend the first meeting of all the first-year course offerings and decide which ones would be taken for credit, which ones audited, and which ones bypassed for second-year courses. Since I had already taken Dick Howey's course in Imperfect Competition, I thought I would probably not need to take Chamberlin's course, but I attended the first meeting to get a better idea of whether I was correct in this estimation. At Harvard your main task was to pass the prelim examinations, and to do that, courses were not required, although they were relevant to achieving the economic maturity necessary to deal with the questions you would have to answer. For example, I had impressive classmates such as Otto Eckstein, who had come from Princeton, where he had been such a superior student that he had taken many of the graduate courses before getting his B.A. At Harvard, Otto essentially bypassed the entire set of standard first-year courses.

Many generations of Harvard graduate students had been exposed to E. H. Chamberlin's beginning graduate course in Monopolistic Competition. On the first day, he would set the stage for the semester using a classroom demonstration experiment intended to demonstrate that competitive price theory was an unrealistic and unworkable idealization of the real world. In his classroom experiment, he gave half the class buyer reservation values, and the other half seller reservation costs. The value/cost environment was like Bohm-Bawerk's *Capital and Interest* (1884/1959) representation of supply and demand in a horse market with multiple buyers and sellers in two-sided competition—perhaps Chamberlin's source of inspiration. I highly recommend that you read only five pages, 217–222, in Bohm-Bawerk's book, and challenge you to find its five-page equal, as a market description, anywhere in economics. I knew of Bohm-Bawerk's work because of Dick Howey's course, but I read little of it, and it had no influence on me at the time. I did not associate its very close parallel with Chamberlin's experimental supply-and-demand protocol until decades later. Chamberlin, unlike Bohm-Bawerk's description, had the buyers and sellers circulate, form pairs, and bargain over a bilateral trade; if the pair succeeded in reaching an agreement, Chamberlin would post the price on the blackboard; if unsuccessful, each would seek a new trading partner. This continued until the market was closed. The prices in sequence were volatile and failed to support the equilibrium prediction.

Chamberlin used this first-day exercise—showing that competition did not work—to pave the way for teaching his theory of monopolistic competition, which was devised to replace the "failed" standard model of competition. It would be several years before I would fully appreciate the obvious: Chamberlin's strategy, showing that Theory A (supply and demand) did not work, said nothing about whether Theory B (monopoly or monopolistic competition) would work. Thus, when I did monopoly experiments, using the incomplete information condition as above, I found little support for the monopoly price and output prediction. As is said of any field, economics is "storytelling." It is unconscionable, though, that some of the stories should be so patently false, or at least not shown to be credible.

Wide awake in the night, I decided that I would use a variation on the generic value/cost setup used by Chamberlin, but change the institution. (This story was actually published: Ted Bergstrom. "Vernon Smith's Insomnia and the Dawn of Economics as Experimental Science" *Scandinavian Journal of Economics* 105.2 (2003): 181–205.) I also decided to repeat the experiment for several trading periods to allow the traders to obtain experience and to adapt over time, as in Marshall's conception of the dynamics of competition—that is, equilibrium was envisioned by Marshall as a state that would be approached only if the conditions defining it remained stationary long enough for the equilibrium to be established. But Chamberlin had run only one trading period. Without repeat trading, there was no opportunity for Marshallian adjustment over time. No one understood the dynamic institutional diffusion process which determined how long was "long enough" or how that process worked, but experiments might make it possible to learn. For the trading institution, I reasoned that if you were going to show that the competitive model did not work, then you should choose a more competitive trading procedure, so that when the competitive model failed to predict the outcomes, you would have a stronger case than had been made by Chamberlin. I did not doubt that Chamberlin's hypothesis would be confirmed, but his approach seemed too blatantly committed to verification of what he believed.

I figured that if there were competitive markets anywhere, the stock and commodity markets in New York and Chicago would qualify. I needed to find out how they traded in these markets. I went to the Purdue Library and found a great textbook by George Leffler, *The Stock Market* (1951; the second edition, 1957, is the one enshrined on my shelf today), giving details on the bid/ask "double auction" used in the stock and commodity exchanges.

For years I thought incorrectly that I had learned the term "double auction" (for the two-sided bid-ask stock market auction process) from Leffler's book, but, searching through it, apparently he nowhere makes use of that term. I seem to have first used the term in 1976, in a paper "Bidding and Auctioning Institutions: Experimental Results," in a book *Bidding and Auctioning for procurement and Allocation*, edited by Y. Amihud (New York: New York University Press, 1976). Perhaps this marks the point in time when I was becoming attuned to the significance for market behavior of different trading procedures and began needing names to identify and distinguish them.

Leffler's book was published well before the two revolutions in finance: the first proving that, rationally, the value of a firm was independent of the mix of debt and equity financing, except that if you believed this theorem, all financing should be from debt, since debt payments are tax free; the second revolution showing that all information relevant to share value was quickly incorporated into the price of the stock, and therefore all the information relevant to determining a stock's value was already in the price, unless you had an inside track on undisclosed information (which disclosure you knew would affect prices negatively or positively).

Because Leffler's book was in a much older tradition it heavily emphasized the operational details of trading in securities. That made it just right for my purposes. It turned out that widespread professional disenchantment with these first two "revolutions" would threaten to return finance to square one.

Financial economists in particular—at least in some quarters—would encounter new skepticism as a consequence of the Great Recession.

In January 1956 I carried out my nocturnal plan, but to my amazement the experimental market converged quickly, at least relative to my expectations, to near the predicted equilibrium price and exchange volume, although there were "only" twenty-two buyers and sellers, none of whom had any information on supply or demand except their own private cost or value. I thought something must be wrong with the experiment, perhaps that it was an accident of symmetry in the buyer and seller surpluses. I shot that idea down with an experiment at the beginning of class the following fall, using a design in which the seller surplus was much greater than that of the buyers.

Had I somehow stumbled upon an engine for testing ideas inside and outside the prescriptions of traditional economic theory?

More recently, John List at Maryland has replicated the Chamberlin experiments and found them to converge over time to efficient outcomes, and Erik Tallroth ("Institutional Choice in Experimental Markets," 2003, PhD dissertation, George Mason University) has compared double auction (DA) with bilateral exchange (BE), where people choose each other blind with no feedback of information except on their own sequential contracts. Erik finds that both institutions are efficient in yielding competitive outcomes in a randomly shifting supply-and-demand environment, although price volatility is much lower with the DA. After nearly a half century, we continue to learn from variations on these elementary early experiments.

Over the years 1956 through 1960, I created many variations on this original experiment by altering the supply-and-demand environment, examining shifts in the demand or supply, varying the double auction trading rules, and introducing cash rewards for the participants. The latter introduction accelerated convergence on the predetermined equilibrium in supply-and-demand designs where the buyer and seller profits from trade were very asymmetrical. I gradually became persuaded that the subjects, without intending to, had revealed to me a basic truth about markets—a law of nature—that was completely foreign to the standard literature of economics. I reported my early experiments—crude as they were compared with what I would later learn to do—in a paper, accepted for publication in *The Journal of Political Economy* in 1962. That publication process involved an initial rejection, four negative referee reports, and two revisions. (See my *Papers in Experimental Economics, Cambridge University Press,* 1991, pp. 157–158, for a discussion of that experience.)

At this juncture "experimental economics" was a personal research program of mine that was gradually becoming a way of life. I would have no idea then or for many more years that a field within economics was in the making. After that nocturnal experience in 1955, it would be sixty years before a definitive history and evaluation of the development of experimental economics is written from the perspective of a scholar on the "outside" looking in, Andrej Svorencik. Andrej is a historian of ideas and of economic thought whose dissertation, compeleted in early 2015, *The Experimental Turn: A History of Experimental Economics*, documents the emergence of the field and his accounting for its rise then and not earlier.

During these years, most of my research and teaching dealt with capital and investment theory and corresponding dynamic pricing problems (*Investment and Production*, Harvard University Press, 1961). In 1961 and 1962, I was a visiting associate professor at Stanford, and at the beginning of the autumn quarter I had the truly significant experience of meeting Sidney Siegel and discovering that we had both been doing "experimental economics." Unknown to both of us at the time, Reinhard Selten had also been pioneering economics experiments in Germany. Sid was a truly powerful experimental intellect who strongly influenced me in becoming committed to experimental economics, but he died unexpectedly at age forty-five, on November 29, 1961, probably within three months of our meeting. Eventually, I read all of his publications, including his classic, *Nonparametric Statistics*, and his two books co-authored with Lawrence Fouraker. Sid was far more than a master experimentalist; he also used theory and statistics with great skill in the design and analysis of experiments. I am persuaded that if Sid had lived he would not only have been the deserving Nobel Laureate, well out in front of the rest of us, but also the timetable for the recognition of experimental economics would have been expedited, perhaps by many years. It is important to be long-lived if you are to obtain such recognition.

I met Sid Siegel in the autumn of 1961 at a dinner party at Marc Nerlove's house. Marc had a number of guests at his house in celebration of several visitors at Stanford and the Center for Advanced Study in the Behavioral Sciences. Sid was there with his wife, Alberta Siegel, who was connected with the medical school while Sid was at the Center. Jack Hirshleifer was also a visitor at the Center and was in attendance with his wife, Phyllis. Many were there from the Economics Department. I recall that in the course of discussion Sid and I discovered that we were both doing "experimental economics," although I have no memory of whether we used that term. In fact, I do not recall when the term was first used, although we did use that designation to describe the first Ford Foundation Faculty Workshop at Carnegie Tech in the summer of 1964.

We were both very excited to learn that we were each doing experiments in economics. Somehow, at Marc's event, Sid got into talking about his origins and childhood—growing up poor on the streets of New York. His family—father, mother, and one brother—lived in a two-bedroom apartment somewhere in New York City. Because his brother "was a genius who played the violin," he needed to have every advantage, the best that the family could provide. So his brother slept in the second bedroom, and Sid was relegated to sleeping on the living room couch. He recounted that he was essentially loose on the streets of New York, got into trouble with the police, and served some time in jail (this I may have learned later). He failed to finish high school (until years later), hung out in pool halls, and supported himself as a pool shark.

A pool shark drifts around from one pool hall to another and plays with newcomers, but always underperforms. He comes off as a fairly skilled but not spectacular player, prone to reckless betting beyond his ability to deliver. When a new player challenges him to games, he wins some, loses more, and plays well enough to be a challenge, but not a threat. Pool sharks play for dollars. Sid used to get behind, up the stakes, feigning a need to win back his losses; he would get ahead, lose erratically, and soon the unwary victim would be suckered into some very large bets and then would be slaughtered, with Sid demonstrating cue skill surpassing anything he had shown up to that point.

Sid was later inducted into the Army, which "saved him" as he described it from a wasted existence. He signed up for the U.S. Army Signal Corps, learned the principles of electricity, communication, and its associated physics. (See his wife, Alberta's memoir on Sid in *Decision and* Choice, McGraw-Hill, 1964). His mastery of the material enabled him to teach in the Signal Core program. This had qualified him for a temporary special California teaching credential. After his discharge from the Army, he began teaching in a San Jose secondary school. But his credential expired and the school principal suggested that he enroll in some college courses, thereby justifying continuance of his teaching credential. Sid noted that this plan had a slight problem: He had never graduated from high school! They found a way around this bureaucratic hurdle that enabled him to get a high school degree by examination. Sid finished his B. A. at San Jose State College in 1951, when he was thirty-five, and completed his PhD at Stanford three years later. His book *Nonparametric Statistics,* a classic still in print, was published in 1956; Sid died five very productive years later on November 29, 1961. What a short, volatile, and distinguished career.

Many years later I attended a small Psychology and Economics conference at Caltech. It was attended by the distinguished cognitive psychologists Danny Kahneman and Amos Tversky. In the context of one of the discussions, wherein the rigor of some experimental study came up, it was natural for me to blurt out, "Whatever became of the tradition of Sidney Siegel in psychology?" In reply, Amos Tversky quipped, "You're it!" This was intended as a put-down, a *touché*. Siegel was seen by the emerging cognitive psychology school as part of the Skinner animal behaviorist tradition in psychology, a tradition that approached decision behavior as an objectivist "black box" study of the choices made by animals and people under various controlled experimental conditions. It eschewed the idea of studying decision-making in humans as part of cognitive processes, and using introspection, surveys, and subject oral and written reports, which are then interpreted by the scientist in terms of models of cognition. Skinner had rejected this methodology as unreliably subjectivist.

Cognitive psychologists, in turn, rejected Skinner's behaviorism as devoid of all attempts to understand mental thought processes. This is typical academic maneuvering: They are both right (and both wrong). Obviously, you use all the instruments at your disposal, recognizing the hazards of subjectivism and the dead-end extreme of the behaviorist's unwillingness to delve into that "black box" called the brain.

For me, the quip by Amos was a compliment in the extreme. I am happy, indeed honored, to be thought by someone as "it" in the Siegel tradition, and also to embrace the learning from cognitive psychology while still recognizing its subjectivist hazards and its many weaknesses in depending heavily on people's conscious cognition. The self-aware mind has little appreciation of the brain's ability to function effectively outside our control. We now have brain-imaging technologies and neuroscience, which is in the process of burying traditional psychology—while reinterpreting and building upon, the earlier traditions of psychology. The neuroscientist Mike Gazzaniga says that psychology, as we have known it, is dead. He is right, but I think much of the earlier learning will survive in a transformed, deeper understanding. I think that is happening even as I write.

Something entirely new and challenging happened before my leave of absence at Stanford. My experiments had aroused my interest in applications to stock and commodity trading, and the possibilities for shareholders trading via computer. Recall that it was the Leffler book that had helped to fuel my interest in the mechanics of stock trading. My idea was that it was feasible for shareholders, say, on the New York Stock Exchange, to trade by submitting bids to buy and offers to sell to a computer in a periodic "call" market for the shares of a listed company. The bids would be ordered from highest to lowest price, the asking prices from lowest to highest price, and the market cleared of those bids that were above and those that were below the uniform price at which the bid array crossed the offer array. As I envisioned the procedure, the bid/ask list would look just like the specialist's book of limit orders shown in Leffler's text except that the supply-and-demand arrays could overlap. Also, you could shift the two schedules to the right by adding in buy and sell orders "at market" that did not specify a limit price. It did not occur to me that you might have an ongoing electronic double auction in continuous "real" time (that prospect would come in 1975–1976, at Arizona, with our development of e-commerce in the lab and the new "real time" computer network technology), because in those days our thinking about computers was very much influenced by batch-processing procedures. You loaded data on cards or tapes, fed it into the computer, and waited until it chugged through the data analysis. In my conception, the computer would do the sorting of the bids and asks, and then chug out the price and the list of buys and sells that traded at that price.

Sometime before the fall of 1960, I had occasion to visit the Chicago Board of Trade, where I met some traders. At lunch, I mentioned the idea to one of them, and I quickly learned that the trader and the CBOT were thoroughly allergic to any notion of using computers in commodity trading. The guy really put down any such utility for computers in his business. I did not get his message, nor did I guess that they would not be prepared for that message for another fifteen years. (The Toronto Stock Exchange would become the first to introduce computer trading in 1976. The TSE system, however, would be strictly limited to the list of thinly traded stocks. There was no way that the TSE members were going to relinquish to some computer, their control over the lucrative, heavily traded, stocks that enabled them to collect big execution fees.) Looking back from the perspective of much later experience, I realized that I was probably lucky to get out of the CBOT without being tarred and feathered!

I related the idea to Em Weiler one day, and he said it sounded like the kind of idea that would interest the Sperry Rand Corporation. This was the same Sperry Corporation that had built the fire-control system on the B-29, but it had merged with Rand. Then he explained to me that Purdue had an exchange agreement with Sperry Rand, which had given a supercomputer of the day to Purdue. I knew about the computer because Ed Ames was learning to program it—a tough task, as in those days you had to program directly in machine language. There were no higher-level operating programs like those that came online later and are everywhere today. New forms of specialization, and the markets necessary to support them, have occurred in wave after wave of innovation in that industry. The Sperry Rand computer was in a large air-conditioned room and was used only by the few specialists on campus who were proficient in machine language.

The exchange agreement, as Em related it, was such that Purdue faculty could bring ideas to the Sperry Rand table for discussion. Sperry Rand was one of the few companies that had extensive experience with real-time computer systems because it was, for decades, a major contractor for the military. Em thought, and I agreed, that what I was talking about was technologically a natural fit for them. Working from the computer business end, rather than the exchange end with which I had failed to get off the ground, seemed like a better way to go.

I had more education ahead of me, and so did Em Weiler!

Em wrote Dause Bibby, President of the Remington Rand Division in the Sperry Rand Corporation, in September 19, 1960. Bibby and Weiler had had lunch shortly before. Weiler wrote:

> On this occasion I am writing to you in connection with another project. One of my staff members, Professor Vernon Smith, has been engaged in an economic study of the competitive trading process in organized markets such as the stock and commodity exchanges. As a result of these studies he has developed an idea for a computer program that would fully automate the trading process in any organized market. The program requires further study, exploration, and testing, but he believes it to be entirely feasible. The system might be potentially very profitable to a computer company because of the savings in manpower and clerical procedures that would be possible in the commodity and stock exchanges.
>
> The next stage of his work on such a program is to secure the cooperation of a computer company and the officials of an organized exchange market for the purpose of writing and testing a program for that market. If you think your Univac Division would be interested in this program, possibly you could have the appropriate person meet with me or Professor Smith to explore the idea and see if a cooperative arrangement can be made.

The upshot was a meeting in New York with executive and board-level personnel. We flew into New York on October 27, 1960, and met with them the following morning. I had put together a presentation showing in great detail how the mechanism would work. I put up a limit order cross on the blackboard and then shifted them over to accommodate orders "at market." I also gave some examples of contingent orders—for example, a "stop-loss" order that is converted to a "market" order to sell, contingent on a trade occurring at a stated higher price.

There were questions, and a discussion ensued. One of the executives invited to the meeting was a former NYSE trader. His view was that it was infeasible to get the NYSE to change; it was simply not practical. Also, we were told that the basic position of the company's management was that there were so many uses of computers out there in the world that Sperry Rand was well advised to wait until people in a particular industry came to them with a problem they wanted to solve, and then the company would work on it. I was learning. We packed up and flew back to West Lafayette. On November 14, Em received an official follow up letter from H.R. Hungerford, Manager Advertising and Training, Remington Rand Univac, noting that "…strong traditions in markets like the stock and commodity exchanges indicate a reluctance to delegate to a data processing system some of the routine functions now being carried out by market specialists."

I thought of this meeting years later as IBM grew rapidly to dominate the computer business and Sperry Rand declined. But regarding the question at hand, I have no doubt that Sperry Rand's reading of the securities industry was dead right. IBM did not leap ahead by selling computers to the stock exchanges that would be used for trading.

The growth of my research interests in experiment, together with a modest literature by myself, others by Siegel, Fouraker and Siegel, and by Ward Edwards in choice under uncertainty, by Anatol Rapoport in prisoners' dilemma games, and miscellaneous others in social psychology who were studying behavior in experimental matrix games, led me to initiate a graduate seminar in experimental economics at Purdue in 1963. The lecture format was not appropriate for the graduate seminar. More appropriate were presentations and discussions of existing papers and projects that students and faculty participants were interested in executing. That got me started: I continued to teach the seminar until my departure in 1967.

In that first seminar, I had thirteen students, including Don Rice, Hugo Sonnenschein, Norm Weldon, and Tom Muench, whose careers I have followed. I published new papers in experimental economics in 1964 (on Bayesian interpretations of experimental methods with Don Rice), another in 1964 (comparing two variations on double auction rules), in 1965 (effect of incentive rewards on convergence; tests of the "Walrasian hypothesis"), and 1967 (uniform vs. discriminative pricing in Treasury Bill auctions). In the seminar, from 1963 to 1965, I developed and taught what I called the "theory of induced valuation" and its extension to multiple-unit purchases or sales by an individual participant. Induced valuation was simply a technique that enabled the experimenter to use monetary rewards to control the economic environment (incentives) and motivate choice in the laboratory study of markets and in all other group-decision and management problems. The problem was explaining and defending why I was doing experimental economics, what it was, and why it was that economics had drawn me to an interest in articulating its methodological foundations. The idea of "induced valuation" was the beginning of that methodological effort.

A key component was this idea of inducing value (cost) onto abstract goods in the laboratory. If (x, y, z) are quantities of three goods (private or public), and we pay subjects $M(x, y, z)$ dollars cash for their end-of-period holdings (x, y, z), the level (constant total payout) curves of the function M are also the indifference curves of the standard postulated preference theory, provided only that the utility of money is strictly increasing in M. M does not have to be money; anything of value to each person will do, like extra-credit grade points. Hence, if we assume that U(M) is the monotone increasing utility function of money rewards, then U[M(x, y, z)] is the utility value induced on the vector (x, y, z). That was the geometry that linked experimental methods to economics and to the standard theory of choice. The same considerations applied to production and cost functions on the supply side of exchange.

Several working papers by students and faculty were also spawned by this workshop effort. In 1964 and again in 1965, under the enabling and supporting influence of Dick Cyert, Jim March (and probably Herb Simon in the background), Lester Lave (an early contributor to experimental games) and I conducted Ford Foundation faculty summer research workshops at Carnegie Mellon. Since I had several experimental papers in the pipeline and a seminar going, experimental economics was becoming much more than a hobby for me. It had a good solid start by the end of the 1960s and took off in the 1970s when Charlie Plott, along with other people at Caltech, and I, with the people at Arizona started to move in step, though following different routes. Thus, at Arizona in 1975–1976, experiments became computer based. By the 1980s, the whole field was on a significant growth path based on a developing body of techniques for running experiments. The methodology consisted of several key features that distinguished experimental economics from experimental psychology: (1) incentive payments to subjects for profits earned as a consequence of their decisions; (2) no deception—we wanted subjects to believe and act on whatever the experimenter specified in the instructions; and (3) the use of written instructions.

The Purdue program in economics was built upon a simple homegrown principle: You keep good faculty by providing them with opportunities for self-fulfilling accomplishment. As they build their careers, this success rubs off on the department and the University, whose reputations are derived from those of the faculty. You build university reputations the way you develop economies—from the bottom up. For those he wanted to keep, Em somehow raised the money to keep pay increases ahead of the competition. When the Harvard Business School approached me again after a few years at Purdue, its representatives complained about the salary structure that Em had created. He constantly importuned us to keep him informed on outside expressions of interest in hiring those of us on his faculty, as well as the offers (and offers of offers) that we got, whether or not we were interested in them, and what our scholarship needs for staying at Purdue were.

All this information was passed on by Em to President Fred Hovde. When Em swung his bat, he was always ahead of the curve. He was a legend, and people everywhere wondered how in the hell anyone could build a distinguished economics faculty in the cornfields of northern Indiana. But we built bloody tall mansions in those corn fields. Purdue produced people with newly created knowledge, and it grew them right there between the cornrows.

In 1959 or 1960, I was invited to give a seminar at Chicago. In your first seminar presentation at Chicago, you learn first-hand what it must have been like to be a Christian in a Roman lions' den. Apparently, I passed muster, since I received an offer. George Stigler was very supportive, but somehow he had gotten the idea that the way to recruit me was to fill me in on some bruising facts. He let me know in no uncertain terms that while Purdue had done wonders, it could not last. It was not possible in the long run to build a prominent economics department outside a major metropolitan area. I should leave Purdue and come to Chicago. I knew in my bones that he was probably right, but I resented being told that in 1960, and it just pissed me off. I was not going to be part of any exodus that fulfilled George's imperious forecasts at that time. I went back to Purdue and conveyed notice of the offer to Em, but I turned it down. We kept Purdue all together in one magnificent piece from 1955 to 1967. We left an enduring legacy, and, more important, helped to change a lot of things that badly needed changing in this sorry ass world, so I make no apologies for any of us. Purdue gave me an honorary Ph.D. in 1989 and then renamed its lab for me in 2003. For me, there could be no greater academic honors—the first before the Nobel award, the other after.

During the period 1956–1957, a group of us at Purdue had a research contract with the Saint Louis and San Francisco Railroad (SLSF, but long known to me, coming from a railroad family, as the "Frisco"). The group included me; Abe Charnes, who left Carnegie Tech to move to Purdue in 1955; and Rubin Saposnik. Abe was looking to develop a train-scheduling routine and perhaps other applications using linear programming. We began with brainstorming sessions in meetings with management. In retrospect, for me, this was a device for enabling us to become familiar with the operations of the railroad, its problems, and the way the minds of the managers worked—and vice versa. It would foreshadow the way we engaged practitioners much later in using experiments to design and develop new market and auction systems for electricity, natural gas and pipelines, water and spectrum licenses.

This was all new to me at the time, and it was a great personal learning experience. I did not come to the meetings with any tool, such as linear programming, that I was looking to apply—an answer in search of a question, a solution in search of a problem. I learned that not having a preconceived tool was an advantage when searching for raw material to shape. It was more useful to focus on how things worked on the Frisco and then ask what modified rules, policies, and procedures could make them work better. The sessions were of intense interest to me, and I soon found myself absorbed in the Frisco's numerous management problems and with discovering how "economic thinking" could help in addressing each problem.

The central problem of the railroads and the decline in their freight business was increasing competition from over-the-road truck trailers. Also of concern to management was the general problem of obtaining more efficient internal operations, an issue that emerged in a series of cases or examples in which internal human and organizational resources were being poorly allocated. There were three key people on the management side with whom I had the most interaction. The vice president of marketing (hereafter VPM, as I do not recall his name), the vice president of operations (Victor "Vic" Gleaves, I believe, but call him VPO), and a bright and intriguing younger man, A. R. "Art" Lindeman, who knew Japanese and had served in intelligence operations with the US Army in the Pacific during World War II. Art had a title that I do not remember, but essentially he was a troubleshooter looking for operating inefficiencies that could be corrected.

I will begin with an issue in the internal organization of the railroads, then address a solicitor/sales problem, and then rate making and piggybacking issues. I will talk about my thoughts and contributions on each issue or problem at that time and present the essence of the various discussions in the form of conversations that approximate the interactions we had in countless meetings around a conference table. Some of this thinking was embodied in the final report to the Frisco that is now in the Vernon L. Smith Archives at Duke University.

Internal Organization

A large regulated railroad has a bureaucracy not unlike that of a large state university. The usual profit criteria applying to any business are modified by ICC regulations, and hence the conditions that create a heavy university-like bureaucracy.

A university's primary mission is research and education, and the delivery of these products to students, professionals, and the larger community. Ideally, for each subordinate activity there is the need to ask how that activity contributes to the mission, and whether the activity should be executed via the university's direct investment or delivered by external entities—in business it's called the "make-or-buy" decision. Such university activities include food handling, custodial services, maintenance of a fleet of automobiles, hotel facilities, bookstores, bowling alleys, pool halls, the capacity to renovate and remodel offices and classrooms using plumbers, electricians, carpenters, painters, and so on. The question is to what extent, given its mission, a university should also develop, in-house, the expertise to develop and manage all these subordinate activities. Exactly the same issues arose in the regulated railroad, and it was fascinating.

The Frisco's operations center was in Springfield, Missouri. Its main tracks formed a cross: one track-bed from Kansas City to Birmingham and the other from St. Louis to Dallas, with the two crossing in Springfield.

Art was in a small town in southeast Kansas, with a Frisco train depot, doing his job: looking around and asking questions of the depot manager. It should be transparent that Art had a great deal of authority—carte blanche, shall we say—to intervene and make changes. "*What is in this warehouse?*" Reply: "*Furniture.*" "*Let's open it and have a look,*" Art says, and inside finds heaps of dusty junk furniture, broken and in disrepair.

"*Why are you keeping it?*" Reply, "*Eventually it will be sent to Springfield for repair in the Frisco furniture repair facility, but they have a backlog.*" "*And you need it?*" Reply, "*No, but one of the other departments in the railroad might.*" So Art said, "*You got a couple of day laborers available? Send them to me.*" When the laborers showed up, Art told them to move all the junk in that storehouse out on the open railroad siding area. Then he poured gasoline over the pile and burned it to ash.

The furniture policy here is a classic make-or-buy decision. Should all the furniture storage and repair facilities be shut down, the assets put to work elsewhere in the company, and furniture purchases and maintenance contracted out to other parties? I emphasized the principle that every policy or activity needs to be tested against one or more alternatives to determine whether to institute a change. This was not a natural way for management to think about its task, although Art clearly understood it and was trying to reduce inefficient furniture inputs to an inefficient repair facility. I found it amazing to learn that a large, regulated railroad, facing intense competition and a decline in its transportation business, was also perpetuating an internal furniture-repair business.

The Solicitor/Sales Problem

Art also reported that he had been investigating commodity-handling operations and had found that the sales force was soliciting uneconomical business that cost more to handle than it was worth. He had several examples, but here is one of the most glaring. A salesman had solicited the movement of some huge steel I-beams that were too long to put on a single flatcar. You had to string the beam across two flatcars. The flatcars would jiggle up and down, rarely in unison, as they sequentially negotiated bumps and unaligned rails in the roadbed. This stressed the beam and escalated maintenance and repair of the flatcar. Art investigated it and noted that the salespeople were judged on the basis of tonnage solicited. As Art reported it, from the salesmen's perspective this solicitation was a coup, and they were giving away whiskey to get the business!

I proposed the following solution to the solicitors' incentive problem: Take every item published in the railroad's rate book, and estimate the out-of-pocket cost of handling that item from pickup to delivery, including any unique equipment needs or costs and maintenance arising from the special handling. For every quoted rate, the salesman is provided this associated out-of-pocket cost. The difference between the load's gross revenue and this cost I called the load's "contribution to overhead" (CTO) from that business. Put every salesman on a commission incentive, stated as a percentage of CTO. And any free whiskey would come out of the salesman's pocket.

The proposal had a mixed reception. The VPM and Art were very favorable, but the VPO, a longtime railroad man, said, "I don't think we can do it. We are a common carrier, and if we publish an ICC approved rate on anything, we cannot refuse to accept some of the business offered." Hmmm. Some thought, however, that there was nothing to prevent salesmen from dragging their feet on the low CTO stuff and expediting the high CTO business. After all, there are always equipment availability problems, especially for I-beams that cross two flatcars! I liked this comment, as it was a fresh new example of the emerging Vernon Smith theorem: Every bureaucratic question has a bureaucratic answer.

It turned out that in railroad rate making there indeed was a significant regulatory issue. Any time a railroad filed new rates, any shipper or competitor could challenge that rate. Furthermore—and this tells you how pernicious such regulations can be—one test that was to be applied was the following: *Does the new rate divert traffic from competitors to the railroad?*

Give me a break, I argued. Why would you want to change the rate if you did not hope to divert traffic, or at least prevent diversion away from the railroad? How had the truckers been making inroads into the rail movement of goods if not by diverting traffic away from the railroads? Apparently, it was possible for the lawyers to argue that the truckers were getting the business by providing faster service, rather than by charging lower prices. But the faster service had a lower price equivalent, which is the counter-argument that should have been used by the Frisco's lawyers. What mattered was the net price to customers, and that should have been the focal point of competition. Ultimately, this thoroughly constructivist and adversarial hearing process was relieved by the deregulation of the trucks and railroads, early in the last quarter of the twentieth century, under Jimmy Carter, but in the 1950s it was all in full destructive swing.

The discussion with Frisco rested with that interchange, and there was no final resolution at the time. We did, however, turn to the question of the commodities that were transported by the Frisco. We looked at some manifests, and two things struck me. (1) Many of the items were low-value, bulky agricultural products such as beans and potatoes. I pointed out that these were likely "inferior goods," defined as those whose consumption declines as individual incomes rise. That turned out to be an eye-opener for management. The VPO thought of those items as growing with population, with no offsetting decline in per capita consumption, so this turned out to be an important if pretty elementary issue. (2) The railroad was hauling commodities that were growing slowly, or even declining, and I realized that the growth of a transportation company is obviously just a weighted average of the growth rates of the industries whose products it hauls. The implication was that one should look at the growth rates of what truckers are hauling, and I was ready to bet they were heavy into hauling new, high-growth industry stuff. That led to an immediate policy change. The Frisco put its marketing staff to work on researching growth rates by industry to earmark high-growth industries on which to focus its solicitation effort.

Rate Making

As background to the discussion, recall that the overarching problem was railroad business decline brought on by increasing competition from over-the-road trucking. Not only were the trucks taking shipment volume away from the rails, but they were also taking the high-value commodities, such as consumer electronics, for which the transportation rates were highest, because the demand was the most inelastic—in economics jargon, but that jargon was not needed to have a meeting of minds across the table. Truckers were able to provide faster service, reducing inventories in transit, and with savings in inventory costs particularly beneficial to the shippers of high valued goods.

So, I asked, "How are rates made?"

The ensuing discussion of rate making noted that besides variable and commodity-specific handling costs, much of rate making was concerned with how to allocate fixed costs to individual movements of goods. Of course, the essence of fixed costs is that they *cannot* be attributed (allocated) to individual movements of commodity, as I explained at one of the meetings in St. Louis. Inventing arbitrary ways to allocate non-allocable fixed costs was, however, the regulatory ICC approach to rate making. Thus, the capital cost of a railroad's track-bed is independent of particular shipments; similarly for track maintenance, except that higher speed trains (passenger trains and express freight) require higher maintenance than slow freight trains. The point-to-point cost of moving an individual train—fuel, crew, car and track maintenance—is a joint fixed cost for all the commodities moved in the train.

But economically, how should the rates be determined to serve the interest of the company? I proposed a simple procedure. Don't begin by looking at your own costs, and certainly not at your fixed costs. That is the wrong end of the telescope. Start by looking at the commodity rates charged by the truckers (or other competing alternatives). You price based on the competition with allowances for speed of delivery and other service elements. Thus, if the Frisco is slower, offer a lower price, but also look into more express trains and other expedited movements for certain commodity groups, weighing the extra costs against the revenue benefits. Does the additional cost of express trains enable higher prices to compete with the truckers? Given a price that is competitive, look at assignable out-of-pocket costs and determine whether the business makes a net contribution to overhead—so we were able to revisit the earlier discussion about associating a CTO with every rate published by Frisco. If CTO is not positive, let that business go to the truckers; otherwise, go for it yourself.

Piggybacking

By the 1950s, a technology had been developed to easily ship semi-trailers on railroad flatcars. A truck tractor picks up the loaded trailer from a shipper, moves it to the nearest rail terminal, and sets the trailer onto a flatcar.

At the destination rail terminal, the trailer is picked up by a local truck tractor that delivers the trailer to the final customer. The railroad provides the long-distance movement of the shipment at low cost, and truck tractors are used for flexible, low-cost local pickup and delivery on each end. The best of both transportation modes are combined. The flatcar movement of a trailer is called piggybacking. If a trailer goes shipboard, as later it did, it was called fishy-backing.

In 1956–1957 individual railroads were considering whether to use the new piggybacking mode of transportation. The VPO took the position that if Frisco did enter the piggybacking business, it would help the truckers who were already snapping up railroad business. Why should Frisco help them? I argued that there were gains from trade using the new mode that would be shared by both entities, and it all boiled down to the terms on which Frisco provided long-haul service for the truckers. The gross gain for Frisco was in the price at which it moved the shipment. And if that price reflected the inherent railroad efficiencies in long-haul movements, then it would be in the interest of truckers to buy piggybacking services from the railroad. It could be an important means of recovering lost business. I was sure that this was the way for the Frisco to go.

But there was a wrinkle, unique to the Frisco, that placed it in a strategic position relative to most railroads, and this would sweeten the whole project. The Frisco had a wholly owned trucking subsidiary, the Frisco Transportation Company (FTC), authorized by the ICC, as a common-carrier trucker. The Frisco used the FTC for substitute service, enabling it to abandon unprofitable rail service in more remote areas served by spur lines. This had been the rationale under which the ICC had allowed the Frisco to escape the standard regulatory must-serve requirement then prevailing. In effect, regulation forced profitable segments of a business to cross-subsidize the losing segments. An unintended consequence was that the existence of the FTC enabled the Frisco to compete with truckers on regular road routes. It could serve as a wedge to expand the FTC in the Frisco operating territory by soliciting traffic in competition with other truckers, while piggybacking the trailers point-to-point at a lower cost. It could also serve the cause of competition with other railroads who had no such subsidiary. That was a promising strategy, but I argued that it did not preclude offering point-to-point piggyback rates to all common-carrier truckers, provided that the Frisco could obtain a favorable rate for such movements.

The above was pretty much the gist of our final report delivered in August 1957. We bid each other good-bye after our last meeting, as we had all become friends in a common unifying purpose. I returned to my hotel room for later departure on a return flight to Los Angeles. It had been a demanding month: Mom's suicide, home to Wichita for the arrangements, the funeral, then to St. Louis for these business meetings. I was relieved and thought it was all over, but it wasn't quite over. The hotel phone rang and it was the vice president of marketing, who wanted to talk with me if I had time to come over to his office. I did and walked right over. He got right to the point, saying, "I want to hire you to be in charge of rate making at the Frisco." I replied, "But I have no experience or knowledge of making railroad rates." He said, "Yes, I know, and that is precisely why I want to hire you. What rate making needs on this damn railroad is someone who thinks like you, not someone who knows all about the regulated world of rate making."

I was not ready to leave Purdue in 1957, but I have sometimes wondered what direction Joyce and I would have taken if we had pulled up stakes and left for St. Louis. I would have followed my maternal side of the family and become a railroad man! And likewise for Joyce, whose father was a Whitewater, Kansas, telegrapher on the Rock Island and Pacific Railroad (the "Rock Island Road" as it was known, was another ambitiously named railroad that had so far not come close to making it to the Pacific). At the moment, it was tempting, exciting, and challenging. Soberly, at that time I thought my comparative advantage was in academia, where I had an unfinished agenda, rather than the railroad business. Still, I felt unusually honored by the VPM. I had privately felt that I had brought value to the railroad and that I was leaving satisfied customers behind in St. Louis. Unexpectedly, the VPM had confirmed this perception in spades. I felt really good about St. Louis and the Frisco project. The month had brought trials, but there had been successes in the midst of failures that had been inevitable, unavoidable, and a bit heartrending. It was now all history; you cannot change it, but it can change you, and in a small way it probably did change me.

I became something of an outdoorsman in the 1960s. By 1964 I'd bought a new International Harvester Scout 80 from the IH dealer in Lafayette for $2750. Before I sold it in Tucson in July 2006 on eBay (for $5800, with an odometer reading somewhere north of 100,000 miles), we regularly fired it up for trips down to Starbucks and other local hangouts, sometimes including the Maverick or some other country-western music hall. (As the fella said, "There's just two kinds of music: Country and Western.") It had been retired for many years from active four-wheel driving on back-country trails that required all-wheel drive. The steel top had long ago been unbolted and discarded, a bikini canvas top installed, the exterior freshly painted, a roll-bar installed, and chromium wheels and bumpers installed. And, not to go unmentioned, a new plate glass windshield was installed—the old one was pockmarked with chips and cracks. In Tucson, it had been transformed from off-road duty into a drugstore, rhinestone cowboy four-wheeler, but it still carried many dents (scars of off-road duty) underneath on the steel "skid plate" installed to protect all the underside cables, springs, transmission, transfer case, and so on. The vehicle weighed over 4800 pounds with all the protective armor and before I discarded the steel top.

In 1964 Joyce, Eric, Deborah, Torrie, our two dogs, and I drove it to Utah, pulling a thirteen-foot travel trailer for upscale camping, complete with dining-room table and propane stove, upper and lower bunks, and a side bunk, sleeping five people in all. We explored southeast Utah and liked Monticello, near the Four Corners border. We settled into Buckboard Flat, a campground, straight up the mountain road west from town, where we unhooked the trailer for living, the Scout for four-wheeling, and turned out the dogs—King, the accomplished hunter of uncertain lineage; and Tanya, the AKC-registered Alaskan malamute. We left the dogs and trailer, drove down the mountain to the highway, and turned left toward Moab. This is a beautiful drive. This area is a very scenic mix of semi-desert, mountains, and the country of "standing up rocks." About halfway to Moab, we came to the entrance to Canyon Lands on the left, at the Church Rock turn—it's impossible to miss a massive rock formation that looks like a church. We were well armed with BLM topography maps covering the whole area, and the region is loaded with crisscrossing four-wheel trails that we were hell-bent to explore: Salt Creek, Elephant Hill, the Staircase, Chesler Park, SOB Hill, Bobby's Hole, and so on, with switchbacks so tight you have to back up the next one rather than try to make a turn so close to the edge.

Past the Canyon Lands entrance, the first landmark you pass is Six Shooter peak on the left. If you saw the movie *Thelma and Louise*, you watched the heroines drive past it in their attempted escape from the Utah State Police. Just past the peaks, there is a four-wheeler trail to the right, but for its first few miles, two-wheel drive is all the traction you need. That is how Thelma and Louise were able to get to the high, flat meadow on the north bank of the Colorado River, downstream from Moab and just upstream from Colorado's confluence with the Green River, where all hell breaks loose as the river cascades through Cataract Canyon. Joyce and I have been on Thelma and Louise's back trail all the way to Moab, and it is the worst trail we have ever negotiated. But they drove only a short distance, because they had a convertible, and you do not have to drive far to get to the movie set up for a grand leap off the edge into the Colorado River, way, way below.

Back in 1964, at our Canyon Lands off-road initiation, we drove to the next landmark, a trail on the left up the middle of Salt Creek. This was before the Canyon Lands National Park and recreation area existed. It was BLM country, and near Salt Creek was a small BLM mobile home, set amidst a few trees of precious shade and occupied by a very pleasant retired builder and his wife from the East Coast, smack in the midst of living out their dreams. The BLM had set him up as the keeper of an imaginary gate at the entrance to all these remote and wonderful trails. His job was to give advice, and we filed our four-wheel exploration plan with him. That way he knew when to expect us, and if we did not show up at the expected time, he would come looking for us. It's easy to get stranded in there, there is no food or water, and there is precious little shade except under the high rock ledges. He was sitting in most of what shade there was.

"So what's your plan?" he asked, and I replied, "We would like to drive in by Chesler Park to Bobby's Hole, up the Hole to the back side of Mt. Abajo, and return to Buckboard Flat." He said, "Nobody can get up Bobby's Hole; it's too steep, and you have to negotiate rocks that are close to the boulder category. A winch does not help, as there is nothing to hook the winch to. But you can creep down it if you've a mind to." So I said, "OK, then today we will go up Salt Creek for a shorter jaunt, get some practice, and return to our campground this evening. Tomorrow morning we will start early, go up and over the saddle here on the to-pog map, find the trail to Bobby's Hole, and drive down it. How long will that take?" He estimated we would be back where we then stood by about 3:00 p.m. if we started at 7:00 a.m. So we went up Salt Creek, and the Scout did its thing masterfully. We got up as far as Angel Arch, a great closed arch of sandstone that does indeed look like an angel with head bowed playing a great harp, with the imaginary strings in abstract representation. Years later I read in a Park Service brochure that Angel Arch was not discovered until the 1940s. Bullshit: As will be related below by Pete Steele, it was the BLM and Park Service bureaucrats that did not discover it until then; it was long known by the Mormon cowboys who *decades earlier* had run cattle on Chesler Park grass.

The next day we managed to get down Bobby's Hole, creeping slowly and negotiating small-scale boulders. In one long morning, the Scout picked up half its lifetime supply of protective armor-plate dents. If you want to do Utah, you never buy an RV without a full skid plate to protect engine, transmission, transfer case, and front and rear differential gears. We stopped at Chesler Park, a huge ring of towering standing rocks. Inside the massive natural stone, enclosure is a meadow of grassland in soil deep enough to hold moisture. It is a natural canyon-walled cattle range. Then up S.O.B. Hill, many stops, and finally, running a little late, we encountered the BLM ranger in his CJ-5 jeep coming into find us. It's the Fourth of July, 1964. There is one other party that we passed on the trail in a jeep. We were told that the entire BLM Canyon Land area contained only the two vehicles. We had maybe several hundred thousand acres all to ourselves on that great day, out of a past that cannot ever be rerun except in memory. Somewhere I have slides, many of them washed out by the intense sunlight. I just now included some of them in this Chapter. No wonder I have had three skin surgeries in the last four years with four more to be added!

But you can live it vicariously: Start by renting and enjoying the movie *Thelma and Louise.* Thelma and Louise, abused a bit by their husbands, decide to take a vacation on their own, and the first stop is a country music bar. A first category jerk hits on Louise, she rebuffs him and the girls decide to leave. Louise goes to the parking lot first and the jerk followers her. Thelma, delayed by a pit stop, comes on the jerk preparing to rape Louise. Thelma pulls her pistol, the jerk pulls back scared, but Thelma, angry though no longer being resisted, pumps two shots into him. This is the start of a great Hollywood movie chase.

Then get a paperback copy of *The Monkey Wrench Gang* and follow Hayduke's jeep chases all over Canyon Lands, from the Maze to Salt Creek, and you will be on all those great trails, originally blazed by Mormons, on which Joyce and I four-wheeled, sometimes with the kids but never the dogs, who preferred to stay back in the cool shade, the streams, and among the small game of Buckboard Flat. You have to learn Hayduke's measure of driving distance: As I recall, Tucson to Flagstaff took a six pack and half to drive. Have fun.

The Scout had one problem: On a very steep upgrade the engine started to cough and choke, and we had to slip the clutch to maintain steady power. When we returned to Lafayette, I drove to the dealership and reported my problem. A mechanic checked out the engine and found nothing wrong. I figured it was a design defect and any Scout would do it, but the dealer denied that could be the case because IH had a proving test ground in Arizona and everything was thoroughly tested to keep such defects from surviving. More BS, but it could be challenged.

Of course, no proving tests are that good. The local guy was just making up the facts to protect his beliefs—humanities favorite pass-time. It's like the people who believed the world was flat: The ships that went out and never returned were said to have fallen off the edge; the ships that returned were said to have never gone far enough.

I got the name of the IH President from the Standard and Poor Corporate records at the Purdue Library, resolving to vault over all the dedicated employees making up the facts, and wrote him a letter explaining my problem. He answered, thanking me profusely for the information, and said the regional division head from engineering would be in touch with me as he would want to hear all about any defects. Clearly, top management was in the business of selling Scouts, and you cannot do that without satisfied customers good-mouthing you. Soon I got a call, and we set up an appointment with the regional director to meet at the local IH dealer.

After some discussion, I said that I could demonstrate the Scout's problems if I could get on a steep-enough incline. The dealership had a flatbed truck with a hydraulic adjustable bed that could be tilted into an incline, and I indicated that would work. Watching me, he tilted it until I indicated that it was poised at a steep-enough angle, about 35 degrees, take or leave a degree. He got in the Scout with me and I began the ascent. Then he said, "Wait, I think I will get out and watch you!" So I stopped. He bailed out, and I resumed. As all four wheels reached the bed, and I started up, the engine started to cut out, with black smoke coming out of the exhaust—black smoke indicates that the fuel mixture is too rich. The fuel-to-air ratio of gas vapor coming into the cylinders was too high for complete fuel combustion.

The head of the regional division said that I would be hearing from the Holly Carburetor representative who was assigned to the IH plant in Ft. Wayne, Indiana. In fact, a man identifying himself as representing Holly called me shortly afterward, made an appointment, and came down to see me and the Scout in Lafayette. He said he knew about the problem, that any Scout off the assembly line would do it, and he showed me why. With the hood up, he pointed out that the gas line comes into the rear of the carburetor. On a steep incline, the gasoline in the carburetor bowl is tilted backward, and the float, which was hinged to the rear of the bowl, drops down. The valve for controlling the inflow of gasoline into the bowl opens, and the bowl is flooded. He said that Holly had been trying to get IH to buy into a new carburetor with a spring-loaded needle valve and a gas line coming in from the side, but IH had balked as it would add $50 to the price of the Scout. So he and I had coincident interests, and from there it was all downhill. He would fix my Scout and he thought the customer complaint meant that IH would be convinced they should change carburetors.

In fact, IH would end up convinced and, beginning sometime afterward, all Scouts had the new design. In 1972 I bought a second new Scout, keeping the old one because I could not bear to give it up, especially since I had the only one known to me that did not have the carburetor flooding problem. The first thing I did in the display room was to lift the hood on the 1972 model and check the carburetor intake line—it was attached to the side of the bowl.

His idea for fixing my 1964 Scout was to build an adapter kit for increasing the tension on the float device and making some other modifications. When it was ready, I would drive to Fort Wayne, Indiana, he would install it, and we could drive to a local gravel pit for testing. He said that if it did not work he could always just turn the carburetor around 180 degrees, which would solve the problem except where you might have to go up a wall in reverse. He made the device and installed it, but it failed my test in the local Fort Wayne gravel pit.

I stayed over that night in a motel. (Here is a sidelight on life in the truck manufacturing region of the city: Upon retiring someone calls me from the desk. Would I like female company sent to my room? "No thank you." "You are welcome, sir. Have a nice sleep.") The next day the carburetor was turned around and passed the test in forward drive, doing its hiccupping only in reverse, and I drove back to West Lafayette quite satisfied. Until 2006 I owned the only 1964 Scout that can climb anything forward. This means that it encounters a problem on only two trails known to me: One of the switchbacks on Black Bear trail above Telluride has to be negotiated in reverse—at 13,000 feet, as you ascend just below the waterfall; there is a similar switchback on Elephant Hill in Canyon Lands. My 1972 Scout could handle either one, but it had a longer wheelbase than the 1964 Scout 80, so it would have dragged its tail on the rocks if I had tried to come down Bobby's Hole.

The lesson here is simple: Don't listen to the stories you hear from the local dealer. Contact the company at a high level. All the companies known to me want satisfied customers—if you find one that does not consider selling its shares short—and the top management wants to know of any problems that its information channels may protect them from hearing about. Lower-level managers are sometimes reluctant to tell their bosses anything but good news, so the president is the last to learn of a problem that needs attention. It's much like a university. In fact, customer-oriented companies now have hotlines for this purpose, so you can bypass the local franchised dealer whose incentives may not be completely coincident with those of the manufacturer. In fact, this disconnect in incentives explains why hotlines exist now, and illustrates how institutions adapt over time if people are alert to the needs for change.

There are, however, completely contrary examples to this one. Institutions can also quite effectively be developed by employees who are committed to problem-solving for their customers, and thereby also serve their managers. Indeed, because of their better local information and on-the-ground interaction with customers, I would expect this to be more common than I found to be the case with international Harvester and my Scout 80. The clear lesson is that management must actively seek to develop and reward that commitment. Thus, ideally, the local IH dealer in Lafayette would have felt a strong obligation to see that my concerns were addressed and that new information passed up the line to illuminate top management policies; i.e., he would want his management to learn of my problem from him; not from me.

Here is a nice example of committed local employees out-maneuvering company procedures to obtain a better outcome for their customers and for their company—an example of ecologically rational adaptation. The company is American Airlines (AA), with whom I have been a loyal frequent flyer member since about 1980. At some cost in inconvenience, we always fly AA and its One World partners.

It was in 2007. Candace and I flew AA to Brussels, but held a paper ticket on Brussels Airlines to Milan, our final destination area; so our bags were not checked through to Milan. Because of a ground delay program in effect at New York's Kennedy, we ended up with a tight connection between our DCA to NY to Brussels flight. We only just made it, but as you can imagine, our bags did not. Upon learning this we went to the AA Brussels desk to file a lost baggage form. They said to wait until we arrived in Milan, file there with instructions to deliver to the hotel 1.5 hours away. We were going to call the Executive Platinum desk in the USA—our usual procedure for getting quality expedited service. The local desk advised us not to get them involved. In retrospect, this turned out to be a valuable warning.

So we followed the instructions, but later that evening, nervous about our bags, we decided to call the US AA desk to see if their trace system, which we had found so good on domestic flights, could tell us where the bags were. They had no record of lost bags and did not know where they were. So we explained that we had filed in Milan, and were told that was completely wrong, always file within 30 minutes in the city of arrival. I called the next day and they still had no record of where the bags were. So now we called the AA person in Brussels who had given us her number and name. Politely, she said, "Your bags are on the way, because it was done before your call to the USA had a chance to screw everything up!" She then logged into the AA baggage record system and "fixed it." Next, she explained to us that the AA rules work fine in the USA but not there. "In Europe we have all these different airlines, procedures and languages, and we have worked out a means of dealing with these cases directly, and we just do it!" So there you have it; how European AA employees use their local knowledge to adapt to local conditions and better serve their customers; all of it well under the AA management radar, but nevertheless in the interest of both (Figs. 11.1, 11.2, 11.3, 11.4, 11.5, 11.6, 11.7, and 11.8).

Fig. 11.1   Angel Arch. The soul can split the sky. 1964

Fig. 11.2   Chesler Park. Waste high grass enclosed in a circle of standing up rocks

Fig. 11.3   Down Bobby's Hole to trail below

Fig. 11.4   Elephant Hill staircase jeep trail

Fig. 11.5 Thelma & Louise chase ends here

Fig. 11.6 Scout retired for rhinestone cowboy duty 1964

Fig. 11.7 Sid at blackboard 1961

Fig. 11.8   Sid at desk 1961

12

The People

Em always was in a position to see it differently from the rest of us. He was the quarterback, and we were the ones carrying the ball and doing the blocking and tackling … None of us saw it the same way, obviously. We each mainly saw the others through the dust of our own work.

—John Hughes

Joy is greatest in those moments in which man is aware that his individuality and creative energy are at their highest pitch.

—W. von Humbolt, *The Limits of State Action*

During our early years at Purdue, 1955–1957, many of us discovered that we shared a common dissatisfaction with substantial portions of our own graduate educations. Our dissatisfaction led to an emergent commitment to create a graduate program that would reflect our own aspirations for new experience and to teach from that experience. By design, the foundation of the program was the product of the work, the methodology, and the content of the faculty's research and thinking. We didn't recruit to fields of economics, with the program structured and predefined by the fields. That was, and is still, what is wrong with economics and economic education, and it is why even the new stuff is so much like carbon copies of the old. Breaking the mold for over a decade is what made Purdue work and why it will not readily be replicated elsewhere. We recruited people we thought were promising and were doing innovative work. The program was then defined by what these young faculty additions wanted to accomplish professionally. What we taught grew out of our own professional problem-solving: Stan Reiter (1925–2014) in mathematical economics—he was self-taught, having

© The Author(s) 2018
V. L. Smith, *A Life of Experimental Economics, Volume I*,
https://doi.org/10.1007/978-3-319-98404-9_12

audited graduate mathematical courses at Stanford and applied his learning to unsolved problems in price and equilibrium theory; Ed Ames (1921–1998) in quantitative methods, also self-taught in topics well beyond his formal degrees; and Lance Davis (1928–2014), John Hughes (1928–1992), and Nate Rosenberg (1927–2015) in economic history; theory, quantitative methods, and economic history were the three "fields," or legs of the program. Within this framework, I would later develop experimental economics, but up into the 1960s I was doing my brand of quantitative methods in the form of what the graduate students would come to call enginomics. We did monetary economics because we had George Horwich (1924–2008) and that was his research. We needed applied economics, but we got that with economic history and experimental economics. The economic historians did monetary economics, macroeconomics, labor economics, international trade, growth, and specialties such as innovation and technological change. So why recruit an international trade economist, a macroeconomist, a labor economist, and so on? Just recruit a stable of economic historians like Lance Davis, John Hughes, and Nate Rosenberg who knew those topics and have an integrative perspective.

In 1957–1958, we inherited a handful of graduate students at Purdue, but not enough to have a program. We proceeded to build it through a direct recruitment effort by members of the faculty, particularly Ed Ames and John Hughes, who visited various New York and other universities. This is how we jump-started the PhD program, and over the years we recruited Hugo Sonnenschein, Tom Muench, Nancy Schwartz (1939–1981), John Ledyard, John Wood, Mort Kamien (1938–2011), Gene Silberberg, Pat Hendershott, and many more. Since the initial students we had inherited were weak in mathematics, we taught a remedial course in mathematical economics, and we emphasized the recruitment of new students who were mathematical majors or minors. If they looked good, and seemed to be motivated, we did not care if their grades were not high, and some were indeed not high—Hugo, Mort, and John Ledyard surely could not have gotten into most graduate programs, any more than I could have gotten into Caltech based on my high school record and courses. They represented the kinds of risks we took that paid off. All produced outstanding careers. Mort went to Carnegie and Northwestern and became both a productive scholar and a dedicated, thoughtful teacher. Tom and Hugo, both Stan Reiter's students, became mathematical economists par excellence. Hugo made important contributions to general equilibrium theory, became a rising administration star, and then became president of the University of Chicago. While a graduate student at Purdue, Tom Muench was teaching a mathematical economics course at Wabash College, when John Ledyard showed up in his class. John was Tom's best student, although he had dropped out of Chicago as an undergraduate and Tom told him to apply to the Purdue graduate program, which he did. Tom told us to just ignore his record and take him, which we did. So John was one of our star graduate students, received his Purdue PhD, went to Northwestern and Caltech, made path-breaking contributions all over the place, and became division head at Caltech—the latter a crazy aberration, but you have to be forgiving of the few mistakes that your best students make.

Two students who were in my first experimental economics course had come out of the MS in Management program: Don Rice and Norm Weldon. As students using the case method, their favorite sport was busting open the punch line of the case in the first fifteen minutes of class. So the professor would be standing there with an hour to go, and the Socratic discovery process of learning the lessons from the case was displayed right at the start.

But Don and Norm each had a very serious side, a practical down-to-earth side, and from the beginning, we all knew that these two guys were destined to run organizations. Don had been in the ROTC program and upon finishing his degrees was required to do service in the military. We got him accepted into a position at the U.S. Department of Defense when McNamara was the Secretary. He became a valuable member of that strategy team—the "whiz kids" with Alain Enthoven and others—and after the Johnson years went to the Rand Corporation as president. Subsequently, he served as Secretary of the Air Force and then returned to the private sector in high-technology business.

Norm went with the CTS Corporation (Chicago Telephone Supply, but it had become a leading electronics component manufacturer and had long abandoned its telephone roots as the world rapidly changed) as head of research in its newly opened research facility in the Purdue Industrial Park of West Lafayette on Yeager Road, which then was out in the country, across the road from where Joyce and I had built our first house. CTS manufactured electronic components, a brutally competitive business in which you signed major supply contracts for innovative new products with companies like IBM at prices below the unit cost at which you could currently produce the item. The research task was to engineer techniques enabling you to lower the unit cost and glide into profitability while the contract still had some distance to go. Norm was made for this sort of challenge. He met it, rose in the ranks, and became president of the company. He later took that company into medical technology, subsequently moved to other companies, and today is a venture capitalist in funding new medical device technologies.

As chairman of the Economic Policy Committee, Ed was a key person behind all the younger people we hired in economics. Ed interviewed all the candidates at the American Economics Association meetings, had a great eye for talent, and was unimpressed by the usual credentials approach to hiring. None of us believed in the credentials approach, so we gave Ed a long leash on which to operate and to make mistakes. He never made any that I recall. That is how we got Charlie Plott; the story also illustrates Ed's *modus operande*, both in recruiting and in plain talk with the candidate and everybody else.

Ed described to the committee all the top interviewed candidates that year. When asked whom he thought was best, he said it was Charlie. Yet, on paper, Charlie did not look like anyone who would be a natural fit with the Purdue crowd. So, aware of this, Ed explained that he did not think Charlie was well trained for doing contemporary research—not much mathematics, quantitative methods, or theory—but he had an inquisitive and creative mind, common sense, and he was likely to do important original work, not potboiler stuff. We decided to move on him, and Ed made him a good offer, but he also informed Charlie that he was basically uneducated, untrained, and had to make up for it, and he told him how to do that. Charlie learned mathematical economics the way Lamont Marsh had learned the machinist's trade. He made his way into a summer program teaching mathematics. If you gotta teach it, you gotta learn it. Just stay a day ahead of the class! That is also how I learned some American economic history at the University of Kansas, except that I took the course for one year and taught it the next. Charlie was easily one of the best young faculty members we ever hired, and contrary to Ed's initial opinion, he in fact had a great background under Jim Buchanan that slowly revealed itself and was part of the creativity that Ed had seen.

I can't leave the subject of my Purdue years without talking about the friendships that were forged in the twelve years that I lived in West Lafayette, 1955–1967.

First, I must mention Kirby Davidson and Jay Wiley (1914–2005). The three of us wrote a textbook, *Economics: An Analytical Approach* (1958, revised 1962). It was designed and written around our teaching of Purdue undergraduates in engineering and science, and made use of the tools of mathematics that were part of these students' studies, and contained lots of applications, particularly of the theory of production—engineering economics ("enginomics") examples. At the time, this was a fun course to develop and to write about in a real-time textbook—written on stream, as it was being taught day to day. Jay was already at Purdue when I came and was a mainstay over the years in helping to build the department and advising graduate students. Kirby was one of our bright new faculty hires who, along with Lance Davis and John Carlson, had completed PhD work at Johns Hopkins. John remained active at Purdue for a great many years and is now Emeritus. Lance ended up at Caltech continuing the development of his reputation as a really distinguished economic historian. I've lost track of Kirby, who left Purdue to work for the Rockefeller Foundation.

The dedication we wrote for that textbook said something about our perception of the Purdue environment:

> This book is respectfully dedicated to all the members of the Departments of Economics and Industrial Management of Purdue University and to the continued growth and professional attainment of the community of friendly scholars which they represent and of which the authors are privileged to be a part.

There was Floyd Gillis, an older member of the new PhD faculty, and one who had been a classmate of mine at Harvard. One of my first papers was co-authored with Floyd, "An Economic Analysis of Contributions Under the Income Tax Laws," published in the *Journal of Political Economy* in October 1958. Floyd's original training had been in accounting, but he had decided to go into economics and ended up at Harvard.

One day he pointed out to me that there was a loophole in the income tax laws as they applied to the firm. Gifts in kind to a charity were deductible from income for determining taxable income. But there was no adjustment applied to the normal deductibility of the cost of goods sold. Items given to a qualified charity could therefore be deducted twice: You could deduct the full cost of producing them, but you could also deduct them at fair market value—defined as the price you could get in your most favorable market at the time of the gift. Hence, depending on the marginal cost of producing the item, your income tax bracket, and taxable income, you could determine at the end of your tax year how many items to give away to maximize your after-tax income. Depending upon the indicated parameters, you could actually improve your bottom line by giving some of your product away. Of course, it might not pay if the gift displaced sales in your own market. Therefore, the gift would have to be to a non-competing market—for example, a foreign market in which the firm did not sell goods. Give some of your shoe output to the people in Belgium where you sell no shoes.

I wrote out the mathematical equations and derived the maximizing solution, and we came up with what the engineers would call a nomograph that enabled a firm, with a given set of parameters, to read off the total dollar value of goods to give away. It was correct, practical, great fun, and the JPE

(*Journal of Political Economy*) loved it! It had a useful message for all private companies, and one as well for public policymakers. I don't know how many firms might have used it, but a few years later we noted that the Treasury modified the law. The modification required the taxpayer to adjust "cost of goods sold" for gifts in kind, thus eliminating the double deduction and the main force of the anomaly.

Floyd had a great maxim, which is sometimes worth quoting in reference to standard economic theories: "If a frog had wings, he wouldn't bump his butt so much." Floyd had emphysema from heavy smoking (4.5 packs a day). He also drank heavily, but you would never know it, so well did he "hold it," as they say—famous last words. His physician said he had to cut back to only one drink per day. So, Floyd bought a double old-fashioned glass, and every evening made himself one and only one martini in that glass. Later, on two different occasions, he was hospitalized with pneumonia. He told me that one night in the hospital bed he had had a strong feeling that he was dying. So he said, "I got up out of bed and was able to stand by leaning against the wall: People don't die standing up!"

Shortly after I left Purdue, Floyd died of pneumonia. So it wasn't like George Burns, who, at age ninety, was told by his doctor that he had to quit smoking cigars. A friend asked, "What did your doctor say when you didn't quit?" Burns said, "I don't know—he died."

Ed Ames, who had "three proper degrees from Harvard," as John Hughes loved to put it, and Stan Reiter, who had a PhD from Chicago, had arrived in West Lafayette in 1954, the year before I got there. John, a Rhodes Scholar and D.Phil. from Oxford, came the year after I arrived. Ed became a legend in everything he did: the classroom, his research, and as an administrator. He knew the Russian language and had full credentials as a Russian economic specialist but did not really pursue that track at Purdue. Early on, when we were developing a school of management and hiring people in accounting, finance, marketing, etc., we elected *not* to form departments. Instead, each area had a faculty policy committee with a chairman—composed of members in and outside of the committee's field— reporting directly to the dean. It worked well, and in the 1960s, it served as a cross-disciplinary integrating form of structure. That integration is what produced PhDs such as Don Rice and Norm Weldon, who came to Purdue for the MS in Management, but pursued PhDs in economics and business and had great careers in business management.

Ed also took the initiative as Economic Policy Committee Chairman to reform the undergraduate program. The Purdue economics department had been a small teaching department, serving the engineering and other technical programs with introductory economics and business classes. The program for majors was not strong. Ed noted that any Midwestern university with 25,000 students had to have scattered through it plenty of first-rate students. So he said, "We will start an Honors program in economics, taught by our best people, and find those best students. We will guarantee that any undergraduate at Purdue who wants an education in economics will get one; for all the others, we will run a hotel, and they will get degrees if they pass minimum standards." And that is what we did. Some of those students in the hotel saw what was going on, checked out of the hotel, and joined us in the honors program.

Ed had unusual skills, not only professional, but also neurological. While writing a longhand sentence with one hand, he could write its mirror image with the other. Later I discovered others who had this aberrant ability. Two decades later, I was sitting in Tucson's Bar M Cattle Company one Friday night as the country-western band was getting ready to play. I was talking with my chemist friend Judy Hooper, a remarkable intuitive biochemical scientist. I was talking about Purdue and its bizarre faculty, and to give it a down-home twist, I related Ed's ambidextrous feat. Judy replied, "Oh, I can do that." With her right hand (I think she is right handed) she wrote on a napkin, "I write like Leonardo" (De Vinci had the same ability). With her left hand she wrote its mirror image. Then, she asked if Ed could do it either way. "What do you mean?" Whereupon Judy wrote, "I write like Leonardo," from left to right with her left hand and simultaneously its mirror image with her right. Hmmm. I didn't know whether Ed could do it, or whether he ever tried. Later, I was at a banquet in New South Wales, Australia, making conversation with a lady next to me, and I related the Ed Ames story. She said, "Oh, I can do that," and proceeded to demonstrate. So I said that I had discovered that a friend, Judy Hooper, could do it, and moreover, she could write forward with either of her hands and the mirror image with the other. The lady said, "Well, you know, I never tried it." Going back to the two sheets of paper, she tried, and yes, she could do it either way. I will never know if Ed was locked into the more limited skill, but he sure was a hell of a good economist and a wonderful colleague who could think outside the box with the best of the few who had that skill. Surely, there is a neurological symmetry theorem here that predicts that the brain that can do it one way is likely able to do it the other.

Ed left Purdue in 1969 for the State University of New York, Stony Brook. He had a home also in Old Lyme, Connecticut, where I once visited him. Both John and Stan kept in closer touch with Ed than I did; through them, I was kept abreast of his continued departmental building efforts at Stony Brook.

Here are excerpts from an obituary written by his colleague, Egon Neuberger:
Ed Ames, one of the few Renaissance men in Economics, was one of the early leaders in the study of the Soviet Economy and Comparative Economic Systems but his range of expertise went far beyond this. He was also a major contributor to Economic History, Econometrics, and Macroeconomics. Although trained in Pre-Samuelsonian Economics, he became convinced that the rigorous, mathematical approach was the way Economics should go, both in his own research, and in the graduate programs at Purdue and Stony Brook. Despite his belief in the mathematical treatment of Economics, he combined this with emphasis on the institutional and historical aspects of the subject. In addition to Economics, he also managed to engage in sculpture and in Russian literary criticism. One of his less known accomplishments, one of which I was not aware, was his participation in the preparation of the Marshall Plan....

Ed was a man of tremendous intellectual power, an innate curiosity, infinite patience, and superhuman effort. He was an early leader in affirmative action; he recruited African Americans to Stony Brook, and then devoted great effort to make them successful economists. His organizational talent was challenged when he was forced to bring up four sons as a de facto single parent, while engaging in major research and teaching efforts...

One of his favorite fields was Economic History since he correctly saw that good studies require the combination of rigorous models and historical and institutional knowledge. The article "The Enfield Arsenal in Theory and History," in the Economic Journal, December 1968, which he co-authored with the economic historian Nathan Rosenberg, was a good example of this.[1]

Before Charlie arrived, I had already checked out all the local bass streams from the Tippecanoe and Wildcat Rivers to the Wea, Flint, Deer, and Sugar Creeks. (You can find these streams on a local map of Indiana's Lafayette area.) Charlie was a dedicated fisherman and soon learned to like the challenge of smallmouth bass in the northern Indiana streams. As Stan Reiter used to put it, "Indiana streams are filled with smallmouth bass and largemouth fishermen." Charlie and I discovered that there was a certain time of year, in early spring, when big carp would hit Mepps Spinners. Why not try, the bass were not hitting yet? We rarely landed them because they were big and heavy with soft mouths that a hook would easily tear through. Slightly later in the spring, we would get into channel catfish hitting daredevil spoons—anything challenging on gamy light lines before the bass started up. But there were few thrills like a strike by a two-pound smallmouth bass. Those bass did magnificent tail stands, arching up like lightning and shaking their heads at the top of the stand, two or more feet out of the water, and often hurled the lure back at our feet if we failed to keep a tight line.

---

[1]http://www.freepatentsonline.com/article/Comparative-Economic-Studies/54806257.html.

I had a twelve-foot flat-bottom aluminum Jon boat like the one in Walt Kelly's incomparable *Pogo* comic strip. Bow and stern were both square cut. It drew about two inches of water and was great for floating streams with volatile depths from two inches above a gravel bed to deep running channels and breakout pools and eddies. Charlie and I floated the Tippecanoe River one day and we learned how it might have received its name.

Charlie and I were in opposite ends of the boat, with our fishing gear in the middle. Charlie is substantially heavier than I am, so the boat sat in the water like a teeter-totter off level. Neither of us was maneuvering the oars, because we just let that boat bang around exposed rocks and stumps and through rapids while we concentrated on fishing. We were casting away when we came to a little drop-off of three or four inches—nothing much, just a very tiny waterfall. My end went over first, and I was in a long cast downstream. Behind came Charlie's end. It dropped down deeper than my end did because my end was riding higher—thanks to Charlie's end drawing more water. He dropped down, my end went up, and the boat hung there in the eddy just long enough to start filling with water from the shortfalls. That action brought my end up still higher and further slowed the boat's downstream motion while increasing the fill rate. In no time, his end took a lot of water over the low sides of the Jon boat. We capsized, fish, tackle, rods, hats, lunch, and spare rods all going under, and the stream was a few feet deep. We hung on to our rods, the oars, and the boat and went to shore. Charlie lost his glasses. We recovered some of our gear, but not all of it.

We learned a little physics; it was obvious once we thought of it. We should have positioned the boat with Charlie at the bow. Then, my end, riding higher, would have slipped over the little falls and not been low enough to draw water.

Stan Reiter was, in my view, our leading economist: untraditional, a first-rate theorist, and outstanding in applications done as a consultant, though with little of it published. Stan taught the best general equilibrium theory class in the world. He used Girard Debreu's *Theory of Value*. It was a small class, and the students had to present each theorem in class, prove it, explicate it, and understand it. He just listened, commented, asked penetrating questions, and made sure the students got every line right no matter how many days they were on stage. If you were his colleague, it was always a good idea to find out what Stan thought about whatever you were thinking about or working on. He was still water that ran deep.

The new School of Industrial Management was created in 1958. Working Paper #1 was written by Stan in 1959: "A Market Adjustment Mechanism" known at Purdue and well beyond as the "Sharks and Flounders" paper.

It was published 22 years later as "A Dynamic Process of Exchange" (1981). Stan was never one who rushed into print—he didn't need to.

His topic was market process, information, and exchange, not equilibrium. Stan believed that there would be time enough to be concerned about equilibrium. The first order of business was to understand how information was transmitted and accumulated in a market populated by agents not presumed to know how to be in equilibrium. This characterization of a market was completely foreign to economic thinking at the time. It could not be imagined at the time that markets could be effective in the absence of complete information, or of large numbers of agents. Stan's process model assured movement toward optimality, but that outcome was accidental, not assured. Similarly, and this is testimony to Stan's (and my) influence, my first experiments in 1956–1959 involved agents fully informed only of their own circumstances, and ignorant of that of others except for what could be learned with messages that resulted in less than optimal binding contracts.

As of August 9, 2014, I felt like the last man standing when I received word by email from his daughter Carla that Stan had died. I was thinking narrowly of the four of us—Stan, Ed, John, and me who were the first to arrive at Purdue, 1954-1956, and of all the joy and trials we went through until 1967. But Stan's influence is pervasive, and there is no last standing person. Northwestern University published an obituary which captures some of this sentiment:

"Stanley Reiter was one of the most original and influential theorists of his generation," said Joel Mokyr, the Robert H. Strotz Professor of Arts and Sciences... "He was also an unusually wide-ranging intellectual, with a strong interest in economic history, on which he worked closely with the late Jonathan Hughes in the 1960s. He is credited with coining the term "cliometrics" – the study of economic history using formal and quantitative methods.

The arrival of Reiter to the business school is easily seen as initiating the great renaissance that powered Northwestern's rise in academia, said Donald Jacobs, dean emeritus, ... "The great thing about Stan is that he brought his own intellectual prowess and beliefs, but he also brought with him a group of people that followed him here and came because he was here," Jacobs said...

In 1971, Reiter founded the Center for Mathematical Studies in Economics and Management Science, which became a hotbed for research in economic theory and operations research at Kellogg and Weinberg...

Hugo F. Sonnenschein, a former student of Reiter's at Purdue University, later went on to become a professor of economics and the president of the University of Chicago (1993-2000). Among the many remarkable economists Sonnenschein had the good fortune to work with, Reiter had the most important influence on his professional life, he said.

"He did not teach you what to say, but he taught you how to think," Sonnenschein said. "He was able to communicate his remarkable taste for what was most important by gently coaxing you along." ...

Then there are Jim Quirk and Rubin Saposnik, both students of Leo Hurwicz who also had mentored Stan Reiter. Quirk and Saposnik wrote an expository contemporary theory text based on Debreu's *Theory of Value.* Not everyone could teach it in the masterly style of Stan, so they resolved to write a book that would try to enable more people to benefit from learning general equilibrium theory. Their text introduced many students to the mysteries of mid-twentieth-century mathematical micro-theory using expository devices and many examples.

As reported in the previous chapter, Rubin and I worked on the Saint Louis San Francisco (Frisco) project and did a joint paper based on that work with Art Lindeman at the railroad. Jim Quirk had worked on default risk and financial investment in firms. Jim got it right, very early, in his thesis. The Modigliani-Miller "theorem" did not work, but nobody cared or noticed. It is interesting that when I visited the Cowles Foundation at Yale, I once talked with Joe Stiglitz about the M-M theorem, and he repeated his version of the non-proof that was commonly used.

The basic idea was both simple and dead wrong: The market value of the firm was independent of the mix of debt and equity used to finance it; this was because, as was commonly argued, no matter what the proportion of shares and debt issued, an investor could always achieve his preferred level of risk by buying the securities in the proportions issued, borrowing to buy more shares or debt, and achieving through "homemade leverage" his private desired combination of debt and equity. But to hold true the "proof" required you to borrow at the same rate that the corporation paid on its bonds. The central flaw was that no one would loan you money at the corporate bond rate if you pledged any number of shares along with the corporate debt. The extra shares in the pledge account made it riskier than the bonds. Hence, the homemade leverage argument was a nonstarter, unless someone on the other side of the transaction was an idiot. Joe Stiglitz once told me when I was visiting for a semester at Yale that in his paper "proving" the M-M theorem, he at first had all the results going the other way, but changed them in proofs at the very last minute to the form that was published. As Yogi Berra once said, "When you come to a fork in the road, take it." I wonder if Joe is still taking forks in the road.

Eventually, Mert Miller, Joe Stiglitz, and their fellow travelers conceded the war without acknowledging defeat in any of its battles. They proclaimed from the rooftops that the M-M theorem was correct given its assumptions, but that the theorem ignored bankruptcy, and if bankruptcy and its costs were admitted, it changed the results. Still not quite right. Full-blown bankruptcy isn't required, only risk of default on debt so that you don't recover all of the interest or principal on the bonds. This is not rocket science; it's just simple common sense.

Then, there was George Horwich, a really good and steady friend. His early work was in monetary theory. Contrary to what many thought, his elaborate diagrams were definitely not dirty pictures. George has made quite a reputation in his "retirement" years working in the economics of catastrophes: the recovery process after major disasters such as earthquakes and floods.

John Hughes arrived in 1956, after I did. He had finished his D.Phil. at Oxford and taken a job at the Federal Reserve Bank of New York. New York was heaven for his wife, Mary Gray Hughes. She is the only person I have known from Brownsville, Texas, but I'll bet there are few, if any, others who acquired an English accent. She loved England, where she and John met, and she took on some English ways, including a little of the tongue. For her, the next best place was New York City, NY, but they lasted only one year there. John could not tolerate his New York Federal Reserve Bank boss blue-penciling all his papers. Em made him an offer and to Purdue they came.

The first year they lived in an area of large old houses over the Wabash on the Lafayette side of the river. Then, they bought a farmhouse north of Montmorenci, a little country town not far from West Lafayette. At the time, the "consolidation" movement was leading to a surplus of farm homes because northern Indiana was well stocked with big combines for harvesting hundreds of acres of corn or soybeans. The revolution whose start I recounted above in Chapter 4—the highway combine trains—was still in process. That meant that the land from three farms might be combined into one farm, which was more economical, given the productivity relative to the cost of the combine and other machinery innovations. That left two surplus houses to be sold or torn down.

John loved the country. As a professor he sometimes worked at home, but he would go into Montmorenci at odd times during weekdays. He said this meant that to the local citizens he was like "the town fool—no visible means of support." His house was on a highway, and once when I was out there, I noticed he had a couple of new cats. He said, "Yes, if you live on a highway, you have to have lots of cats." He also raised two St. Bernard dogs—two because the first one was killed on the highway. Mary Gray was good at offbeat names: Gerhardt and Ulrich were the names of the St. Bernards, and the Cocker Spaniel was Ahab. Ulrich, at 180 pounds, could take out half a cake—resting dog-head high on a table—with one swipe of his giant tongue. He once got through the fence to John's garden and ate tomatoes, cantaloupe, and other produce, whether ripe or green, seeds, membranes, and all.

At one point, John's water well stopped functioning. A new pump was not enough. A new well had to be drilled, so he called a driller and got an estimate, and the driller brought his drilling rig out. He looked around and asked John where he wanted it drilled. John said, "I don't know anything about where to drill for water. That is why I am hiring a driller." The guy said, "Well, OK, but have you had your land divined?" (Divining is the "art" of walking over the land with the forked branch of a tree or bush, a fork in each hand, and stopping when one sees the correct bending motion of the branch, indicating the location of water below ground.) John said, "No, I don't believe in that magic stuff." The driller replied, "Neither do I, but it can't hurt."

John had an endless supply of narratives born of his direct experience: running the rapids of Idaho's Bruneau River after World War II, the fly-fishing so good that you could catch trout in the morning without getting out of your sleeping bag; playing jazz clarinet at age sixteen in Fish Haven, Idaho, and in Wells and Elko, Nevada, on Friday and Saturday nights when the miners and cowboys were in town to party and visit the whorehouses; telling Dick Easterlin, the economic historian who studied Western migration patterns, and who wondered why there were so many "seamstresses" in all those Western towns, "Dick, they were hookers, not seamstresses. What the hell were they supposed to report as their employment?"; or overhearing the British economic historian Eric Jones tell a German visitor at Purdue, who was lagging behind the others in a group hike through the Indiana countryside, "No wonder you chaps lost the war." One of my favorites stemmed from a summer that John had worked as an accountant for an Alaskan fish cannery. At the season's end, the "half-Eskimo" night watchman was removing all the locks and chains from the lockers and supply rooms. "Why are you removing all the security locks?" The answer, "Locks and chains are not needed now that the Christians are gone." His cannery boss referred to the Eskimo (among several Alaskan Native groups) as "n-----s." John protested, but it made no difference. He said the guy had a simple dichotomy that covered every person in this world: You were either white or a n-----.

But the best way for you to get to know John is for me to quote some excerpts from his letters to me. I have few copies of letters that I wrote to John so I have no systematic record of the interaction. In January 2015, I wrote to John's son (January 21, 2015), Benjamin Acosta-Hughes, Professor and Chair of the Department of Classics at Ohio State University asking if he knew what happened to John's correspondence. He replied "I don't know what became of my father's correspondence: my mother handled the deposition of his office(s) and his papers after his death, and I know none of this came to us on her sudden death in 1999. The best person to ask would be Joel Mokyr at the Northwestern University Economics dept. I will write to him and will get back to you."

Fortunately, after some investigation, the matter was resolved on March 5, 2015, when Benjamin wrote:

"I finally heard back from Utah State: apparently my mother donated these to Northwestern shortly after my father's death."

John and I were very close, and this is evident in our correspondence: I have about 80 pages of letters from him (available at the Duke Archives of my papers); written when he was away visiting Oxford; when I was a summer consultant at the Rand Corporation; visiting at Stanford; etc. I am sure there are many more in the Duke Archives. Most of them are in typescript but some are handwritten. They are a historical treasure of academic life at Purdue, Oxford, and Northwestern with running commentary on high-profile historical events as they played out in current history.

Here are excerpts from many of these letters.

June 10, 1957 [with Joyce and the children I am at the Rand Corporation for the summer, as a consultant.]

"All goes well here. I have only one more section to write and we will have finished off the first 2000 steamships. Big hassle as to where it ought to be sent. It has too much statistics for JEH [Journal of Economic History]. Stan wants to put it in the JASA [Journal of the American Statistical Association] but that would be casting pearls before swine in my opinion. We must decide on some compromise. If I thought there was a chance I would try the JES. [John must mean Review of Economics and Statistics, RES] But I wonder if it isn't necessary to be Seymour Harris's brother-in-law to get into it? Anyhow, it sure is a good little article. [John's opinion was an understaement: JASA is where it was published as "The First 1,945 Steamships" and it became a landmark contribution to the new field of Cliometrics.]

November 18, 1961 [I am visiting at Stanford]

Well Leontief was here and it all appeared to go off all right. I went with a group to lunch and managed to keep the conversation on fishing [and off Harvard since open fawning would doubtless have nauseated Leontief...]... He should have enjoyed the place a bit. Rubin, Lance and Quirk have some new cliometrica going, an input-output table for USA before the civil war... Leontief gave a paper on the theoretical structure of his regional studies. He is a very deft lecturer, but a real lecturer, nothing informal. You would have been amazed at the turnout. We had to move out of the downstairs room up to the big auditorium. Hell there must have been 200 people...

On a day like this, old Chappy, you can have California. I am sitting here watching the first snowfall. It has snowed about two inches since last night and I've got my corn shocked and the snow is on the shocks with the birds flitting about looking for kernels. There isn't any wind and the flakes come down lazily, sort of floating. I was out wrestling big Ulrich earlier. He likes to be thrown down and covered up with snow.

> *Purdue!*
> *Fairest in the Fields*
> *Our train still runs*
> *The corn still yields.*

I'm sort of hung over this morning as a result of a party over at Rosenberg's last night. We left at midnight—thank God—just as Harley Flanders was getting warmed up (I had already gagged him to stop him from reciting all of Beowulf) and it seems that he gave a one man, unaccompanied rendition of all but two of the Gilbert and Sullivan operas, singing all arias, recitativo's, tuttis etceteras himself. Since he has a voice like a bullfrog with bronchitis it must have been quite a show. Nate said that Mrs Eissinger picked up her husband, marbles, etc., and went home after Nate couldn't "stop that horrid man's singing" Harley's debut in local music circles went on nonstop until 3 A.M, when he was dragged kicking and screaming into the snowstorm still going strong. Jesus what a complete madman. I'm serving a new drink these days. Fill a tumbler with cognac and light it on fire. It's called a "Flanders." Love to Joyce. A Happy Thanksgiving to the kids.

In order to properly balance John's narrative account, I should inform the reader that Harley Flanders was a brilliant young mathematician married at the time to a first-rate economist, June Flanders (1927–2017, "Mother, grandmother and great-grandmother Professor of economics, photographer and actress").

They moved to Israel and June later became head of the economics department at Tel Aviv. Genius is sometimes packaged with what John calls "madness." No one knew that better than John.

April 29, 1962

I'm so far behind on everything that I feel like surrendering. Anyhow, since I can't, I'll try to catch up. First, I saw your article in the JPE [my first experimental paper]. It is great to see it in print after three years. Mark my words, that article is going to make a real stir boy. I guess it already has in fact because someone told me you had got an NSF grant to keep it up. [NSF funding for me started in 1962—over the objection of several referees, I was told. Howard Hines, head of social science at NSF, once told me that NSF support was only possible because they had the flexibility to overrule opinions obviously hostile toward experimental methods, and they did.]

The new building for the school has been announced. We will all look like slick magazine executives now. I don't know whether Purdue is going to be as much fun now that we are travelling in style. The rest of the deal for the K. [Krannert] School of Industrial Administration will be announced in June. Weiler pinpointed how much we've got to change our ways by pointing out that we've literally pissed away about $200,000 so far by only completing two PhD's out of 10 old candidates...

My work is grinding along. I'm working on Carnegie now and hope to get one other besides him, possibly Whitney, done before I go across the water. [John is referring to his manuscript, The Good Land; published under the title, The Vital Few; The Entrepreneur and American Economic Progress. John's monumental study has now been in print for 53 years] That will only leave Edison, Ford and Harriman to do. It is just an enormous book. We have now settled on about 2,000,000 words, or more than double the first estimate. I'm not being particularly long-winded, it just has grown into a big fat book and that's all there is to it. I still have every hope of being done by mid-October which is when things begin across the water.

MG is leaving on 12 July. She is due in early September. I've got the professor of obstetrics to do the delivery so all ought to be as smooth as possible.

August 8, 1962

...I am writing on my new Olivetti portable. It will take some getting used to.

Well England does not resemble the England I knew at all so far as the physical arrangements go. The prosperity is just bursting out in every direction and I have wondered if the net effect of the Socialism of my day was not just to hold this back. It is perfectly clear that the carrot is much more effective than "fair shares."

...I must say that I don't feel any kindlier towards it than I ever did, and that was not very kindly. I thought it an insidious place, pretentious, phony and so forth. The intellectual standards are great but those are, after all, only a small part of Oxford and they don't apply to many people, only the good ones, marked out early to try for "firsts". I think that the much vaunted political activity around here amongst both the students and the faculty is largely a device to get out of work for the second raters of both ranks.

One of the main notions that keeps going through my mind is "What in hell are we doing here?" The only answer I can think of is change for its own sake. Since I am an American I suppose that makes sense. I went into Nuffield yesterday to check into my office space and I must say that it is poshy beyond my wildest dreams! When I was here they were still building it. Now that it is finished, with its cut stone, leaded windows, carved wood, tailored lawns and all, the only thing I can think of is "money." Each college has its coat of arms. I told the secretary that Nuffield coat of arms ought to be simply a £1 note and let it go at that. She didn't quite laugh. Stan saw the place so he knows what I'm talking about...

The trip over was uneventful, as was my stay in New York...My publisher and I see eye to eye about most of the book and the rest will just have to be fought over. I saw Bob Lindsay [A senior economist and chief of domestic research at the Federal Reserve Bank of New York from 1954 to 1964; Bob and I were classmates at Harvard; he also finished his PhD at Harvard in 1955.] in his plush office, with the carpet, carafe, pen set, clock—the whole drill. He makes a splendid big shot and I was so impressed by the quality of his mahogany desk that I refused to put my feet on it even though he had his feet on it and didn't think a thing of it.

August 14, 1962

Nuffield is an astonishing place. There are 20 faculty, a few "visitors" like me, and 40 students. All housed in a multi-million dollar college with kitchen, dining hall, chapel, several lounges, a beer garden, a library, servant catering—the whole lot. It is lavish out of all reason. There is but one secretary available to the faculty (she probably can't type, although I'm not sure of that), there are no "supplies," the "computing room" consists of one hand-driven calculator, two electric ones, a typewriter, a 9 button adding machine, hand-driven. In short, the whole thing is the opposite of Purdue. This is a place designed for "gentlemen" and leisure. It would be very difficult to really pour out the work here. If the Purdue hotshots were installed at Nuffield they would tear it apart, literally, at the seams. Purdue is organized for work, on the assumption that the faculty have homes to go to, and homes in which they would prefer to do their entertaining.

...The fact that the colleges are organized for leisure instead of work is a hangover from the days of the monastery. I don't suppose it will ever change. I find that the idea of this college being England's great center of Social Sciences is slightly absurd. Good work comes out of Oxford, but it is partly in spite of the college system rather than because of it. In my own case that was absolutely true. It was only by not having anything to do with the college excepting using it as a hotel that I was able to do my work here.

September 13, 1962

...Clower [Robert] is here...this term...I spent a couple of hours with him yesterday (he is also at Nuffield). He naturally offered me a job. I think we ought to hire him. I'm sure Weiler would go along if he accepted. Anymore when two American economists meet, they first try to hire each other, and then they ask about the wife and kids...

I have been canvassing for talent here and have already turned up... an American, Cliff Lloyd [In time we would hire him at Purdue.] He is a theorist (micro) trying to do a D. Phil under Hicks. He was Clower's student once at Northwestern, has...already published a little bit. Is in the market for next year...Clower likes him, offered him a job...

On Monday I'm going to Birmingham to see the people there to find out about their management program. I'll send a memo to Em and he can decide if we ought to have an international subsidiary there. Birmingham is known among the few who think here is a place where there is some intellectual curiosity. Alan Walters seems to be the coming noise there now. [Alan subsequently visited for a year at Purdue; became Sir Alan Walters, and special advisor to Margret Thatcher in Downing Street; in 1989 he advised successfully against Britain joining the European Exchange Rate Mechanism that evolved into the euro, a magnificent decision in the light of subsequent history; Alan died January 3, 2009 at age 82.]

We are fine. About two weeks to go, two of MG's doctors think it is twins. She has 4 (four) obstetricians! You know "Socialized Medicine," where there is no doctor-patient relationship!

September 15, 1962

Would you pass the following information on to: Reiters, Ameses, Saposniks, and McDougall's and anyone else...

MG had twins last night. They are fine. The girls look like carbon copies of MG and her mother...That is the family. Two for the price of one, and now MG and I can get out of what is clearly a kid's game and settle into a comfortable middle age. Brrrr. Pregnancy should be entered into before 30, or so it appears to me, a helpless, if not completely innocent bystander...

MG looks like she had 10 rounds with Joe Louis last night. One breech and one with instruments. Labor time just under four hours.

O.K. now our vacation year in England—together—can begin. [John is not being sarcastic; they will hire nannies]...I needn't tell you two what the last two weeks of sweating out twins was like. MG looked increasingly like a barrage balloon. [Except that Joyce, her doctor and I had no warning that twins were coming; in our day if the doctor could not pick up a second heartbeat, you did not know in advance whether you had twins or a boy with a big bag of water.]

September 28, 1962

...One twin is still in the hospital and ought to be out next week.

The other one is home now and is a real doll. I was amused to see the old sibling rivalry in Benjamin. It is mixed of course with other things, but he obviously is not to be trusted alone with his little sisters for awhile. He might just accidentally push one or both into the fire. Now is the time when our being in England pays off. I have a full time nurse for the little girls. I have engaged her for six weeks. She costs us £8-8-0 or $32.52 a week in wages. She is with us all the time and with the nurse, for a total labor outlay of say $250 for six weeks...

Little BBH is a lot of fun. He is in school! At two years of age, so help me he goes every day to a nursery school and "plays with the boys and girls." The other day he promoted himself into the pre-schooler class...He is also pig headed as hell...

Nuffield College...(is) lavish...But in the older colleges, well it's strictly Louis XIV and is just criminal, but nice. By God Vernon, liveried waiters and footmen, fine wines, superb cuisine. Whiskey in the senior Common room after dinner (after the coffee). After desert comes the port and nuts. All carried off in the medieval manner with the chaps wearing their gowns and all. It isn't part of this world but us hard working Hoosiers ought to get to enjoy a bit of it before the Bolsheviks come and sweep it all away.

October 3, 1962

...I am following the events in Mississippi aghast. [Southern segregationists were protesting the enrollment of James Meridith, black US Military veteran at the University of Mississippi; two killed some 70 wounded.] Who is replacing Morrissett and Rosenberg? [John is referring to faculty activists on racial issues with some exaggeration shall we say?] I presume they have gone off to enlist. This is what they've been straining for, Federal troops in the Deep South. OK, now what? If that poor bastard [James Meridith] is alive in a month he'll be lucky.

If he gets an "education" at Ole Miss it will be a miracle in more ways than one. I don't know what he could learn even if he weren't surrounded by an armed bodyguard. Without the bodyguard I wouldn't think his skin would be worth much. Oxford [Mississippi] isn't a very large town, and my suggestion is to turn it into a permanent garrison. It will be a lot cheaper than finally pulling the troops out and having a slaughter. I hope they put that damned governor in Fort Leavenworth and let him rot there. God knows how many will die over this (at this time the toll is two). Anyhow now that the army is there, they may as well stay. I presume that no hearts in Mississippi are going to suddenly turn liberal and law abiding out of gratitude for a military occupation. Hence, now that the fire has been stirred up good it seem to me that it is the Federal government's obligation to the citizens, both black and white, to protect them from the reign of terror what will come if the soldiers leave. Did you read about the arms taken out of cars and off guys trying to get into Oxford?

Jesus. Why don't people try to find out a little about southerners...The deed is done now...So I hope to hell they stay in Oxford for good. Call it Fort Oxford and let it go at that...

One grand piece of entertainment was General Walker. It looks like he's done for now, they're going to give him a psychiatric examination. The tailors might just as well start cutting his Napoleon suit.[2]

We will get our other twin home in a couple of days. BBH is acting up a little bit. But it is not because of the baby so much as the disruption. Our nannie turns out to be a nitwit and I think that upsets him. You know friendly one minute, wild the next. We'll fire her a mile high just as soon as MG has her strength back. She is making a good recovery but will need a couple of more weeks.

My work is going grand and I want to get back to it right now, so I'll sign off.

---

[2]If you are unfamiliar with the tragic events John is writing about, and the polarization of people on segregation issues, see: http://partners.nytimes.com/library/national/race/100262race-ra.html.

October 6, 1962

...I am at work on Edison now, so the whole damned business will be wrapped up in a couple of months. I won't know how to act on a sane time schedule again...I should have been an electrical engineer, I was able to deduce a workable definition of Ohm's Law by looking up volts, amperes and Ohms in the Oxford dictionary! Not bad eh? I am now reading [John] Jewkes on innovations and find it stimulating as hell. [It is; John got me to read John Jeweks, The Sources of Invention, 1958. I did, and it is a great study of 19th and 20th century innovation.] He is sort of an outcast around here because he is a conservative [sic, classical liberal—did the Brits then know the difference?] I'll arrange to have lunch with him and flatter him a bit. It ought to be good for his ego.

Today is election day at home. My only hope is that Tricky Dick [Richard Nixon] gets clobbered. But I wouldn't bet on it. The bastard has always been able to get votes in California.

...We're ready to come home now. But there are still seven months to go. Damn! As I told Weiler, ten minutes with Lance Davis is more intellectual stimulation than I've received here. Perhaps we've got to be English to find Oxford stimulating. I find it backward, careless, provincial and boring. Still, the countryside is beautiful next week we will go to London for some Ballet.

October 11, 1962

I am now working on Edison and that is the end of the book. Meanwhile, for the edification of the English, I am going to give the opening Nuffield economics seminar paper. (They have a college seminar, which is possible because there are no Lances here wrecking it all with irresponsible guerila action). I have chosen as my title "The Economics of Henry Ford" which will give them education in several different ways. I am taking out a couple of days right now to write the paper. I hate to give papers, but it is the only way one can have any impact in a short time. I could whip several of these out of the book. In fact, I have now agreed with J.R. Hicks to give a "public lecture" in the spring term. For that I have chosen "Economic Development–The American Example". In that I am going to point out that the most efficient development that ever occurred was capitalism operating within an open society characterized by individual liberty. Around here that is revolutionary information. A public lecture is fun because of all the formality. Nevertheless, I'm glad to do it because this book has a lot of important stuff in it, as you know. By the way, the publisher now thinks we can get the Pulitzer Prize. Ha! Not without footnotes. If they'd let me spray it with a minimum of ibids and op cits we'd be in business.

October 23, 1962

For two cents I'd abandon ship and fly us home today. Kennedy just announced the Cuba blockade. I don't know if this is an election gimmick or that he really didn't think that the Russians were building missile sites there.

Am I just simple Vernon? I have always assumed that the Russian were in Cuba to put up missile bases, just as I have always assumed that the Russian space and nuclear experiments were for military purposes only. I mean man they ain't got any other purposes. Well I don't know what Kennedy does to the Russians but he sure scares hell out of me. The thing is that there is more to come. A blockade is no solution to the problem...The argument that the Russians are only doing it because of our effort is totally ridiculous. I suppose even India has been able to figure out what the communists of Russia and China are up to. It will probably even reach West Lafayette, Indiana in a few months. I would rather be vaporized at home than over here...

I always said that if I lived to be 25 I'd be satisfied. That was when WW II was on and a lot of my friends were not living to see their 18th birthdays. I would still hold to that. The trouble is that you'd like your kids to live to 25 too. That makes you greedy...

October 24, 1962

Wow, I just heard that Khrushchev has asked for a parley with Kennedy... Has this ever been a nervous three days for us. I don't know how the Cuba matter will now be settled, and it is clear that Kennedy wants those bases out of there. The Russians have got a negotiating point with that fait accompli so it is possible that we'll do some horse-trading about it all. It is one hell of a world, but you've got to live in it, you can't just put your head in the sand. That is what India did and now the Chinese have got them by the throat. I should think that even the blind can now see that any policy besides the one we've followed would now have us sitting ducks under a bunch of Russian missiles. Hell no wonder they've been stalling at Geneva. The clever bastards just about got the whole farm. They've got some of it now, but with fully installed bases there our "deterrent" would have been posthumous. I had assumed right along that they were building missile bases, but I hadn't thought of the difference between "defensive" and the kind they have in fact been building,

I suppose that we'll all survive and live to joke about these last three days. But it has sure been a strain. Three kids, two of them infants, isolated in a foreign country, with an odd-even chance of ending up some kind of undesirable alien... In case of Nuclear War, Britain, full of bases is not a place where one would do too much calculating about survival unless the British government bugged out, and to my astonishment they came right out and backed Kennedy. Then the French and the Germans followed suit. I hope Americans remember that. But it has been wild, man, just sitting here in front of this radio listening about those two bunches of ships converging and knowing, as I do, that the Americans are willing to go to war, the whole hog, over this thing. That, after all, is the reason we got to be a free and independent country in the first place. I have never been impressed with the hysterical academics because I know too many "ordinary" people at home and they have been just as determined about this thing as ever they were during World War II. I would sit around Purdue last year listening to all the "let's be reasonable and surrender" talk and then go out to Cyclone Hill and talk to my neighbors and realize that I live in two sep-

arate and distinct worlds in Lafayette, the academic one and the real one. Out in the country no one feared the Russians. In town not only were the Russians nine feet high but you got the impression that some people yearned to feel the Soviet whip across their backs.

It is all so damned corny. But it is just true, in this world it seems that if you aren't prepared to die for your freedom you can't have it. Not that it has been any compensation, but I have amused myself thinking about certain people I know in Lafayette who were all for "using military force" in the South to integrate the schools, who must have been singing an hysterically different tune these last two days about using force in Cuba.

Well I don't know if we're out of the woods on this. But there is hope to night and there wasn't much last night. Love to Joyce, it looks like we'll meet again after all.

[Well, John, we got out of those woods clean, because we manage to muddle through. But 53 years later the press and the public have sweated through the first year of the Trump Presidency—the candidate who could not win. Confrontations on race, immigration, drug use, and war with North Korea have continued, but are less unsettling than your graphic, grim and accurate reports from October-December, 1962. Cuba continues to wallow in unnecessary poverty, and North Korea can barely feed itself. Venezuela cannot feed itself, and is one of the richest nations in oil reserves. They all have only one problem—no freedom—and constitute proof of the proposition that where there is no freedom little is left for life.

December 6, 1962

Tonight I am dining at Merton College with John Jewkes...He is a complete outcast here and I have never been able to find out just why. I hold to my first re-impressions of Oxford and the system....you ought to come here, or to Cambridge and experience these medieval splendors before someone seizes them in the name of the people. It is a real land of make-believe, the dons in there gowns, the table groaning with food and wine by candle-light. The port and nuts afterward in the common room. It is just like, it is, a scene out of C. P. Snow...

Since, as you know, I am a man of conscience, I cannot fully enjoy these evenings of debauch knowing that poor Mary Gray is in our freezing-cold little home battling three babes to bed. Still I grit my teeth and carry on, in the higher interests of science, culture and scholarship. We are just now having fantastically vicious weather. We've had a freezing fog most of the week which has snarled old England up from one end to the other. In London visibility for several night has been down to 5 yards and the streets are apparently strewn with abandoned automobiles...

I talked awhile with Frank Fisher this afternoon. He is over here from Holland, where I take it he is making the usual pilgrimage to Theil. He said that when he stepped ashore the English immigration officer asked him what his business in England was. When he said he was a tourist, the guy looked at him incredulously and said: "Are you mad?"

I got J. R. Hicks to read Davis, Hughes and MacDougal. He seemed to like it, but complained and I quote "The thing about the earlier chapters that makes me a bit nervous is the amount of use you make of these 'macro' figures over long periods. I should have liked a little more warning than I found of the index-number troubles that are involved in such comparisons." What can I say to him? It isn't really fair to our readers, after having eliminated, explicitly, all tools of historical analysis except economic theory itself to add, "oh yeah, we're not sure of the facts either!" The poor devils would never know what to believe. We leave it to people like Hicks to know that none of us knows what in hell he is talking about. The students have to believe <u>something</u> in order to be "educated."

Right?...

We are all well enough. The twins are thriving. We would have been down to London to the Ballet again except for the fog. We will go there next week just to bum around. I want to hit the bookstores again. On the last trip I got an eight volume <u>Pepys Diary</u> for £2-2-0. That was damn near worth the trip over here. I have still to make any interesting buys in old Economics books. It looks like too damn many American economists have been over here on sabbatical leaves and have cleaned it all out.

December 31. 1962

Happy New Year. Tonight will be a big party somewhere in New Athens and a good time by all...I ended 1962 by delivering my manuscript to a typist. I could have done it 10 days ago but couldn't find anyone who would take my money. It is gigantic and I'm having it typed in pica type (script) and on English paper. The result will probably be a 1200 page typescript and cause my publisher to faint. It has been a long, long grind but there is something awfully nice, as you know, in the feeling you have when you wrap up a big piece of work. There is always a terrible letdown and a feeling of being lost afterwards, but it is better to keep grinding out different things than staying on the same one all one's life. Anyhow, I'm glad I wrote this book. I've got a lot of things said that I wanted to say. It will make me a lot of enemies I fear since people like me are getting fewer in the profession, those who really do prefer to see the economy as a mirror of its people's lives instead of a blacksnake whip directing their lives. The government should do its part of course, but it won't get any more output than its people will produce. A lot of people forget that...

There has been a great change in things since the Cuba crisis and I can't pretend that I comprehend it all. On the face of it now it would appear that the tide has turned on an enormous scale in our favor. But I think perhaps that in the past the Russians have really won <u>all</u> the hands and so we got a pair of kings and it looked like a royal flush...

January 18, 1963

...I have been working on my public lecture, which is essentially a big hairy thing on methodology. I am trying to work out the advantages of studying the past through conceptual categories like mine as opposed to the chronological stages. The differences are interesting but are not even obvious to me until I sweat over them. This is typical I think. I have written this book with ease, but it is terribly difficult to explain in a critical way what I've done, to turn intuition

into formal methodology. I'm reminded of Horwich's retort to Reiter one day at lunch after Reiter proved that none of us knew what we were doing methodology-wise. George said "All right, I don't know what I am doing. But I'm right!"

In 1966, John and Mary Grey moved to Northwestern, living in Evanston. We talked more often by phone than via letters.

November 15, 1966

Northwestern has a lot to say for it as a place to work. But Mainly Evanston is a lovely place to live and the schools are better than we had hoped for or even imagined. That part of our decision to sell Cyclone Hill and move up here was certainly sound. I could stay here happily for life I think. The town is just lovely, although it is hellishly expensive. We live like millionaires, whether we want to or not.

My hope of "retiring" here from the academic rat race has been dashed. I was put on the Personnel Committee, more or less against my wishes. And as a result I have been involved in my share of Warfare here. I regret this. You know how Northwestern has always worked, who is big, (make offers) and who can you get from Harvard, MIT and Chicago (make offers). For this sort of operation they don't need me on the committee. By Purdue standards Northwestern does this sort of thing completely "blind." I wouldn't care if I weren't on the committee. But being on the committee I've had to make suggestions, stand up for them and all. You can easily guess the results. It has been something like having all of my Purdue battles in a three-month period...

Some of the colleagues are delightful...Irma Adelman is a splendid economist, some of the younger men are very able, and some of the older ones congenial. I miss my old Purdue colleagues a good deal. But the past cannot be relived, and was well over with by the time we left. It was a grand experience though...

September 1, 1978

I have just finished my paper for the SEA meetings in DC. In it I raise the issue, yet again, about the government. This time from the viewpoint of the private entrepreneur, and what the hell kind of future this economy can have with that force reduced to arbitrage. [John is referring to my letter using the term tax arbitrage—actions that enable a company to make a profit from tax incentives without generating any new productive service. For example, Jim Tobin in those days had sold the policy idea that investment could be stimulated by an investment tax credit up to a maximum of 7% of the cost of the capital goods purchased. So a company A, whose business—insurance—required little in the way of capital goods, could not benefit from the tax subsidy; another company, B—an airline—could not benefit beyond the 7% limit. So A would invest in a Boeing 727, take the investment credit, and lease the airliner to B. The lease price enables each company to share the increased *after-tax profit, but no net value is produced for consumers. You don't create new wealth by inducing people to profit from tax savings by moving money from one pocket to another. I mentioned this example once to Jim Tobin; his response was that "the policy works."] Have you read Israel Kirzner's book on entrepreneurship? ... the entrepreneurial role is not Schumpeter's ... more like Stanley's sharks in the sharks and flounders paper [John refers here to the Purdue School of Industrial Management Working Paper #1 (1959): "A Market Adjustment Mechanism"]....*

I spent ten days at the Buchanan and Tullock show in Blacksburg ... one of three speakers. The other two speakers were [Bill] Niskanen, whose views of government make me sound like an optimist. But he is prepared to do something, a whole lot of things, about it. ... Tullock reminds me of Ed Ames, so god damn smart he thinks up the decisive counter example to his own argument before he makes it. ... Our old student from Purdue, Paul Rubin, was one of the participants. He was very good. ... Buchanan ... is an intellectually honest and honorable man. I find that impressive after the bitter cynics I've spent so much of my career with, those and wise guys.

I wonder if all this conservative stuff I've been around these past months adds up to anything? [John's publication of The Governmental Habit led to an unaccustomed surge in conference invitations.] Most of them are as muddled (not the ones in Blacksburg) as the lefties one ordinarily meets [or what John called the "totalitarian liberals"]. I don't know what Howard Jarvis is, most likely a shady character. ... It is the simplicity of his view that matters. "You take money from A and give it to B. Why? Shouldn't A have something to say about it? Let's ask him." Man did that approach to public finance ever ring a bell! We were over to Galbraith's for lunch, and Mary Gray asked him what did he think about Proposition 13. He said: "Mass hysteria." You don't ask the great man hurtful questions. But the obvious question is: "Why do you think the people have become hysterical?"

September 19, 1978

In my opinion our real problem with government comes down to two factors:

1. The urge to redistribute.
2. The belief that government spending is "better" than private spending.

As I see it the really effective way to reduce the government is to counter these two. Nothing else is going to work. I don't believe appeals to personal freedom—libertarian arguments—can get enough votes.

May 20, 1979

Today Stan and I made the trek down to Lafayette to say goodbye to Em [Weiler]. A sad occasion, but, always the gentleman, he made it easy for us.

He introduced immediately the awkward fact that he will soon be dead, and that his time is now extremely limited. Honest to God but he made a pleasant conversation of it. What a class guy, right to the end.

Just as we were ready to go he thanked us for our years on the faculty and for what we all did there. He then embraced both of us and he said goodbye. Just like that.

We were with him a bit more than half an hour. I watched a friend of mine go from Hodgkins disease some years ago. On that basis I would say a week. But it is hard to tell for a layman who has only watched one person go from cancer. Em is pretty well wasted away now, but still bright and in control of all his mental facilities.

He says that he is ready. That he has had an active life, made the most of it while he had it, and has few regrets. He is extremely pleased that he is leaving Cathy well fixed, and with all in order. He joked a bit about leaving the IRS with some problems trying to rob them.

I was thinking, looking at the other two, and thinking of myself, that it really hasn't been all that long. Life really is pretty short. He is proud of what we all did, and the way the old Purdue influence has spread out and carried on. It really was touching as hell. It made me feel pretty good about the accomplishment there as well as all the fun we had in the midst of all the pain and trouble.

Em always was in a position to see it differently from the rest of us. He was the quarterback, and we were the ones carrying the ball and doing the blocking and tackling.

All the way back we reminisced about the entire experience, each from his own perspective. None of us saw it the same way, obviously. We each mainly saw the others through the dust of our own work. I never regretted the time I spent there, and the way it affected the rest of my career. I've done more since I left Purdue, than I did when I was there. But that is partly due to the fact that what I learned there was so damned forceful when I came to apply it elsewhere, with other people and other problems. ...

For me the biggest use I made of Em himself was when I was chairman here. I did it just like he instructed me there when I was Chairman of the policy committee—decide what you are going to do, and then go ahead and do it. Don't just sit. I laughed a good deal about my "dictatorial" methods. Stan did the same cut with MEDS (Management, Economics and Decision Sciences in the Kellogg School at Northwestern).

So it goes on. Em is, was, a complex person to me. I didn't figure him out today—my last chance—and I never figured him out before either. He was terribly hurt when I left Purdue, but I didn't know he would be! Well, God rest him. [Deidre McClosky has said that for a decade Purdue had the best economics department in the world.]

August 2, 1979

Mary Gray called me the night you told her that Em had died. I'm glad the Festschrift [Essays in Contemporary Fields of Economics In Honor of Emanuel T. Weiler, edited by George Horwich and James P. Quirk, Purdue University Press, 1979] is well along. It will be a nice tribute and a reminder of what we *did. I don't know about the rest, but the Purdue experience gave me enough food for thought to last the rest of my days. When I became Chairman at Northwestern I moved the place, fast. By the time the departmental deadbeats could get together an opposition, the job was done. I operated just like Weiler, as near as I could. Stan did essentially the same thing with MEDS and by the time we were retired back to "civilian life" NW was on the map in economics as something more than just an outpost. If I ever had to do it again, I could.*

Most guys in academic life have no idea what it takes to move a place, people ... look at Don Jacobs [Dean of the Kellogg School] at NW. Hell, he wouldn't be anyone's idea of a Dean. But look what he has done! Most academics want the quiet life, and I do too, when I can get it. [Bullshit. John had a dream about getting it, but his urges were its constant enemy, down to the last.] But silence is no way to build. Old Weiler was like Henry Ford, movement, movement, keep it moving, don't let it rest.

Well, he meant a great deal to some of us. When I last saw him there was still that unspoken understanding there always was. It wasn't true, I guess, of his dealings with everyone. There were people at Purdue who hated him, and some who came to know how wrong they had been, too. The trouble is that life only goes 'round once, and a lot of things can't be re-run that mattered.

Like it was yesterday, I recall when Em Weiler was selected as dean of the newly minted School of Industrial Administration, later the Krannert School, a position and program sought aggressively by two schools: Agriculture and Engineering. With the president's backing, he beat out the two most powerful schools at Purdue, either one of which would have blown the opportunity big time. At the end of his brutal first year as dean, he told me it had been the most difficult of his life, but that if you could count on only one supporter for your program, you wanted that to be the president; it was Hovde, a Purdue innovator who did many unpopular things—such as to create the Engineering Science program over powerful internal objections. The program became absolutely first rate; it attracted the best students who got the best offers, and that competition galvanized all the other engineering programs into major upgrades.

February 4, 1980

When I decided to see if Mary Gray would marry me it was a very self-centered decision. I had finally found a woman who was in all ways congenial to me, and I feared that she would drift off and I would never find another. Women were one thing; a wife something else. Time proved the wisdom then hidden in my young brain. I trust she doesn't regret it. Here we are 26 years and many hard blows later, still, for the most part congenial.

The bliss, with us, lasted a long time. About bliss, my big brother said something wise last summer. We had a big family reunion on my mother's 80th *birthday. My brother was in the middle of his 3rd divorce. His first wife was, as mother and grandmother, invited and came up from Utah. She was in the process of leaving her 6th husband for the second time. My brother was her first. For both of them nothing had been like that first marriage. Anyhow, someone asked my brother if she still looked as good to him as she did in 1945? He thought about that for awhile, and answered slowly, "Nothing ever looked that good again." That's how it goes with bliss. For most people it is only once around. One pities only those who never experienced it!*

April 21, 1982

I meant to write to you about the paper you sent to me summarizing the results of experimental economics. As they say, from little acorns mighty oak trees grow. You'll probably get a Nobel Prize for experimental economics, but many moons from now, when you're so old you won't remember it, or maybe even your name. That seems to be the way we work in Economics.

October 3, 1984

NU is a fine place to work, always was. But you can't build and hold a department here. We were really going to town, then Strotz decided to get back his deficit from faculty salaries. He was reported to have said, "Where will they go?" Answer:

Truman Bewley--Yale
Kip Viskusi--Duke
Mark Pauly--Penn
Marc Nerlove--Penn
Mike Scherer--Swarthmore
Betsy Hoffman--Purdue

And there were more. We got creamed in about 3 years, when the salaries fell behind. Moreover, it is still going on. Even Cornell is trying to get Mortensen and Domowitz. We lost people to Stanford too, out of MEDS. But Stanford more or less can have anyone they want, like Harvard. So anyhow, Stan and I worked for ten years building NU's department, and it was blown away in three years or so...

May 24, 1989

I am doing just fine with my recovery from surgery, and am taking my chemotherapy without undue interference with my normal life. They give me the stuff intravenously once a week (it takes two hours to drip into my veins) and when I get to feeling "toxic" (sort of like a bad hangover, but without the headache) they lay off for two weeks. Then go at it again. This will go on for a year. Modern medicine.

The events in China are truly stupendous. One sees, written in English, the words of Abraham Lincoln, Thomas Jefferson, and Lord Acton ["Power corrupts absolute power corrupts absolutely"] on the banners being carried by the chanting students. I wondered about that. I have a student here from Shanghai, Jianxin Wang, and I asked him where the students in Red China ever learned such subversive [to communism] stuff, and he said from their English lessons! He said the government had been encouraging the students to learn English as part of their programs of economic modernization. Apparently the ideas of the English-speaking world cannot be kept out of the reading matter. ... The students are learning the English language, but to read English beyond the elementary level the texts are full of—what else?—FREEDOM. I had never thought of it that way. But it does explain why Marxism was such a losing proposition in the English-speaking world.

One would expect western European culture, including democracy, finally to surface in Russia, since the Russians are Europeans and even seventy years of communism could not erase the civilization planted there at such great cost by the Tsars in the past, and I anticipate Marxism to vanish from Chinese thought without a trace in another generation. [In fact, China has moved remarkably far in that direction in the generation since John wrote these lines, recently with much backsliding.]

[But] one cannot pretend to know what will happen in China, even from day to day. Gorbachov will apparently become a sort of unofficial President of the World. He is a hero everywhere except in the Soviet Union. They are angry with him there because they can't get their economy moving, and they blame him. The Chinese, who don't need to be told how to organize and run business enterprises, are going to town on their own. They may have to give the Russians lessons! After all, it cannot be easy to unravel a command economy and put it on a market basis in any reasonable length of time [as indeed we found out in the Russian experiment]. The Chinese have been terribly skillful at it, compared to their Russian comrades.

The ultimate right of private property transferred to this country in the 17th century in the tenure, free and common socage, was the right of "waste." A few months back I bought, through the mail for $99.00, an electronic gadget, a little black box that is a speller, dictionary and thesaurus, with 250,000 words. The idea is that I would carry it with me, and Mary Gray could too, on our travels, when we are usually writing things in addition to sight-seeing. My gadget was defective. I 'phoned the distributor—the thing is manufactured in Korea—to complain. They said that they would have to have proof that I owned the thing before they would honor their guarantee. Acting on a professorial impulse, I sent them the gadget and said: "As proof of ownership, if you cannot repair this thing, then you keep it." Right of waste; I was destroying my property without compensation. Two days ago a new one came to me in the mails, without comment! Education is not always worthless.

Mary Gray has now finished her novel, upon which she has been working for eight years. I read it straight through, and couldn't put it down. Our procedure is that we don't bother each other with "work in progress" so I had no idea what it was about. I am not a fiction reader, so when I read a book of fiction straight through, it must be good. I think she will send it off to her agent in another week or so. Then she must wait for a publisher to bite. In anticipation of that agony, I remind her that my book, <u>The Vital Few</u>, was turned down by nine publishers, and has been in print for a quarter of a century [Now more than fifty-three years, and continuing as a classic!]. Publishers often don't know what they are doing. But I maintain that any reasonable book can find its publisher, ultimately, so you just have to suffer out the waiting.

February 17, 1990

If you don't mind, I am using you as a reference. The Dean of CAS here is putting up my dear old book, The Vital Few, for some kind of an award for writing about entrepreneurs. I don't know more about it than that. ... It has been a long time since I needed a reference for anything, and most of my old teachers are either dead or retired. But you were there when it was first written, and can attest that entrepreneurship wasn't exactly a hot topic when I wrote the book back in 1962. I took a chance, then, and it certainly paid off for me in the long run. The thing is still in print ... and sells right along at a couple of thousand copies a year. ... I added two more biographies in 1986 to the expanded addition. I think that may be what causes it to keep selling.

All is well with us. I have finished with my chemo therapy, and so far so good. It is not a process I would recommend, but if you have cancer, and the oncologists want that, you would be a fool, or a big risk taker, not to go along. ...

I don't know if you have seen any of Stan's sculpting. He is a regular Michelangelo. Mary Gray bought me a small statue for Xmas. I didn't ask what it cost, but it was enough that he apparently gave the proceeds to charity! He does sell them. And has commissions. I have told him to stop worrying about economics and just sculpt. Someone else will think of the theorems, but no one else will be able to sculpt that way. If I had that much talent at something, I would be exploiting it. One doesn't live forever, and one has no tenure on one's talent. It can just stop some day, as it did with Sibelius, leaving him with a half century to just stare into space before he died.

John

I miss John, and it will always be so. He was one of those rare friends—an intellectually intimate brother who both lightens and enlightens your way. He always had probing questions about why, how, where, and when. But mixed in with the serious scholarship, there were always laughs and good cheer. Mary Gray told me that when I sent him a copy of my book, *Papers in Experimental Economics* (1991), he was in the next room tearing apart the mailing carton, then let out one of his famous trademark laughs and some chuckles. Mary Gray asked, "What is it, John?" And John replied, "It's a Nobel Prize, that's what it is: a Nobel Prize." I am not sure that book made any difference, but it was symbolic to John, who had unbounded confidence in his friends. He was personally thrilled with their every success and always discounted the downers and disappointments. No one dared to squelch his enthusiasm about a project, a friend's project, or a friend or loved one. His happiness for others was always genuine.

If anyone could have survived cancer, detected too late, it was John. He fought for his life and would not concede until the very end, bearing out Dr. Hertzler's observation that irrespective of belief systems, people in the end accept the inevitable in quiet peace. John was a Jack Mormon, defined by Howard Jarvis of California Proposition 13 fame as an "ex Mormon who smokes and drinks." But his Mormon heritage, combined with his intellectual endowment, served him well as a scholar and as a man—here was a man who loved, and was loved by, those he befriended. He had great faith, if not always conventional faith. However, I recently learned from Bartell Jensen, one of our early Purdue PhDs that John visited Logan, Utah, in his last months and his spirit had returned "home" to his wonderful Mormon heritage. I doubt not for a moment, the truth of Bartell's witness.

Here is a short excerpt from the Deseret News obituary *"Death: Jonathan R. T. Hughes"* on June 3, 1992.

Jonathan Roberts Tyson Hughes, a native of Twin Falls, Idaho, died of cancer May 30, 1992, in Evanston, Illinois.

...A graduate of Twin Falls High School, John played football and was one of the region's finest clarinetists. He attended Utah State University, graduating in economics in 1950. After two years at the University of Washington, he received a Rhodes Scholarship to Oxford, where he earned a D. Phil. in economics in 1955, studying with the finest economists in England.

At Oxford, John met Mary Gray Stilwell, a Texan studying anthropology, and they were married in 1953. A son, Benjamin, was born in 1960, and twin daughters, Charis and Margaret, were born in 1962.

John worked for the Federal Reserve Bank of New York, Purdue University, Columbia University, University of California at Berkeley, and spent the last 30 years as a professor of economic history at Northwestern University in Evanston, Illinois. He has been a Distinguished Professor of Economics and Robert E. and Emily King Professor of Business Institutions there since 1989. A productive scholar, Dr. Hughes has written widely in the field of economic history, producing a dozen books and more than one hundred professional articles. His book, "The Vital Few: The Entrepreneur and American Economic Progress," won a $25,000 prize from the Kenan Enterprise Center for its celebration of American entrepreneurship. His writing was witty and insightful. He has been a Guggenheim Fellow, Ford Foundation Faculty Fellow, Fellow of All Souls College, Oxford, and president of the Economic History Association. In 1990 he was given an honorary Doctor of

Social Science degree from Utah State University. The same year, his former students and colleagues published a festschrift in his honor entitled "The Vital One: Essays in Honor of Jonathan R. T. Hughes."...

One of my most treasured experiences was to write a tribute to him and to savor the moment as I read it at the gathering to celebrate the life, influence, and accomplishments of this wonderful person. It took me months to write it. I wrote a draft, revised it, set it aside, returned to edit it some more, over and over and over again, until there were no more additions, edits, subtractions, or fine-tunings left in me, and I finally let it be. That exercise, conducted over the months from his death in the spring until he was honored at Northwestern the following October 1992, gutted and cleansed me of all grief. I was free at last, thank God almighty, free at last, happy to have known and loved this great friend, colleague and confidant. I now look back on this expressed sense of relief and am aware that you are never free of such deep connections, but I was free of it as a steady weight, free to get on with all that had to be done.

Jonathan Roberts Tyson Hughes
A Memorial

On this occasion
we are privileged to celebrate
the memory of a wonderful life;
one that spanned sixty-four years;
one that touched and altered
dozens, likely hundreds, of other lives.

In his life John taught us how to live
with energy, splendor, joy, and hope.
In his death he taught us how to die
with stubborn resistance, candor,
optimism, and inspiration.

I am awash with delightful memories,
but I will remember best and miss most
his unflagging personal support;
no one else could get as genuinely excited
about your work as about his own.

He believed in his friends,
as he would have them believe in themselves.
He never allowed me not to believe in myself,

nor other friends not to believe in themselves.
He awakened the hidden strength within you.

When he wrote of the history he had learned
it was as if he had experienced it,
much as he spoke and wrote
of the history he had truly lived:
down the white water rapids
of Idaho's Bruneau River;
playing jazz clarinet in
Ely, Wells, Elko, and Fish Haven;
the Great Strike of 1951 at Nushagak Station.

I first read *The Vital Few*,
and its masterful essay on Brigham Young,
in manuscript, then entitled *The Good Land*.
I was astonished for it read
like he had been there, lived it all.
That's when I knew how
good writing is born of personal—
even if vicarious—experience
that draws the reader into the phenomena, as it lived.

I was disheartened that the title was changed
to the colorless,
though accurate *The Vital Few*,
thus eliminating John's ringing text from Exodus 3:8:
"And I come down to deliver them
out of the hand of the Egyptians,
and to bring them up out of that land
unto a good land and a large,
unto a land flowing with milk and honey."

John loved the land, because he was of the land: Idaho,
Utah, Nevada, Washington, Indiana, Illinois, Vermont.

His heroes were most especially
of the Good Land
that flowed with the milk and honey
of nineteenth-century opportunity.

John catapulted himself into your life,
a fact that, shall we say, was not universally appreciated.
I welcomed and blossomed from this warm intrusion
for he was the brother I never had,
the confidant who nourished so very deeply,
and meaningfully.

He came to Purdue for one reason:
he told me that he could no longer tolerate
his Federal Reserve Bank superior
blue-penciling all his work.
Such was his fierce Mormon independence.

After Purdue,
although there were sometimes long spaces
between our encounters,
somehow we managed always to pick up
where we had ended,
as if it had been but an hour, or a day.
With John there were no beginnings or endings;
just the flow of experience shared.

It was this continuity, this dependability
and reliability in the face
of unimportant interruption,
that most significantly
defined our relationship.

Others, I think, must have shared
a similar experience,
because of who he was.
That continuity defined and gave sustenance
to an enduring thirty-six-year bond between us.
I shall miss that bond dearly,
but without repining,
because of the strength he inspired.

His works,
his personal influence,
will of course live,
as resistant to extinction as was his spirit to the end.
This is assured by those of us here,
on this day, and elsewhere,
who were touched so intimately by him,
for with John there were no beginnings or endings.

Now it is for each of us,
the living, privately,
as well as through this congregation,
to find whatever meaning for our lives,
that is contained in his death.

He came
as dust

delivered of the good land;
he chose to return
as dust, for renewal,
unto a land made sweeter by his coming.

—Vernon Smith
Delivered at Northwestern University
Alice Millar Chapel October 25, 1992

See Figs. 12.1, 12.2, and 12.3.

Fig. 12.1 Vernon's nearby escape at Purdue

Fig. 12.2 Purdue honorary degree 1989

Fig. 12.3 Tanya and her 7 Pups Cincinnati, 1965–1966

Author Index

Subject Index